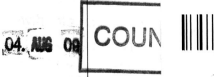
...onsin, USA, in
...about two and a half years of his early life
... where his father was Consul-General. He re-
...to California, graduated from Yale, and then spent a
year at the American Academy at Rome. From this experience came his first novel, *The Cabala*, published in
1926. He taught French and was a Housemaster of Lawrence-
ville School, a boys' preparatory school in New Jersey,
and for six years taught English at the University of
Chicago. During the war Thornton Wilder worked in the
Intelligence Branch of the US Army Air Force and served
in North Africa and Italy. In 1950–51 he held the post as
C. E. Norton Professor at Harvard.

In 1927 came publication of *The Bridge of San Luis Rey*,
which established Thornton Wilder as one of the leading
novelists of the twentieth century. His novels include: *The
Woman of Andros* (1930), *Heaven's My Destination* (1935),
and *The Ides of March* (1948). Amongst his plays, *Our Town*
(1938) and *The Skin of Our Teeth* (1942) both won the
Pulitzer Prize; he also published *The Merchant of Yonkers*
(1938) and two volumes of short plays, *The Angel that
Troubled the Waters* (1928) and *The Long Christmas Dinner*
(1931); and two of his plays, *The Matchmaker* (1954)
and *A Life in the Sun* (1955), were first performed
at the Edinburgh Festival. *Three Plays* was published in
1958, and *Plays for Bleecker Street* in 1962. In 1967 he
published *The Eighth Day*, his first novel for twenty
years, which won the National Book Award in
1968. Thornton Wilder died in December 1975.

THORNTON WILDER

OUR TOWN
THE SKIN OF OUR TEETH
THE MATCHMAKER

PENGUIN BOOKS

PENGUIN BOOKS

Published by the Penguin Group
Penguin Books Ltd, 27 Wrights Lane, London W8 5TZ, England
Viking Penguin, a division of Penguin Books USA Inc.
375 Hudson Street, New York, New York 10014, USA
Penguin Books Australia Ltd, Ringwood, Victoria, Australia
Penguin Books Canada Ltd, 2801 John Street, Markham, Ontario, Canada L3R 1B4
Penguin Books (NZ) Ltd, 182–190 Wairau Road, Auckland 10, New Zealand

Penguin Books Ltd, Registered Offices: Harmondsworth, Middlesex, England

Our Town first published in the USA 1938
Copyright 1938 by Thorton Wilder
Copyright © Thornton Wilder, 1957
The Skin of Our Teeth first published in the USA 1942
Copyright 1942 by Thornton Wilder
The Matchmaker first published in the USA 1955
Copyright © Thornton Wilder, 1955, 1957
First published together in Great Britain by Longmans 1958
Published in Penguin Books 1962
23 25 27 29 30 28 26 24

Printed in England by Clays Ltd, St Ives plc
Set in Monotype Bembo

The amateur performing rights in these plays are controlled by Samuel
French Ltd, 52 Fitzroy Street, London W1P 6JR, and no performance may
be given unless a licence has been obtained. Fees will be quoted on request.
  It should be noted that Thornton Wilder has instructed that no performance of any excerpts from any of his plays may be given: this instruction
applies in all circumstances.

CONTENTS

PREFACE
BY THORNTON WILDER

TOWARD the end of the twenties I began to lose pleasure in
going to the theatre. I ceased to believe in the stories I saw
presented there. When I did go it was to admire some secondary aspect of the play, the work of a great actor or director
or designer. Yet at the same time the conviction was growing
in me that the theatre was the greatest of all the arts. I felt that
something had gone wrong with it in my time and that it was
fulfilling only a small part of its potentialities. I was filled with
admiration for presentations of classical works by Max Reinhardt and Louis Jouvet and the Old Vic, as I was by the best
plays of my own time, like *Desire Under the Elms* and *The
Front Page*; but at heart I didn't believe a word of them. I was
like a schoolmaster grading a paper; to each of these offerings
I gave an A+, but the condition of mind of one grading a
paper is not that of one being overwhelmed by an artistic
creation. The response we make when we 'believe' a work of
the imagination is that of saying: 'This is the way things are.
I have always known it without being fully aware that I knew
it. Now in the presence of this play or novel or poem (or
picture or piece of music) I know that I know it.' It is this
form of knowledge which Plato called 'recollection'. We have
all murdered, in thought; and been murdered. We have all
seen the ridiculous in estimable persons and in ourselves. We
have all known terror as well as enchantment. Imaginative
literature has nothing to say to those who do not recognize –
who cannot be *reminded* – of such conditions. Of all the arts
the theatre is best endowed to awaken this recollection within
us – to believe is to say 'yes'; but in the theatres of my time I

7

did not feel myself prompted to any such grateful and self-forgetting acquiescence.

This dissatisfaction worried me. I was not ready to condemn myself as blasé and over-fastidious, for I knew that I was still capable of belief. I believed every word of *Ulysses* and of Proust and of *The Magic Mountain*, as I did of hundreds of plays when I read them. It was on the stage that imaginative narration became false. Finally, my dissatisfaction passed into resentment. I began to feel that the theatre was not only inadequate, it was evasive; it did not wish to draw upon its deeper potentialities. I found the word for it: it aimed to be *soothing*. The tragic had no heat; the comic had no bite; the social criticism failed to indict us with responsibility. I began to search for the point where the theatre had run off the track, where it had chosen – and been permitted – to become a minor art and an inconsequential diversion.

The trouble began in the nineteenth century and was connected with the rise of the middle classes – they wanted their theatre soothing. There's nothing wrong with the middle classes in themselves. We know that now. The United States and Scandinavia and Germany are middle-class countries, so completely so that they have lost the very memory of their once despised and ludicrous inferiority (they had been inferior not only to the aristocracy but, in human dignity, to the peasantry). When a middle class is new, however, there is much that is wrong with it. When it is emerging from under the shadow of an aristocracy, from the myth and prestige of those well-born Higher-ups, it is alternately insecure and aggressively complacent. It must find its justification and reassurance in making money and displaying it. To this day, members of the middle classes in England, France, and Italy feel themselves to be a little ridiculous and humiliated. The prestige of aristocracies is based upon a dreary untruth that moral superiority and the qualifications for leadership are transmittable through the chromosomes, and the secondary lie, that the environment afforded by privilege and leisure tends to nurture the flowers of the spirit. An aristocracy, defending and fostering its lie, extracts from the arts only such elements as can further its interests, the aroma and not the sap, the grace and not the trenchancy. Equally harmful to culture is the newly arrived middle class. In the English-speaking world the middle classes came into power early in the nineteenth century and gained control over the theatre. They were pious, law-abiding, and industrious. They were assured of eternal life in the next world and, in this, they were squarely seated on Property and the privileges that accompany it. They were attended by devoted servants who knew their place. They were benevolent within certain limits, but chose to ignore wide tracts of injustice and stupidity in the world about them; and they shrank from contemplating those elements within themselves that were ridiculous, shallow, and harmful. They distrusted the passions and tried to deny them. Their questions about the nature of life seemed to be sufficiently answered by the demonstration of financial status and by conformity to some clearly established rules of decorum. These were precarious positions; abysses yawned on either side. The air was loud with questions that must not be asked. These audiences fashioned a theatre which could not disturb them. They thronged to melodrama (which deals with tragic possibilities in such a way that you know from the beginning that all will end happily) and to sentimental drama (which accords a total license to the supposition that the wish is father to the thought) and to comedies in which the characters were so represented that they always resembled someone else and not oneself. Between the plays that Sheridan wrote in his twenties and the first works of Wilde and Shaw there was no play of even moderate interest written in the English language. (Unless you happen to admire and except Shelley's *The Cenci*.) These audiences, however, also thronged to Shakespeare. How did they shield themselves against his probing? How did they smother the theatre – and with such effect that it smothers us still? The box set was already there, the curtain, the proscenium, but not taken 'seriously' – it was a convenience in view of the weather in northern countries. They took it seriously and emphasized and enhanced everything that thus removed, cut off, and boxed the action; they increasingly shut the play up into a museum showcase.

Let us examine why the box-set stage stifles the life in drama and why and how it militates against belief.

*

Every action which has ever taken place – every thought, every emotion – has taken place only once, at one moment in time and place. 'I love you,' 'I rejoice,' 'I suffer,' have been said and felt many billions of times, and never twice the same. Every person who has ever lived has lived an unbroken succession of unique occasions. Yet the more one is aware of this individuality in experience (innumerable! innumerable!) the more one becomes attentive to what these disparate moments have in common, to repetitive patterns. As an artist (or listener or beholder) which 'truth' do you prefer – that of the isolated occasion, or that which includes and resumes the innumerable? Which truth is more worth telling? Every age differs in this. Is the Venus de Milo 'one woman'? Is the play *Macbeth* the story of 'one destiny'? The theatre is admirably fitted to tell both truths. It has one foot planted firmly in the particular, since each actor before us (even when he wears a mask!) is indubitably a living, breathing 'one'; yet it tends and strains to exhibit a general truth since its relation to a specific 'realistic' truth is confused and undermined by the fact that it is an accumulation of untruths, pretences, and fiction. The novel is pre-eminently the vehicle of the unique occasion, the theatre of the generalized one. It is through the theatre's power to raise the exhibited individual action into the realm of idea and type and universal that it is able to evoke our belief. But power is precisely what those nineteenth-century audiences did not – dared not – confront. They tamed it and drew its teeth; squeezed it into that removed showcase. They loaded the stage with specific objects, because every concrete object on the stage fixes and narrows the action to one moment in time and place. (Have you ever noticed that in the plays of Shakespeare no one – except occasionally a ruler – ever sits down? There were not even chairs on the English or Spanish stages in the time of Elizabeth I.) So it was by a jugglery with time that the middle classes devitalized the theatre. When you emphasize *place* in the theatre, you drag down and limit and harness time to it. You thrust the action back into past time, whereas it is precisely the glory of the stage that it is always 'now' there. Under such production methods the characters are all dead before the action starts. You don't have to pay deeply from your heart's participation. No great age in the theatre ever attempted to capture the audiences' belief through this kind of specification and localization. I became dissatisfied with the theatre because I was unable to lend credence to such childish attempts to be 'real'.

*

I began writing one-act plays that tried to capture not verisimilitude but reality. In *The Happy Journey to Trenton and Camden* four kitchen chairs represent an automobile and a family travels seventy miles in twenty minutes. Ninety years go by in *The Long Christmas Dinner*. In *Pullman Car Hiawatha* some more plain chairs serve as berths and we hear the very vital statistics of the towns and fields that passengers are traversing; we hear their thoughts; we even hear the planets over their heads. In Chinese drama a character, by straddling a stick, conveys to us that he is on horseback. In almost every 'No' play of the Japanese, an actor makes a tour of the stage and we know that he is making a long journey. Think of the ubiquity that Shakespeare's stage afforded for the battle scenes at the close of *Julius Caesar* and *Antony and Cleopatra*. As we see them today what a cutting and hacking of the text takes place – what condescension, what contempt for his dramaturgy.

Our Town is not offered as a picture of life in a New Hampshire village; or as a speculation about the conditions of life after death (that element I merely took from Dante's *Purgatory*). It is an attempt to find a value above all price for the smallest events in our daily life. I have made the claim as preposterous as possible, for I have set the village against the largest dimensions of time and place. The recurrent words in this play (few have noticed it) are 'hundreds', 'thousands', and 'millions'. Emily's joys and griefs, her algebra lessons and her birthday presents – what are they when we consider all the billions of girls who have lived, who are living, and who will live? Each individual's assertion to an absolute reality can only be inner, very inner. And here the method of staging finds its justification – in the first two acts there are at least a few chairs and tables; but when she revisits the earth and the kitchen to which she descended on her twelfth birthday, the very chairs and table are gone. Our claim, our hope, our despair are in the mind – not in things, not in 'scenery'. Molière said that for the theatre all he needed was a platform and a passion or two. The climax of this play needs only five square feet of boarding and the passion to know what life means to us.

The Matchmaker is an only slightly modified version of *The*

Merchant of Yonkers, which I wrote the year after I had written
Our Town. One way to shake off the nonsense of the nineteenth-century staging is to make fun of it. This play parodies
the stock-company plays that I used to see at Ye Liberty
Theatre, Oakland, California, when I was a boy. I have already
read small theses in German comparing it with the great
Austrian original on which it is based. The scholars are very
bewildered. There is most of the plot (except that our friend
Dolly Levi is not in Nestroy's play); there are some of the
tags; but it's all 'about' quite different matters. My play is
about aspirations of the young (and not only of the young) for
a fuller, freer participation in life. Imagine an Austrian
pharmacist going to the shelf to draw from a bottle which he
knows to contain a stinging corrosive liquid, guaranteed to
remove warts and wens; and imagine his surprise when he
discovers that it has been filled overnight with very American
birch-bark beer.

The Skin of Our Teeth begins, also, by making fun of old-
fashioned playwriting; but the audience soon perceives that
he is seeing 'two times at once'. The Antrobus family is living
both in prehistoric times and in a New Jersey commuters'
suburb today. Again, the events of our homely daily life – this
time the family life – are depicted against the vast dimensions
of time and place. It was written on the eve of our entrance into
the war and under strong emotion and I think it mostly comes
alive under conditions of crisis. It has been often charged with
being a bookish fantasia about history, full of rather bloodless
schoolmasterish jokes. But to have seen it in Germany soon
after the war, in the shattered churches and beerhalls that were
serving as theatres, with audiences whose price of admission
meant the loss of a meal and for whom it was of absorbing
interest that there was a 'recipe for grass soup that did not
cause the diarrhoea', was an experience that was not so cool.

I am very proud that this year it has received a first and over-whelming reception in Warsaw. The play is deeply indebted to James Joyce's *Finnegans Wake*. I should be very happy if, in the future, some author should feel similarly indebted to any work of mine. Literature has always more resembled a torch race than a furious dispute among heirs.

The theatre has lagged behind the other arts in finding the 'new ways' to express how men and women think and feel in our time. I am not one of the new dramatists we are looking for. I wish I were. I hope I have played a part in preparing the way for them. I am not an innovator but a rediscoverer of forgotten goods and I hope a remover of obtrusive bric-à-brac. And as I view the work of my contemporaries I seem to feel that I am exceptional in one thing – I give (don't I?) the impression of having enormously enjoyed it.

Our Town

The first performance of this play took place at the McCarter Theatre, Princeton, New Jersey, on 22 January 1938. The first New York performance was at the Henry Miller Theatre, 4 February 1938. It was produced and directed by Jed Harris. The technical director was Raymond Sovey; the costumes were designed by Madame Hélène Pons. The role of the Stage Manager was played by Frank Craven. The Gibbs family were played by Jay Fassett, Evelyn Varden, John Craven and Marilyn Erskine; the Webb family by Thomas Ross, Helen Carew, Martha Scott (as Emily) and Charles Wiley, Jr. Mrs Soames was played by Doro Merande; Simon Stimson by Philip Coolidge.

CAST
(in the order of their appearance)

STAGE MANAGER

DR GIBBS

JOE CROWELL

HOWIE NEWSOME

MRS GIBBS

MRS WEBB

GEORGE GIBBS

REBECCA GIBBS

WALLY WEBB

EMILY WEBB

PROFESSOR WILLARD

MR WEBB

WOMAN IN THE BALCONY

MAN IN THE AUDITORIUM

LADY IN A BOX

SIMON STIMSON

MRS SOAMES

CONSTABLE WARREN

SI CROWELL

THREE BASEBALL PLAYERS

SAM CRAIG

JOE STODDARD

The entire play takes place in Grover's Corners,
New Hampshire.

ACT ONE

No curtain.

No scenery.

The audience, arriving, sees an empty stage in half-light.

Presently the STAGE MANAGER, *hat on and pipe in mouth, enters and begins placing a table and three chairs downstage left, and a table and three chairs downstage right. He also places a low bench at the corner of what will be the Webb house, left.*

'Left' and 'right' are from the point of view of the actor facing the audience. 'Up' is towards the back wall.

As the house lights go down he has finished setting the stage and leaning against the right proscenium pillar watches the late arrivals in the audience.

When the auditorium is in complete darkness he speaks.

STAGE MANAGER: This play is called *Our Town*. It was written by Thornton Wilder; produced and directed by A. . . . (cr: produced by A. . . .; directed by B. . . .). In it you will see Miss C. . . .; Miss D. . . .; Miss E. . . .; and Mr F. . . .; Mr G. . . .; Mr H. . . .; and many others. The name of the town is Grover's Corners, New Hampshire – just across the Massachusetts line: latitude 42 degrees 40 minutes; longitude 70 degrees 37 minutes. The First Act shows a day in our town. The day is 7 May 1901. The time is just before dawn.

 [*A rooster crows.*]

 The sky is beginning to show some streaks of light over in the east there, behind our mount'in.

 The morning star always gets wonderful bright the minute before it has to go – doesn't it?

 [*He stares at it for a moment, then goes upstage.*]

Well, I'd better show you how our town lies. Up here –

[*That is: parallel with the back wall*]

is Main Street. Way back there is the railway station; tracks go that way. Polish Town's across the tracks, and some Canuck families.

[*Towards the left*]

Over there is the Congregational Church; across the street's the Presbyterian.

Methodist and Unitarian are over there.

Baptist is down in the holla' by the river.

Catholic Church is over beyond the tracks.

Here's the Town Hall and Post Office combined; jail's in the basement.

Bryan once made a speech from these very steps here.

Along here's a row of stores. Hitching posts and horse blocks in front of them. First automobile's going to come along in about five years – belonged to Banker Cartwright, our richest citizen ... lives in the big white house up on the hill.

Here's the grocery store and here's Mr Morgan's drug-store. Most everybody in town manages to look into those two stores once a day.

Public School's over yonder. High School's still farther over. Quarter of nine mornings, noontimes, and three o'clock afternoons, the hull town can hear the yelling and screaming from those schoolyards.

[*He approaches the table and chairs downstage right.*]

This is our doctor's house – Doc Gibbs's. This is the back door.

[*Two arched trellises, covered with vines and flowers, are pushed out, one by each proscenium pillar.*]

There's some scenery for those who think they have to have scenery.

This is Mrs Gibbs's garden. Corn . . . peas . . . beans . . . hollyhocks . . . heliotrope . . . and a lot of burdock.

[*Crosses the stage.*]

In those days our newspaper come out twice a week – the Grover's Corners *Sentinel* – and this is Editor Webb's house.

And this is Mrs Webb's garden.

Just like Mrs Gibbs's, only it's got a lot of sunflowers, too.

[*He looks upwards, centre stage.*]

Right here . . .'s a big butternut tree.

[*He returns to his place by the right proscenium pillar and looks at the audience for a minute.*]

Nice town, y'know what I mean?

Nobody very remarkable ever come out of it, s'far as we know.

The earliest tombstones in the cemetery up there on the mountain say 1670 to 1680 – they're Grovers and Cartwrights and Gibbses and Herseys – same names as are around here now.

Well, as I said: it's about dawn.

The only lights on in town are in a cottage over by the tracks where a Polish mother's just had twins. And in the Joe Crowell house, where Joe Junior's getting up so as to deliver the paper. And in the depot, where Shorty Hawkins is gettin' ready to flag the 5.45 for Boston.

[*A train whistle is heard. The* STAGE MANAGER *takes out his watch and nods.*]

Naturally, out in the country – all around – there've been lights on for some time, what with milkin's and so on. But town people sleep late.

So – another day's begun.

There's Doc Gibbs comin' down Main Street now,

comin' back from that baby case. And here's his wife comin' downstairs to get breakfast.

[MRS GIBBS, *a plump, pleasant woman in the middle thirties, comes 'downstairs' right. She pulls up an imaginary window shade in her kitchen and starts to make a fire in her stove.*]

Doc Gibbs died in 1930. The new hospital's named after him.

Mrs Gibbs died first – long time ago, in fact. She went out to visit her daughter, Rebecca, who married an insurance man in Canton, Ohio, and died there – pneumonia – but her body was brought back here. She's up in the cemetery there now – in with a whole mess of Gibbses and Herseys – she was Julia Hersey 'fore she married Doc Gibbs in the Congregational Church over there.

In our town we like to know the facts about everybody.

There's Mrs Webb, coming downstairs to get her breakfast, too. – That's Doc Gibbs. Got that call at half past one this morning.

And there comes Joe Crowell, Jr, delivering Mr Webb's *Sentinel.*

[DR GIBBS *has been coming along Main Street from the left. At the point where he would turn to approach his house, he stops, sets down his – imaginary – black bag, takes off his hat, and rubs his face with fatigue, using an enormous handkerchief.* MRS WEBB, *a thin, serious, crisp woman, has entered her kitchen, left, tying on an apron. She goes through the motions of putting wood into a stove, lighting it, and preparing breakfast. Suddenly,* JOE CROWELL, JR, *eleven, starts down Main Street from the right, hurling imaginary newspapers into doorways.*]

JOE CROWELL, JR: Morning, Doc Gibbs.

DR GIBBS: Morning, Joe.

JOE CROWELL, JR: Somebody been sick, Doc?

DR GIBBS: No. Just some twins born over in Polish Town.

JOE CROWELL, JR: Do you want your paper now?

DR GIBBS: Yes, I'll take it – Anything serious goin' on in the world since Wednesday?

JOE CROWELL, JR: Yessir. My schoolteacher, Miss Foster, 's getting married to a fella over in Concord.

DR GIBBS: I declare – How do you boys feel about that?

JOE CROWELL, JR: Well, of course, it's none of my business – but I think if a person starts out to be a teacher, she ought to stay one.

DR GIBBS: How's your knee, Joe?

JOE CROWELL, JR: Fine, Doc, I never think about it at all. Only like you said, it always tells me when it's going to rain.

DR GIBBS: What's it telling you today? Goin' to rain?

JOE CROWELL, JR: No, sir.

DR GIBBS: Sure?

JOE CROWELL, JR: Yessir.

DR GIBBS: Knee ever made a mistake?

JOE CROWELL, JR: No, sir.

[JOE *goes off*. DR GIBBS *stands reading his paper*.]

STAGE MANAGER: Want to tell you something about that boy Joe Crowell there. Joe was awful bright – graduated from high school here, head of his class. So he got a scholarship to Massachusetts Tech. Graduated head of his class there, too. It was all wrote up in the Boston paper at the time. Goin' to be a great engineer, Joe was. But the war broke out and he died in France – All that education for nothing.

HOWIE NEWSOME [*off left*]: Giddap, Bessie! What's the matter with you today?

STAGE MANAGER: Here comes Howie Newsome, deliverin' the milk.

HOWIE NEWSOME, *about thirty, in overalls, comes along*

*Main Street from the left, walking beside an invisible horse
and wagon and carrying an imaginary rack with milk bottles.
The sound of clinking milk bottles is heard. He leaves some
bottles at Mrs Webb's trellis, then, crossing the stage to Mrs
Gibbs's, he stops centre to talk to Dr Gibbs.]*

HOWIE NEWSOME: Morning, Doc.

DR GIBBS: Morning, Howie.

HOWIE NEWSOME: Somebody sick?

DR GIBBS: Pair of twins over to Mrs Goruslawski's.

HOWIE NEWSOME: Twins, eh? This town's gettin' bigger
every year.

DR GIBBS: Goin' to rain, Howie?

HOWIE NEWSOME: No, no. Fine day – that'll burn through.
Come on, Bessie.

DR GIBBS: Hello Bessie.
   [He strokes the horse, which has remained up centre.]
How old is she, Howie?

HOWIE NEWSOME: Going on seventeen. Bessie's all mixed up
about the route ever since the Lockharts stopped takin' their
quart of milk every day. She wants to leave 'em a quart just
the same – keeps scolding me the hull trip.
   [He reaches Mrs Gibbs's back door. She is waiting for him.]

MRS GIBBS: Good morning, Howie.

HOWIE NEWSOME: Morning, Mrs Gibbs. Doc's just comin'
down the street.

MRS GIBBS: Is he? Seems like you're late today.

HOWIE NEWSOME: Yes. Somep'n went wrong with the
separator. Don't know what 'twas.
   [He passes Dr Gibbs up centre.]
   Doc!

DR GIBBS: Howie!

MRS GIBBS [*Calling upstairs*]: Children! Children! Time to get
up.

26

HOWIE NEWSOME: Come on, Bessie!

    [*He goes off right.*]

MRS GIBBS: George! Rebecca!

    [DR GIBBS *arrives at his back door and passes through the*
    trellis into his house.]

MRS GIBBS: Everything all right, Frank?

DR GIBBS: Yes. I declare – easy as kittens.

MRS GIBBS: Bacon'll be ready in a minute. Set down and
    drink your coffee. You can catch a couple hours' sleep this
    morning, can't you?

DR GIBBS: Hm! . . . Mrs Wentworth's coming at eleven.
    Guess I know what it's about, too. Her stummick ain't what
    it ought to be.

MRS GIBBS: All told, you won't get more'n three hours' sleep.
    Frank Gibbs, I don't know what's goin' to become of you.
    I do wish I could get you to go away someplace and take a
    rest. I think it would do you good.

MRS WEBB: Emileeee! Time to get up! Wally! Seven
    o'clock!

MRS GIBBS [*busy at the stove*]: I declare, you got to speak to
    George. Seems like something's come over him lately. He's
    no help to me at all. I can't even get him to cut me some
    wood.

DR GIBBS [*washing and drying his hands at the sink*] : Is he sassy
    to you?

MRS GIBBS: No. He just whines! All he thinks about is
    that baseball – George! Rebecca! You'll be late for
    school.

DR GIBBS: M-m-m . . .

MRS GIBBS: George!

DR GIBBS: George, look sharp!

GEORGE'S VOICE: Yes, Pa!

DR GIBBS [*as he goes off the stage*]: Don't you hear your

mother calling you? I guess I'll go upstairs and get forty winks.

MRS WEBB: Walleee! Emileee! You'll be late for school! Walleee! You wash yourself good or I'll come up and do it myself.

REBECCA GIBBS'S VOICE: Ma! What dress shall I wear?

MRS GIBBS: Don't make a noise. Your father's been out all night and needs his sleep. I washed and ironed the blue gingham for you special.

REBECCA: Ma, I hate that dress.

MRS GIBBS: Oh, hush-up-with-you.

REBECCA: Every day I go to school dressed like a sick turkey.

MRS GIBBS: Now, Rebecca, you always look *very* nice.

REBECCA: Mama, George's throwing soap at me.

MRS GIBBS: I'll come and slap the both of you – that's what I'll do.

[*A factory whistle sounds.*
The CHILDREN *dash in and take their places at the tables. Right,* GEORGE, *about sixteen, and* REBECCA, *eleven. Left,* EMILY *and* WALLY, *same ages. They carry strapped schoolbooks.*]

STAGE MANAGER: We've got a factory in our town too – hear it? Makes blankets. Cartwrights own it and it brung 'em a fortune.

MRS WEBB: Children! Now I won't have it. Breakfast is just as good as any other meal and I won't have you gobbling like wolves. It'll stunt your growth – that's a fact. Put away your book, Wally.

WALLY: Aw, Ma! By ten o'clock I got to know all about Canada.

MRS WEBB: You know the rule 's well as I do – no books at table. As for me, I'd rather have my children healthy than bright.

28

EMILY: I'm both, Mama: you know I am. I'm the brightest girl in school for my age. I have a wonderful memory.

MRS WEBB: Eat your breakfast.

WALLY: I'm bright, too, when I'm looking at my stamp collection.

MRS GIBBS: I'll speak to your father about it when he's rested. Seems to me twenty-five cents a week's enough for a boy your age. I declare I don't know how you spend it all.

GEORGE: Aw, Ma – I gotta lotta things to buy.

MRS GIBBS: Strawberry phosphates – that's what you spend it on.

GEORGE: I don't see how Rebecca comes to have so much money. She has more'n a dollar.

REBECCA [*spoon in mouth, dreamily*]: I've been saving it up gradual.

MRS GIBBS: Well, dear, I think it's a good thing to spend some every now and then.

REBECCA: Mama, do you know what I love most in the world – do you? – Money.

MRS GIBBS: Eat your breakfast.

THE CHILDREN: Mama, there's first bell – I gotta hurry – I don't want any more – I gotta hurry.

[*The* CHILDREN *rise, seize their books and dash out through the trellises. They meet, down centre, and chattering, walk to Main Street, then turn left.*

The STAGE MANAGER *goes off, unobtrusively, right.*]

MRS WEBB: Walk fast, but you don't have to run. Wally, pull up your pants at the knee. Stand up straight, Emily.

MRS GIBBS: Tell Miss Foster I send her my best congratulations – can you remember that?

REBECCA: Yes, Ma.

MRS GIBBS: You look real nice, Rebecca. Pick up your feet.

ALL: Good-bye.

[MRS GIBBS *fills her apron with food for the chickens and comes down to the footlights.*]

MRS GIBBS: Here, chick, chick, chick.

No, go away, you. Go away.

What's the matter with *you*? Fight, fight, fight – that's all you do.

Hm ... *you* don't belong to me. Where'd you come from?

[*She shakes her apron.*]

Oh, don't be so scared. Nobody's going to hurt you.

[MRS WEBB *is sitting on the bench by her trellis, stringing beans.*]

Good morning, Myrtle. How's your cold?

MRS WEBB: Well, I still get that tickling feeling in my throat. I told Charles I didn't know as I'd go to choir practice tonight. Wouldn't be any use.

MRS GIBBS: Have you tried singing over your voice?

MRS WEBB: Yes, but somehow I can't do that and stay on the key. While I'm resting myself I thought I'd string some of these beans.

MRS GIBBS [*rolling up her sleeves as she crosses the stage for a chat*]: Let me help you. Beans have been good this year.

MRS WEBB: I've decided to put up forty quarts if it kills me. The children say they hate 'em, but I notice they're able to get 'em down all winter.

[*Pause. Brief sound of chickens cackling.*]

MRS GIBBS: Now, Myrtle. I've got to tell you something, because if I don't tell somebody I'll burst.

MRS WEBB: Why, Julia Gibbs!

MRS GIBBS: Here, give me some more of those beans. Myrtle, did one of those second-hand-furniture men from Boston come to see you last Friday?

MRS WEBB: No-o.

MRS GIBBS: Well, he called on me. First I thought he was a patient wantin' to see Dr Gibbs. 'N he wormed his way into my parlour, and, Myrtle Webb, he offered me three hundred and fifty dollars for Grandmother Wentworth's highboy, as I'm sitting here!

MRS WEBB: Why, Julia Gibbs!

MRS GIBBS: He did! That old thing! Why, it was so big I didn't know where to put it and I almost give it to Cousin Hester Wilcox.

MRS WEBB: Well, you're going to take it, aren't you?

MRS GIBBS: I don't know.

MRS WEBB: You don't know – three hundred and fifty dollars! What's come over you?

MRS GIBBS: Well, if I could get the Doctor to take the money and go away someplace on a real trip, I'd sell it like that – Y'know, Myrtle, it's been the dream of my life to see Paris, France – Oh, I don't know. It sounds crazy, I suppose, but for years I've been promising myself that if we ever had the chance –

MRS WEBB: How does the Doctor feel about it?

MRS GIBBS: Well, I did beat about the bush a little and said that if I got a legacy – that's the way I put it – I'd make him take me somewhere.

MRS WEBB: M-m-m ... What did he say?

MRS GIBBS: You know how he is. I haven't heard a serious word out of him since I've known him. No, he said, it might make him discontented with Grover's Corners to go traipsin' about Europe; better let well enough alone, he says. Every two years he makes a trip to the battlefields of the

Civil War and that's enough treat for anybody, he says.

MRS WEBB: Well, Mr Webb just *admires* the way Dr Gibbs knows everything about the Civil War. Mr Webb's a good mind to give up Napoleon and move over to the Civil War, only Dr Gibbs being one of the greatest experts in the country just makes him despair.

MRS GIBBS: It's a fact! Dr Gibbs is never so happy as when he's at Antietam or Gettysburg. The times I've walked over those hills, Myrtle, stopping at every bush and pacing it all out, like we were going to buy it.

MRS WEBB: Well, if that second-hand man's really serious about buyin' it, Julia, you sell it. And then you'll get to see Paris, all right. Just keep droppin' hints from time to time – that's how I got to see the Atlantic Ocean, y'know.

MRS GIBBS: Oh, I'm sorry I mentioned it. Only it seems to me that once in your life before you die you ought to see a country where they don't talk in English and don't even want to.

[*The* STAGE MANAGER *enters briskly from the right. He tips his hat to the ladies, who nod their heads.*]

STAGE MANAGER: Thank you, ladies. Thank you very much.

[MRS GIBBS *and* MRS WEBB *gather up their things, return into their homes and disappear.*]

Now we're going to skip a few hours.

But first we want a little more information about the town, kind of a scientific account, you might say.

So I've asked Professor Willard of our State University to sketch in a few details of our past history here.

Is Professor Willard here?

[PROFESSOR WILLARD, *a rural savant, pince-nez on a wide satin ribbon, enters from the right with some notes in his hand.*]

May I introduce Professor Willard of our State University.

A few brief notes, thank you, Professor – unfortunately our time is limited.

PROFESSOR WILLARD: Grover's Corners ... let me see ... Grover's Corners lies on the old Pleistocene granite of the Appalachian range. I may say it's some of the oldest land in the world. We're very proud of that. A shelf of Devonian basalt crosses it with vestiges of Mesozoic shale, and some sandstone outcroppings; but that's all more recent: two hundred, three hundred million years old.

Some highly interesting fossils have been found ... I may say: unique fossils ... two miles out of town, in Silas Peckham's cow pasture. They can be seen at the museum in our University at any time – that is, at any reasonable time. Shall I read some of Professor Gruber's notes on the meteorological situation – mean precipitation, et cetera?

STAGE MANAGER: Afraid we won't have time for that, Professor. We might have a few words on the history of man here.

PROFESSOR WILLARD: Yes ... anthropological data: Early Amerindian stock. Cotahatchee tribes ... no evidence before the tenth century of this era ... hm ... now entirely disappeared ... possible traces in three families. Migration towards the end of the seventeenth century of English brachiocephalic blue-eyed stock ... for the most part. Since then some Slav and Mediterranean –

STAGE MANAGER: And the population, Professor Willard?

PROFESSOR WILLARD: Within the town limits: 2,640.

STAGE MANAGER: Just a moment, Professor.

[*He whispers into the professor's ear.*]

PROFESSOR WILLARD: Oh, yes, indeed? – The population, *at the moment*, is 2,642. The Postal District brings in 507 more, making a total of 3,149 – Mortality and birth rates: constant – By MacPherson's gauge: 6·032.

STAGE MANAGER: Thank you very much, Professor. We're all very much obliged to you, I'm sure.

PROFESSOR WILLARD: Not at all, sir; not at all.

STAGE MANAGER: This way, Professor, and thank you again.

[*Exit* PROFESSOR WILLARD.]

Now the political and social report: Editor Webb – Oh, Mr Webb?

[MRS WEBB *appears at her back door.*]

MRS WEBB: He'll be here in a minute. . . . He just cut his hand while he was eatin' an apple.

STAGE MANAGER: Thank you, Mrs Webb.

MRS WEBB: Charles! Everybody's waitin'.

[*Exit* MRS WEBB.]

STAGE MANAGER: Mr Webb is Publisher and Editor of the Grover's Corners *Sentinel*. That's our local paper, y'know.

[MR WEBB *enters from his house, pulling on his coat. His finger is bound in a handkerchief.*]

MR WEBB: Well . . . I don't have to tell you that we're run here by a Board of Selectmen – All males vote at the age of twenty-one. Women vote indirect. We're lower-middle class: sprinkling of professional men . . . ten per cent illiterate labourers. Politically, we're eighty-six per cent Republicans; six per cent Democrats; four per cent Socialists; rest, indifferent.

Religiously, we're eighty-five per cent Protestants; twelve per cent Catholics; rest indifferent.

STAGE MANAGER: Have you any comments, Mr Webb?

MR WEBB: Very ordinary town, if you ask me. Little better behaved than most. Probably a lot duller.

But our young people here seem to like it well enough. Ninety per cent of 'em graduating from high school settle down right here to live – even when they've been away to college.

STAGE MANAGER: Now, is there anyone in the audience who would like to ask Editor Webb anything about the town?

WOMAN IN THE BALCONY: Is there much drinking in Grover's Corners?

MR WEBB: Well, ma'am, I wouldn't know what you'd call *much*. Satiddy nights the farmhands meet down in Ellery Greenough's stable and holler some. We've got one or two town drunks, but they're always having remorses every time an evangelist comes to town. No, ma'am, I'd say likker ain't a regular thing in the home here, except in the medicine chest. Right good for snake bite, y'know – always was.

BELLIGERENT MAN AT BACK OF AUDITORIUM: Is there no one in town aware of –

STAGE MANAGER: Come forward, will you, where we can all hear you – What were you saying?

BELLIGERENT MAN: Is there no one in town aware of social injustice and industrial inequality?

MR WEBB: Oh, yes, everybody is – somethin' terrible. Seems like they spend most of their time talking about who's rich and who's poor.

BELLIGERENT MAN: Then why don't they do something about it?

[*He withdraws without waiting for an answer.*]

MR WEBB: Well, I dunno. . . . I guess we're all hunting like everybody else for a way the diligent and sensible can rise to the top and the lazy and quarrelsome can sink to the bottom. But it ain't easy to find. Meanwhile, we do all we can to help those that can't help themselves and those that can we leave alone – Are there any other questions?

LADY IN A BOX: Oh, Mr Webb? Mr Webb, is there any culture or love of beauty in Grover's Corners?

MR WEBB: Well, ma'am, there ain't much – not in the sense you mean. Come to think of it, there's some girls that play the piano at High School Commencement; but they ain't happy about it. No, ma'am, there isn't much culture; but maybe this is the place to tell you that we've got a lot of pleasures of a kind here: we like the sun comin' up over the mountain in the morning, and we all notice a good deal about the birds. We pay a lot of attention to them. And we watch the change of the seasons; yes, everybody knows about them. But those other things – you're right, ma'am, – there ain't much – *Robinson Crusoe* and the Bible; and Handel's 'Largo', we all know that; and Whistler's *Mother* – those are just about as far as we go.

LADY IN A BOX: So I thought. Thank you, Mr Webb.

STAGE MANAGER: Thank you, Mr Webb.

[MR WEBB *retires.*]

Now, we'll go back to the town. It's early afternoon. All 2,642 have had their dinners and all the dishes have been washed.

[MR WEBB, *having removed his coat, returns and starts pushing a lawn mower to and fro beside his house.*]

There's an early-afternoon calm in our town: a buzzin' and a hummin' from the school buildings; only a few buggies on Main Street – the horses dozing at the hitching posts; you all remember what it's like. Doc Gibbs is in his office, tapping people and making them say 'ah'. Mr Webb's cuttin' his lawn over there; one man in ten thinks it's a privilege to push his own lawn mower.

No, sir. It's later than I thought. There are the children coming home from school already.

[*Shrill girls' voices are heard, off left.* EMILY *comes along*

36

Main Street, carrying some books. There are some signs that she is imagining herself to be a lady of startling elegance.]

EMILY: I can't Lois. I've got to go home and help my mother. *I promised.*

MR WEBB: Emily, walk simply. Who do you think you are today?

EMILY: Papa, you're terrible. One minute you tell me to stand up straight and the next minute you call me names. I just don't listen to you.

[*She gives him an abrupt kiss.*]

MR WEBB: Golly, I never got a kiss from such a great lady before.

[*He goes out of sight.* EMILY *leans over and picks some flowers by the gate of her house.*

GEORGE GIBBS *comes careening down Main Street. He is throwing a ball up to dizzying heights, and waiting to catch it again. This sometimes requires his taking six steps backwards. He bumps into an Old Lady invisible to us.*]

GEORGE: Excuse me, Mrs Forrest.

STAGE MANAGER [*as Mrs Forrest*]: Go out and play in the fields, young man. You got no business playing baseball on Main Street.

GEORGE: Awfully sorry, Mrs Forrest – Hello, Emily.

EMILY: H'lo.

GEORGE: You made a fine speech in class.

EMILY: Well ... I was really ready to make a speech about the Monroe Doctrine, but at the last minute Miss Corcoran made me talk about the Louisiana Purchase instead. I worked an awful long time on both of them.

GEORGE: Gee, it's funny, Emily. From my window up there I can just see your head nights when you're doing your homework over in your room.

EMILY: Why, can you?

37

GEORGE: You certainly do stick to it, Emily. I don't see how you can sit still that long. I guess you like school.

EMILY: Well, I always feel it's something you have to go through.

GEORGE: Yeah.

EMILY: I don't mind it really. It passes the time.

GEORGE: Yeah – Emily, what do you think? We might work out a kinda telegraph from your window to mine; and once in a while you could give me a kinda hint or two about one of those algebra problems. I don't mean the answers, Emily, of course not . . . just some little hint. . . .

EMILY: Oh, I think *hints* are allowed – So – ah – if you get stuck, George, you whistle to me; and I'll give you some hints.

GEORGE: Emily, you're just naturally bright, I guess.

EMILY: I figure that it's just the way a person's born.

GEORGE: Yeah. But, you see, I want to be a farmer, and my Uncle Luke says whenever I'm ready I can come over and work on his farm and if I'm any good I can just gradually have it.

EMILY: You mean the house and everything?

   [*Enter* MRS WEBB *with a large bowl and sits on the bench by her trellis.*]

GEORGE: Yeah. Well, thanks . . . I better be getting out to the baseball field. Thanks for the talk, Emily – Good afternoon, Mrs Webb.

MRS WEBB: Good afternoon, George.

GEORGE: So long, Emily.

EMILY: So long, George.

MRS WEBB: Emily, come and help me string these beans for the winter. George Gibbs let himself have a real conversation, didn't he? Why, he's growing up. How old would George be?

EMILY: I don't know.

MRS WEBB: Let's see. He must be almost sixteen.

EMILY: Mama, I made a speech in class today and I was very good.

MRS WEBB: You must recite it to your father at supper. What was it about?

EMILY: The Louisiana Purchase. It was like silk off a spool. I'm going to make speeches all my life – Mama, are these big enough?

MRS WEBB: Try and get them a little bigger if you can.

EMILY: Mama, will you answer me a question, serious?

MRS WEBB: Seriously, dear – not serious.

EMILY: Seriously – will you?

MRS WEBB: Of course, I will.

EMILY: Mama, am I good-looking?

MRS WEBB: Yes, of course you are. All my children have got good features; I'd be ashamed if they hadn't.

EMILY: Oh, Mama, that's not what I mean. What I mean is: am I *pretty*?

MRS WEBB: I've already told you, yes. Now that's enough of that. You have a nice young pretty face. I never heard of such foolishness.

EMILY: Oh, Mama, you never tell us the truth about anything.

MRS WEBB: I *am* telling you the truth.

EMILY: Mama, were *you* pretty?

MRS WEBB: Yes, I was, if I do say it. I was the prettiest girl in town next to Mamie Cartwright.

EMILY: But, Mama, you've got to say *something* about me. Am I pretty enough ... to get anybody ... to get people interested in me?

MRS WEBB: Emily, you make me tired. Now stop it. You're pretty enough for all normal purposes – Come along now and bring that bowl with you.

EMILY: Oh, Mama, you're no help at all.

STAGE MANAGER: Thank you. Thank you! That'll do. We'll have to interrupt again here. Thank you, Mrs Webb; thank you, Emily.

[MRS WEBB *and* EMILY *withdraw*.]

There are some more things we want to explore about this town.

[*He comes to the centre of the stage. During the following speech the lights gradually dim to darkness, leaving only a spot on him.*]

I think this is a good time to tell you that the Cartwright interests have just begun building a new bank in Grover's Corners – had to go to Vermont for the marble, sorry to say. And they've asked a friend of mine what they should put in the cornerstone for people to dig up . . . a thousand years from now. . . . Of course, they've put in a copy of the *New York Times* and a copy of Mr Webb's *Sentinel*. . . . We're kind of interested in this because some scientific fellas have found a way of painting all that reading matter with a glue – a silicate glue – that'll make it keep a thousand – two thousand years.

We're putting in a Bible . . . and the Constitution of the United States – and a copy of William Shakespeare's plays. What do you say, folks? What do you think?

Y'know – Babylon once had two million people in it, and all we know about 'em is the names of the kings and some copies of wheat contracts . . . and contracts for the sale of slaves. Yet every night all those families sat down to supper, and the father came home from his work, and the smoke went up the chimney – same as here. And even in Greece and Rome, all we know about the *real* life of the people is what we can piece together out of the joking poems and the comedies they wrote for the theatre back then.

So I'm going to have a copy of this play put in the cornerstone and the people a thousand years from now'll know a few simple facts about us – more than the Treaty of Versailles and the Lindbergh flight.

See what I mean?

So – people a thousand years from now – this is the way we were in the provinces north of New York at the beginning of the twentieth century – This is the way we were: in our growing up and in our marrying and in our living and in our dying.

[*A choir partially concealed in the orchestra pit has begun singing 'Blessed Be the Tie That Binds'.*

SIMON STIMSON *stands directing them.*

Two ladders have been pushed on to the stage; they serve as indication of the first storey in the Gibbs and Webb houses.

GEORGE *and* EMILY *mount them, and apply themselves to their schoolwork.*

DR GIBBS *has entered and is seated in his kitchen reading.*]

Well! – good deal of time's gone by. It's evening.

You can hear choir practice going on in the Congregational Church.

The children are at home doing their schoolwork.

The day's running down like a tired clock.

SIMON STIMSON: Now look here, everybody. Music come into the world to give pleasure – Softer! Softer! Get it out of your heads that music's only good when it's loud. You leave loudness to the Methodists. You couldn't beat 'em, even if you wanted to. Now again. Tenors!

GEORGE: Hsst! Emily!

EMILY: Hello.

GEORGE: Hello!

EMILY: I can't work at all. The moonlight's so *terrible*.

GEORGE: Emily, did you get the third problem?

EMILY: Which?

GEORGE: The *third*?

EMILY: Why, yes, George – that's the easiest of them all.

GEORGE: I don't see it. Emily, can you give me a hint?

EMILY: I'll tell you one thing: the answer's in yards.

GEORGE: !!! In yards? How do you mean?

EMILY: In *square* yards.

GEORGE: Oh ... in square yards.

EMILY: Yes, George, don't you see?

GEORGE: Yeah.

EMILY: in square yards of *wallpaper*.

GEORGE: Wallpaper – oh, I see. Thanks a lot, Emily.

EMILY: You're welcome. My, isn't the moonlight *terrible*? And choir practice going on – I think if you hold your breath you can hear the train all the way to Contoocook. Hear it?

GEORGE: M-m-m – What do you know!

EMILY: Well, I guess I better go back and try to work.

GEORGE: Good night, Emily. And thanks.

EMILY: Good night, George.

SIMON STIMSON: Before I forget it: how many of you will be able to come in Tuesday afternoon and sing at Fred Hersey's wedding? – show your hands. That'll be fine; that'll be right nice. We'll do the same music we did for Jane Trowbridge's last month.

Now we'll do: 'Art Thou Weary; Art Thou Languid?' It's a question, ladies and gentlemen, make it talk. Ready.

DR GIBBS: Oh, George, can you come down a minute?

GEORGE: Yes, Pa.

[*He descends the ladder.*]

DR GIBBS: Make yourself comfortable, George; I'll only keep you a minute. George, how old are you?

GEORGE: I? I'm sixteen, almost seventeen.

DR GIBBS: What do you want to do after school's over?

GEORGE: Why, you know, Pa. I want to be a farmer on Uncle Luke's farm.

DR GIBBS: You'll be willing, will you, to get up early and milk and feed the stock ... and you'll be able to hoe and hay all day?

GEORGE: Sure, I will. What are you ... what do you mean, Pa?

DR GIBBS: Well, George, while I was in my office today I heard a funny sound ... and what do you think it was? It was your mother chopping wood. There you see your mother – getting up early; cooking meals all day long; washing and ironing – and still she has to go out in the back yard and chop wood. I suppose she just got tired of asking you. She just gave up and decided it was easier to do it herself. And you eat her meals, and put on the clothes she keeps nice for you, and you run off and play baseball – like she's some hired girl we keep around the house but that we don't like very much. Well, I knew all I had to do was call your attention to it. Here's a handkerchief, son. George, I've decided to raise your spending money twenty-five cents a week. Not, of course, for chopping wood for your mother, because that's a present you give her, but because you're getting older – and I imagine there are lots of things you must find to do with it.

GEORGE: Thanks, Pa.

DR GIBBS: Let's see – tomorrow's your payday. You can count on it – Hmm. Probably Rebecca'll feel she ought to have some more too. Wonder what could have happened to your mother. Choir practice never was as late as this before.

GEORGE: It's only half past eight, Pa.

DR GIBBS: I don't know why she's in that old choir. She

hasn't any more voice than an old crow. ... Traipsin'
around the streets at this hour of the night. ... Just about
time you retired, don't you think?

GEORGE: Yes, Pa.

[GEORGE *mounts to his place on the ladder.*

*Laughter and good nights can be heard on stage left and
presently* MRS GIBBS, MRS SOAMES, *and* MRS WEBB *come
down Main Street. When they arrive at the corner of the stage
they stop.*]

MRS SOAMES: Good night, Martha. Good night, Mr Foster.

MRS WEBB: I'll tell Mr Webb; I *know* he'll want to put it in
the paper.

MRS GIBBS: My, it's late!

MRS SOAMES: Good night, Irma.

MRS GIBBS: Real nice choir practice, wa'n't it? Myrtle Webb!
Look at that moon, will you! Tsk-tsk-tsk. Potato weather,
for sure.

[*They are silent a moment, gazing up at the moon.*]

MRS SOAMES: Naturally I didn't want to say a word about it
in front of those others, but now we're alone – really, it's
the worst scandal that ever was in this town!

MRS GIBBS: What?

MRS SOAMES: Simon Stimson!

MRS GIBBS: Now, Louella!

MRS SOAMES: But, Julia! To have the organist of a church
drink and *drunk* year after year. You know he was drunk
tonight.

MRS GIBBS: Now, Louella! We all know about Mr Stimson,
and we all know about the troubles he's been through, and
Dr Ferguson knows too, and if Dr Ferguson keeps him on
there in his job the only thing the rest of us can do is just
not to notice it.

MRS SOAMES: *Not to notice it!* But it's getting worse.

44

MRS WEBB: No, it isn't, Louella. It's getting better. I've been in that choir twice as long as you have. It doesn't happen anywhere near so often. . . . My, I hate to go to bed on a night like this – I better hurry. Those children'll be sitting up all hours. Good night, Louella.

[*They all exchanged good nights. She hurries downstage, enters her house and disappears.*]

MRS GIBBS: Can you get home safe, Louella?

MRS SOAMES: It's as bright as day. I can see Mr Soames scowling at the window now. You'd think we'd been to a dance the way the menfolk carry on.

[*More good nights.* MRS GIBBS *arrives at her home and passes through the trellis into the kitchen.*]

MRS GIBBS: Well, we had a real good time.

DR GIBBS: You're late enough.

MRS GIBBS: Why, Frank, it ain't any later 'n usual.

DR GIBBS: And you stopping at the corner to gossip with a lot of hens.

MRS GIBBS: Now, Frank, don't be grouchy. Come out and smell the heliotrope in the moonlight.

[*They stroll out arm in arm along the footlights.*]

Isn't that wonderful? What did you do all the time I was away?

DR GIBBS: Oh, I read – as usual. What were the girls gossiping about tonight?

MRS GIBBS: Well, believe me, Frank – there is something to gossip about.

DR GIBBS: Hmm! Simon Stimson far gone, was he?

MRS GIBBS: Worst I've ever seen him. How'll that end, Frank? Dr Ferguson can't forgive him forever.

DR GIBBS: I guess I know more about Simon Stimson's affairs than anybody in this town. Some people ain't made for small-town life. I don't know how that'll end; but there's nothing we can do but just leave it alone. Come, get in.

MRS GIBBS: No, not yet ... Frank, I'm worried about you.

DR GIBBS: What are you worried about?

MRS GIBBS: I think it's my duty to make plans for you to get a real rest and change. And if I get that legacy, well, I'm going to insist on it.

DR GIBBS: Now, Julia, there's no sense in going over that again.

MRS GIBBS: Frank, you're just *unreasonable*!

DR GIBBS [*starting into the house*]: Come on, Julia, it's getting late. First thing you know you'll catch cold. I gave George a piece of my mind tonight. I reckon you'll have your wood chopped for a while anyway. No, no, start getting upstairs.

MRS GIBBS: Oh, dear. There's always so many things to pick up, seems like. You know, Frank, Mrs Fairchild always locks her front door every night. All those people up that part of town do.

DR GIBBS [*blowing out the lamp*]: They're all getting citified, that's the trouble with them. They haven't got nothing fit to burgle and everybody knows it.

[*They disappear.*

REBECCA *climbs up the ladder beside George.*]

GEORGE: Get out, Rebecca. There's only room for one at this window. You're always spoiling everything.

REBECCA: Well, let me look just a minute.

GEORGE: Use your own window.

REBECCA: I did, but there's no moon there. ... George, do you know what I think, do you? I think maybe the moon's getting nearer and nearer and there'll be a big 'splosion.

GEORGE: Rebecca, you don't know anything. If the moon

46

were getting nearer, the guys that sit up all night with telescopes would see it first and they'd tell about it, and it'd be in all the newspapers.

REBECCA: George, is the moon shining on South America, Canada, and half the whole world?

GEORGE: Well – prob'ly is.

[*The* STAGE MANAGER *strolls on.*
Pause. The sound of crickets is heard.]

STAGE MANAGER: Nine-thirty. Most of the lights are out. No, there's Constable Warren trying a few doors on Main Street. And here comes Editor Webb, after putting his newspaper to bed.

[MR WARREN, *an elderly policeman, comes along Main Street from the right,* MR WEBB *from the left.*]

MR WEBB: Good evening, Bill.

CONSTABLE WARREN: Evenin', Mr Webb.

MR WEBB: Quite a moon!

CONSTABLE WARREN: Yepp.

MR WEBB: All quiet tonight?

CONSTABLE WARREN: Simon Stimson is rollin' around a little. Just saw his wife movin' out to hunt for him so I looked the other way – there he is now.

[SIMON STIMSON *comes down Main Street from the left, only a trace of unsteadiness in his walk.*]

MR WEBB: Good evening, Simon ... Town seems to have settled down for the night pretty well. ...

[SIMON STIMSON *comes up to him and pauses a moment and stares at him, swaying slightly.*]

Good evening ... Yes, most of the town's settled down for the night, Simon. .... I guess we better do the same. Can I walk along a ways with you?

[SIMON STIMSON *continues on his way without a word and disappears at the right.*]

CONSTABLE WARREN: I don't know how that's goin' to end, Mr Webb.

MR WEBB: Well, he's seen a peck of trouble, one thing after another. ... Oh, Bill ... if you see my boy smoking cigarettes, just give him a word, will you? He thinks a lot of you, Bill.

CONSTABLE WARREN: I don't think he smokes no cigarettes, Mr Webb. Leastways, not more'n two or three a year.

MR WEBB: Hm ... I hope not – Well, good night, Bill.

CONSTABLE WARREN: Good night, Mr Webb.

[*Exit.*]

MR WEBB: Who's that up there? Is that you, Myrtle?

EMILY: No, it's me, Papa.

MR WEBB: Why aren't you in bed?

EMILY: I don't know. I just can't sleep yet, Papa. The moonlight's so *won*-derful. And the smell of Mrs Gibbs's heliotrope. Can you smell it?

MR WEBB: Hm ... Yes. Haven't any troubles on your mind, have you, Emily?

EMILY: *Troubles*, Papa? *No.*

MR WEBB: Well, enjoy yourself, but don't let your mother catch you. Good night, Emily.

EMILY: Good night, Papa.

[MR WEBB *crosses into the house, whistling 'Blessed Be the Tie That Binds' and disappears.*]

REBECCA: I never told you about that letter Jane Crofut got from her minister when she was sick. He wrote Jane a letter and on the envelope the address was like this: It said: Jane Crofut; The Crofut Farm; Grover's Corners; Sutton County; New Hampshire; United States of America.

GEORGE: What's funny about that?

REBECCA: But listen, it's not finished: the United States of America; Continent of North America; Western Hemisphere; the Earth; the Solar System; the Universe; the Mind of God – that's what it said on the envelope.

GEORGE: What do you know!

REBECCA: And the postman brought it just the same.

GEORGE: What do you know!

STAGE MANAGER: That's the end of the First Act, friends. You can go and smoke now, those that smoke.

ACT TWO

The tables and chairs of the two kitchens are still on the stage.
The ladders and the small bench have been withdrawn.
The STAGE MANAGER *has been at his accustomed place watching the audience return to its seats.*

STAGE MANAGER: Three years have gone by.

Yes, the sun's come up over a thousand times.

Summers and winters have cracked the mountains a little bit more and the rains have brought down some of the dirt.

Some babies that weren't even born before have begun talking regular sentences already; and a number of people who thought they were right young and spry have noticed that they can't bound up a flight of stairs like they used to, without their heart fluttering a little.

All that can happen in a thousand days.

Nature's been pushing and contriving in other ways, too: a number of young people fell in love and got married.

Yes, the mountain got bit away a few fractions of an inch; millions of gallons of water went by the mill; and here and there a new home was set up under a roof.

Almost everybody in the world gets married – you know what I mean? In our town there aren't hardly any exceptions. Most everybody in the world climbs into their graves married.

The First Act was called the Daily Life. This act is called Love and Marriage. There's another act coming after this: I reckon you can guess what that's about.

So:

It's three years later. It's 1904.

ACT TWO

It's 7 July, just after High School Commencement.

That's the time most of our young people jump up and get married.

Soon as they've passed their last examinations in solid geometry and Cicero's *Orations*, looks like they suddenly feel themselves fit to be married.

It's early morning. Only this time it's been raining. It's been pouring and thundering.

Mrs Gibbs's garden, and Mrs Webb's here: drenched.

All those bean poles and pea vines: drenched.

All yesterday over there on Main Street, the rain looked like curtains being blown along.

Hm . . . it may begin again any minute.

There! You can hear the 5.45 for Boston.

[MRS GIBBS *and* MRS WEBB *enter their kitchen and start the day as in the First Act.*]

And there's Mrs Gibbs and Mrs Webb come down to make breakfast, just as though it were an ordinary day. I don't have to point out to the women in my audience that those ladies they see before them, both of those ladies cooked three meals a day – one of 'em for twenty years, the other for forty – and no summer vacation. They brought up two children a piece, washed, cleaned the house – and *never a nervous breakdown.*

It's like what one of those Middle West poets said: You've got to love life to have life, and you've got to have life to love life. . . .

It's what they call a vicious circle.

HOWIE NEWSOME [*off stage left*]: Giddap, Bessie!

STAGE MANAGER: Here comes Howie Newsome delivering the milk. And there's Si Crowell delivering the papers like his brother before him.

[SI CROWELL *has entered hurling imaginary newspapers into*

51

doorways; HOWIE NEWSOME *has come along Main Street with Bessie.*]

SI CROWELL: Morning Howie.

HOWIE NEWSOME: Morning, Si – Anything in the papers I ought to know?

SI CROWELL: Nothing much, except we're losing about the best baseball pitcher Grover's Corners ever had – George Gibbs.

HOWIE NEWSOME: Reckon he is.

SI CROWELL: He could hit and run bases, too.

HOWIE NEWSOME: Yep. Mighty fine ball player – Whoa! Bessie! I guess I can stop and talk if I've a mind to!

SI CROWELL: I don't see how he could give up a thing like that just to get married. Would you, Howie?

HOWIE NEWSOME: Can't tell, Si. Never had no talent that way.

[CONSTABLE WARREN *enters. They exchange good mornings.*]

You're up early, Bill.

CONSTABLE WARREN: Seein' if there's anything I can do to prevent a flood. River's been risin' all night.

HOWIE NEWSOME: Si Crowell's all worked up here about George Gibbs retiring from baseball.

CONSTABLE WARREN: Yes, sir; that's the way it goes. Back in '84 we had a player Si – even George Gibbs couldn't touch him. Name of Hank Todd. Went down to Maine and become a parson. Wonderful ball player – Howie, how does the weather look to you?

HOWIE NEWSOME: Oh, 'tain't bad. Think maybe it'll clear up for good.

[CONSTABLE WARREN and SI CROWELL *continue on their way.*

HOWIE NEWSOME *brings the milk first to Mrs Gibbs's house.   She meets him by the trellis.*]

MRS GIBBS: Good morning Howie. Do you think it's going to rain again?

HOWIE NEWSOME: Morning, Mrs Gibbs. It rained so heavy, I think maybe it'll clear up.

MRS GIBBS: Certainly hope it will.

HOWIE NEWSOME: How much did you want today?

MRS GIBBS: I'm going to have a houseful of relations, Howie. Looks to me like I'll need three-a-milk and two-a-cream.

HOWIE NEWSOME: My wife says to tell you we both hope they'll be very happy, Mrs Gibbs. Know they *will*.

MRS GIBBS: Thanks a lot, Howie. Tell your wife I hope she gits there to the wedding.

HOWIE NEWSOME: Yes, she'll be there; she'll be there if she kin.

[HOWIE NEWSOME *crosses to Mrs Webb's house.*]
Morning, Mrs Webb.

MRS WEBB: Oh, good morning, Mr Newsome. I told you four quarts of milk, but I hope you can spare me another.

HOWIE NEWSOME: Yes'm . . . and the two of cream.

MRS WEBB: Will it start raining again, Mr Newsome?

HOWIE NEWSOME: Well. Just sayin' to Mrs Gibbs as how it may lighten up. Mrs Newsome told me to tell you as how we hope they'll both be very happy, Mrs Webb. Know they *will*.

MRS WEBB: Thank you, and thank Mrs Newsome and we're counting on seeing you at the wedding.

HOWIE NEWSOME: Yes, Mrs Webb. We hope to git there. Couldn't miss that. Come on, Bessie.

[*Exit* HOWIE NEWSOME.
DR GIBBS *descends in shirt sleeves, and sits down at his break-fast table.*]

DR GIBBS: Well, Ma, the day has come. You're losin' one of your chicks.

MRS GIBBS: Frank Gibbs, don't you say another word. I feel like crying every minute. Sit down and drink your coffee.

DR GIBBS: The groom's up shaving himself – only there ain't an awful lot to shave. Whistling and singing, like he's glad to leave us – Every now and then he says 'I do' to the mirror, but it don't sound convincing to me.

MRS GIBBS: I declare, Frank, I don't know how he'll get along. I've arranged his clothes and seen to it he's put warm things on – Frank! they're too *young*. Emily won't think of such things. He'll catch his death of cold within a week.

DR GIBBS: I was remembering my wedding morning, Julia.

MRS GIBBS: Now don't start that, Frank Gibbs.

DR GIBBS: I was the scaredest young fella in the State of New Hampshire. I thought I'd make a mistake for sure. And when I saw you comin' down that aisle I thought you were the prettiest girl I'd ever seen, but the only trouble was that I'd never seen you before. There I was in the Congregational Church marryin' a total stranger.

MRS GIBBS: And how do you think I felt! – Frank, weddings are perfectly awful things. Farces – that's what they are!

[*She puts a plate before him.*]

Here, I've made something for you.

DR GIBBS: Why, Julia Hersey – French toast!

MRS GIBBS: 'Tain't hard to make and I had to do *something*.

[*Pause.* DR GIBBS *pours on the syrup.*]

DR GIBBS: How'd you sleep last night, Julia?

MRS GIBBS: Well, I heard a lot of the hours struck off.

DR GIBBS: Ye-e-s! I get a shock every time I think of George setting out to be a family man – that great gangling thing!

– I tell you Julia, there's nothing so terrifying in the world as a *son*. The relation of father and son is the darndest, awkwardest –

MRS GIBBS: Well, mother and daughter's no picnic, let me tell you.

DR GIBBS: They'll have a lot of troubles, I suppose, but that's none of our business. Everybody has a right to their own troubles.

MRS GIBBS [*at the table, drinking her coffee, meditatively*]: Yes . . . people are meant to go through life two by two. 'Tain't natural to be lonesome.

[*Pause.* DR GIBBS *starts laughing.*]

DR GIBBS: Julia, do you know one of the things I was scared of when I married you?

MRS GIBBS: Oh, go along with you!

DR GIBBS: I was afraid we wouldn't have material for conversation more'n'd last us a few weeks.

[*Both laugh.*]

I was afraid we'd run out and eat our meals in silence, that's a fact – Well, you and I been conversing for twenty years now without any noticeable barren spells.

MRS GIBBS: Well – good weather, bad weather – 'tain't very choice, but I always find something to say.

[*She goes to the foot of the stairs.*]

Did you hear Rebecca stirring around upstairs?

DR GIBBS: No. Only day of the year Rebecca hasn't been managing everybody's business up there. She's hiding in her room – I got the impression she's crying.

MRS GIBBS: Lord's sakes! – This has got to stop – Rebecca! Rebecca! Come and get your breakfast.

[GEORGE *comes rattling down the stairs, very brisk.*]

GEORGE: Good morning, everybody. Only five more hours to live.

[*Makes the gesture of cutting his throat, and a loud 'k-k-k',
and starts through the trellis.*]

MRS GIBBS: George Gibbs, where are you going?

GEORGE: Just stepping across the grass to see my girl.

MRS GIBBS: Now, George! You put on your overshoes. It's
raining torrents. You don't go out of this house without
you're prepared for it.

GEORGE: Aw, Ma. It's just a *step*!

MRS GIBBS: George! You'll catch your death of cold and
cough all through the service.

DR GIBBS: George, do as your mother tells you!

[DR GIBBS *goes upstairs.*

GEORGE *returns reluctantly to the kitchen and pantomimes
putting on overshoes.*]

MRS GIBBS: From tomorrow on you can kill yourself in
all weathers, but while you're in my house you'll live
wisely, thank you – Maybe Mrs Webb isn't used to callers
at seven in the morning – Here, take a cup of coffee
first.

GEORGE: Be back in a minute.

[*He crosses the stage, leaping over the puddles.*]
Good morning, Mother Webb.

MRS WEBB: Goodness! You frightened me! – Now, George,
you can come in a minute out of the wet, but you know I
can't ask you in.

GEORGE: Why not – ?

MRS WEBB: George, you know's well as I do: the groom can't
see his bride on his wedding day, not until he sees her in
church.

GEORGE: Aw! – that's just a superstition – Good morning, Mr
Webb.

[*Enter* MR WEBB.]

MR WEBB: Good morning, George.

GEORGE: Mr Webb, you don't believe in that superstition, do you?

MR WEBB: There's a lot of common sense in some superstitions George.

[*He sits at the table, facing right.*]

MRS WEBB: Millions have folla'd it, George, and you don't want to be the first to fly in the face of custom.

GEORGE: How is Emily?

MRS WEBB: She hasn't waked up yet. I haven't heard a sound out of her.

GEORGE: Emily's *asleep*!!!

MRS WEBB: No wonder! We were up 'til all hours, sewing and packing. Now I'll tell you what I'll do; you set down here a minute with Mr Webb and drink this cup of coffee; and I'll go upstairs and see she doesn't come down and surprise you. There's some bacon, too; but don't be long about it.

[*Exit* MRS WEBB.

Embarrassed silence.

MR WEBB *dunks doughnuts in his coffee.*

More silence.]

MR WEBB [*suddenly and loudly*]: Well, George, how are you?

GEORGE [*startled, choking over his coffee*]: Oh, fine, I'm fine.

[*Pause.*]

Mr Webb, what sense could there be in a superstition like that?

MR WEBB: Well, you see – on her wedding morning a girl's head's apt to be full of ... clothes and one thing and another. Don't you think that's probably it?

GEORGE: Ye-e-s. I never thought of that.

MR WEBB: A girl's apt to be a mite nervous on her wedding day.

[*Pause.*]

GEORGE: I wish a fellow could get married without all that marching up and down.

MR WEBB: Every man that's ever lived has felt that way about it, George; but it hasn't been any use. It's the womenfolk who've built up weddings, my boy. For a while now the women have it all their own. A man looks pretty small at a wedding, George. All those good women standing shoulder to shoulder making sure that the knot's tied in a mighty public way.

GEORGE: But . . . you *believe* in it, don't you, Mr Webb?

MR WEBB [*with alacrity*]: Oh, yes; *oh, yes*. Don't you misunderstand me, my boy. Marriage is a wonderful thing – wonderful thing. And don't you forget that, George.

GEORGE: No, sir – Mr Webb, how old were you when you got married?

MR WEBB: Well, you see: I'd been to college and I'd taken a little time to get settled. But Mrs Webb – she wasn't much older than what Emily is. Oh, age hasn't much to do with it, George – not compared with . . . uh . . . other things.

GEORGE: What were you going to say, Mr Webb?

MR WEBB: Oh, I don't know – Was I going to say something?
   [*Pause.*]
   George, I was thinking the other night of some advice my father gave me when I got married. Charles, he said, Charles start out early showing who's boss, he said. Best thing to do is to give an order, even if it don't make sense; just so she'll learn to obey. And he said: if anything about your wife irritates you – her conversation, or anything – just get up and leave the house. That'll make it clear to her, he said. And, oh, yes! he said never, *never* let your wife know how much money you have, never.

GEORGE: Well, Mr Webb . . . I don't think I could . . .

MR WEBB: So I took the opposite of my father's advice and

I've been happy ever since. And let that be a lesson to you, George, never to ask advice on personal matters – George, are you going to raise chickens on your farm?

GEORGE: What?

MR WEBB: Are you going to raise chickens on your farm?

GEORGE: Uncle Luke's never been much interested, but I thought –

MR WEBB: A book came into my office the other day, George, on the Philo System of raising chickens. I want you to read it. I'm thinking of beginning in a small way in the back yard, and I'm going to put an incubator in the cellar –

[*Enter* MRS WEBB.]

MRS WEBB: Charles, are you talking about that old incubator again? I thought you two'd be talking about things worth while.

MR WEBB [*bitingly*]: Well, Myrtle, if you want to give the boy some good advice, I'll go upstairs and leave you alone with him.

MRS WEBB [*pulling* GEORGE *up*]: George, Emily's got to come downstairs and eat her breakfast. She sends you her love but she doesn't want to lay eyes on you. Good-bye.

GEORGE: Good-bye.

[GEORGE *crosses the stage to his own home, bewildered and crestfallen. He slowly dodges a puddle and disappears into his house.*]

MR WEBB: Myrtle, I guess you don't know about that older superstition.

MRS WEBB: What do you mean, Charles?

MR WEBB: Since the cave men: no bridegroom should see his father-in-law on the day of the wedding, or near it. Now remember that.

[*Both leave the stage.*]

STAGE MANAGER: Thank you very much, Mr and Mrs Webb

– Now I have to interrupt again here. You see, we want to know how all this began – this wedding, this plan to spend a lifetime together. I'm awfully interested in how big things like that begin.

You know how it is: you're twenty-one or twenty-two and you make some decisions; then whisssh! you're seventy: you've been a lawyer for fifty years, and that white-haired lady at your side has eaten over fifty thousand meals with you.

How do such things begin?

George and Emily are going to show you now the conversation they had when they first knew that . . . that . . . as the saying goes . . . they were meant for one another.

But before they do it I want you to try and remember what it was like to have been very young.

And particularly the days when you were first in love; when you were like a person sleepwalking, and you didn't quite see the street you were in, and didn't quite hear everything that was said to you.

You're just a little bit crazy. Will you remember that, please?

Now they'll be coming out of high school at three o'clock. George has just been elected President of the Junior Class, and as it's June, that means he'll be President of the Senior Class all next year. And Emily's just been elected Secretary and Treasurer.

I don't have to tell you how important that is.

[*He places a board across the backs of two chairs, which he takes from those at the Gibbs family's table. He brings two high stools from the wings and places them behind the board. Persons sitting on the stools will be facing the audience. This is the counter of Mr Morgan's drugstore. The sounds of young voices are heard off left.*]

60

Yepp – there they are coming down Main Street now.
[EMILY, *carrying an armful of – imaginary – schoolbooks,
comes along Main Street from the left.*]

EMILY: I can't, Louise. I've got to go home. Good-bye. Oh,
Ernestine! Ernestine! Can you come over tonight and do
Latin? Isn't that Cicero the worst thing – ! Tell your
mother you *have* to. G'by. G'by, Helen. G'by, Fred.
[GEORGE, *also carrying books, catches up with her.*]

GEORGE: Can I carry your books home for you, Emily?

EMILY [*coolly*]: Why . . . uh . . . Thank you. It isn't far.
[*She gives them to him.*]

GEORGE: Excuse me a minute, Emily – Say, Bob, if I'm a little
late, start practice anyway. And give Herb some long high
ones.

EMILY: Good-bye, Lizzy.

GEORGE: Good-bye, Lizzy – I'm awfully glad you were
elected, too, Emily.

EMILY: Thank you.
[*They have been standing on Main Street, almost against the
back wall. They take the first steps towards the audience when
GEORGE stops and speaks.*]

GEORGE: Emily, why are you mad at me?

EMILY: I'm not mad at you.

GEORGE: You've been treating me so funny lately.

EMILY: Well, since you ask me, I might as well say it right out,
George –
[*She catches sight of a teacher passing.*]
Good-bye, Miss Corcoran.

GEORGE: Good-bye, Miss Corcoran – Wha – what is it?

EMILY [*not scoldingly; finding it difficult to say*]: I don't like the
whole change that's come over you in the last year. I'm
sorry if that hurts your feelings, but I've got to – tell the
truth and shame the devil.

GEORGE: A *change*? – Wha – what do you mean?

EMILY: Well, up to a year ago I used to like you a lot. And I used to watch you as you did everything . . . because we'd been friends so long . . . and then you began spending all your time at *baseball* . . . and you never stopped to speak to anybody any more. Not even to your own family you didn't . . . and, George, it's a fact, you've got awful conceited and stuck-up, and all the girls say so. They may not say so to your face, but that's what they say about you behind your back, and it hurts me to hear them say it, but I've got to agree with them a little. I'm sorry if it hurts your feelings . . . but I can't be sorry I said it.

GEORGE: I . . . I'm glad you said it, Emily. I never thought that such a thing was happening to me. I guess it's hard for a fella not to have faults creep into his character.

[*They take a step or two in silence, then stand still in misery.*]

EMILY: I always expect a man to be perfect and I think he should be.

GEORGE: Oh . . . I don't think it's possible to be perfect, Emily.

EMILY: Well, my *father* is, and as far as I can see *your* father is. There's no reason on earth why you shouldn't be, too.

GEORGE: Well, I feel it's the other way round. That men aren't naturally good; but girls are.

EMILY: Well, you might as well know right now that I'm not perfect. It's not as easy for a girl to be perfect as a man, because we girls are more – more – nervous – Now I'm sorry I said all that about you. I don't know what made me say it.

GEORGE: Emily –

EMILY: Now I can see it's not the truth at all. And I suddenly feel that it isn't important, anyway.

GEORGE: Emily ... would you like an ice-cream soda, or something, before you go home?

EMILY: Well, thank you. ... I would.

[*They advance towards the audience and make an abrupt right turn, opening the door of Morgan's drugstore. Under strong emotion,* EMILY *keeps her face down.* GEORGE *speaks to some passers-by.*]

GEORGE: Hello, Stew – how are you? – Good afternoon, Mrs Slocum.

[*The* STAGE MANAGER, *wearing spectacles and assuming the role of Mr Morgan, enters abruptly from the right and stands between the audience and the counter of his soda fountain.*]

STAGE MANAGER: Hello, George. Hello, Emily – What'll you have? – Why, Emily Webb – what you been crying about?

GEORGE [*he gropes for an explanation*]: She ... she just got an awful scare, Mr Morgan. She almost got run over by that hardware-store wagon. Everybody says that Tom Huckins drives like a crazy man.

STAGE MANAGER [*drawing a drink of water*]: Well, now! You take a drink of water, Emily. You look all shook up. I tell you, you've got to look both ways before you cross Main Street these days. Gets worse every year – What'll you have?

EMILY: I'll have a strawberry phosphate, thank you, Mr Morgan.

GEORGE: No, no, Emily. Have an ice-cream soda with me. Two strawberry ice-cream sodas, Mr Morgan.

STAGE MANAGER [*working the faucets*]: Two strawberry ice-cream sodas, yes sir. Yes, sir. There are a hundred and twenty-five horses in Grover's Corners this minute I'm talking to you. State Inspector was in here yesterday. And now they're bringing in these auto-mo-biles, the best thing to do is to just stay home. Why, I can remember when a dog could go to sleep all day in the middle of Main Street and nothing come along to disturb him.

[*He sets the imaginary glasses before them.*]

There they are. Enjoy 'em.

[*He sees a customer, right.*]

Yes, Mrs Ellis. What can I do for you?

[*He goes out right.*]

EMILY: They're so expensive.

GEORGE: No, no – don't think of that. We're celebrating our election. And then do you know what else I'm celebrating?

EMILY: N-no.

GEORGE: I'm celebrating because I've got a friend who tells me all the things that ought to be told me.

EMILY: George, *please* don't think of that. I don't know why I said it. It's not true. You're –

GEORGE: No, Emily, you stick to it. I'm glad you spoke to me like you did. But you'll *see*: I'm going to change so quick – you bet I'm going to change. And, Emily, I want to ask you a favour.

EMILY: What?

GEORGE: Emily, if I go away to State Agriculture College next year, will you write me a letter once in a while?

EMILY: I certainly will. I certainly will, George . . .

[*Pause. They start sipping the sodas through the straws.*]

It certainly seems like being away three years you'd get out of touch with things. Maybe letters from Grover's Corners wouldn't be so interesting after a while. Grover's Corners isn't a very important place when you think of all – New Hampshire; but I think it's a very nice town.

GEORGE: The day wouldn't come when I wouldn't want to know everything that's happening here. I know *that's* true, Emily.

EMILY: Well, I'll try to make my letters interesting.

64

[*Pause.*]

GEORGE: Y'know. Emily, whenever I meet a farmer I ask him if he thinks it's important to go to Agriculture School to be a good farmer.

EMILY: Why, George –

GEORGE: Yeah, and some of them say that it's even a waste of time. You can get all those things, anyway, out of the pamphlets the government sends out. And Uncle Luke's getting old – he's about ready for me to start in taking over his farm tomorrow, if I could.

EMILY: My!

GEORGE: And, like you say, being gone all that time ... in other places and meeting other people. ... Gosh, if anything like that can happen I don't want to go away. I guess new people aren't any better than old ones. I'll bet they almost never are. Emily ... I feel that you're as good a friend as I've got. I don't need to go and meet the people in other towns.

EMILY: But, George, maybe it's very important for you to go and learn all that about – cattle judging and soils and those things. ... Of course, I don't know.

GEORGE [*after a pause, very seriously*]: Emily, I'm going to make up my mind right now. I won't go. I'll tell Pa about it tonight.

EMILY: Why, George, I don't see why you have to decide right now. It's a whole year away.

GEORGE: Emily, I'm glad you spoke to me about that ... that fault in my character. What you said was right; but there was *one* thing wrong in it, and that was when you said that for a year I wasn't noticing people, and ... you, for instance. Why, you say you were watching me when I did everything ... I was doing the same about you all the time. Why, sure – I always thought about you as one of the chief people

65

I thought about. I always made sure where you were sitting on the bleachers, and who you were with, and for three days now I've been trying to walk home with you; but something's always got in the way. Yesterday I was standing over against the wall waiting for you, and you walked home with *Miss Corcoran.*

EMILY: George! . . . Life's awful funny! How could I have known that? Why, I thought –

GEORGE: Listen, Emily, I'm going to tell you why I'm not going to Agriculture School. I think that once you've found a person that you're very fond of . . . I mean a person who's fond of you, too, and likes you enough to be interested in your character . . . Well, I think that's just as important as college is, and even more so. That's what I think.

EMILY: I think it's awfully important, too.

GEORGE: Emily.

EMILY: Y-yes, George.

GEORGE: Emily, if I *do* improve and make a big change . . . would you be . . . I mean: *could* you be . . .

EMILY: I . . . I am now; I always have been.

GEORGE [*after a pause*]: So I guess this is an important talk we've been having.

EMILY: Yes . . . yes.

GEORGE [*taking a deep breath and straightening his back*]: Wait just a minute and I'll walk you home.

[*With mounting alarm he digs into his pockets for the money. The* STAGE MANAGER *enters, right.*

GEORGE, *deeply embarrassed, but direct, says to him*]

Mr Morgan, I'll have to go home and get the money to pay you for this. It'll only take me a minute.

STAGE MANAGER [*pretending to be affronted*]: What's that? George Gibbs, do you mean to tell me – !

GEORGE: Yes, but I had reasons, Mr Morgan – Look, here's

my gold watch to keep until I come back with the money.

STAGE MANAGER: That's all right. Keep your watch. I'll trust you.

GEORGE: I'll be back in five minutes.

STAGE MANAGER: I'll trust you ten years, George – not a day over – Got all over your shock, Emily?

EMILY: Yes, thank you, Mr Morgan. It was nothing.

GEORGE [taking up the books from the counter]: I'm ready.

[They walk in grave silence across the stage and pass through the trellis at the Webb's back door and disappear.

The STAGE MANAGER watches them go out, then turns to the audience, removing his spectacles.]

STAGE MANAGER: Well –

[He claps his hands as a signal.]

Now we're ready to get on with the wedding.

[He stands waiting while the set is prepared for the next scene. STAGEHANDS remove the chairs, tables, and trellises from the Gibbs and Webb houses.

They arrange the pews for the church in the centre of the stage. The congregation will sit facing the back wall. The aisle of the church starts at the centre of the back wall and comes towards the audience.

A small platform is placed against the back wall on which the stage manager will stand later, playing the minister. The image of a stained-glass window is cast from a lantern slide upon the back wall.

When all is ready the STAGE MANAGER strolls to the centre of the stage, down front, and, musingly, addresses the audience.]

There are a lot of things to be said about a wedding; there are a lot of thoughts that go on during a wedding.

We can't get them all into one wedding, naturally, and especially not into a wedding at Grover's Corners, where they're awfully plain and short.

In this wedding I play the minister. That gives me the right to say a few more things about it.

For a while, now, the play gets pretty serious.

Y'see, some churches say that marriage is a sacrament. I don't quite know what that means, but I can guess. Like Mrs Gibbs said a few minutes ago: People were made to live two-by-two.

This is a good wedding, but people are so put together that even at a good wedding there's a lot of confusion way down deep in people's minds and we thought that that ought to be in our play, too.

The real hero of this scene isn't on the stage at all, and you know who that is. It's like what one of those European fellas said: every child born into the world is nature's attempt to make a perfect human being. Well, we've seen nature pushing and contriving for some time now. We all know that nature's interested in quantity; but I think she's interested in quality, too – that's why I'm in the ministry.

And don't forget all the other witnesses at this wedding – the ancestors. Millions of them. Most of them set out to live two-by-two, also. Millions of them.

Well, that's all my sermon. 'Twan't very long, anyway. [*The organ starts playing Handel's 'Largo'.*

The congregation streams into the church and sits in silence. Church bells are heard.

MRS GIBBS *sits in the front row, the first seat on the aisle, the right section; next to her are* REBECCA *and* DR GIBBS. *Across the aisle* MRS WEBB, WALLY, *and* MR WEBB. *A small choir takes its place, facing the audience under the stained-glass window.*

MRS WEBB, *on the way to her place, turns back and speaks to the audience.*]

MRS WEBB: I don't know why on earth I should be crying. I

suppose there's nothing to cry about. It came over me at breakfast this morning; there was Emily eating her breakfast as she's done for seventeen years and now she's going off to eat it in someone else's house. I suppose that's it.

And Emily! She suddenly said: I can't eat another mouthful, and she put her head down on the table and *she* cried.

[*She starts towards her seat in the church, but turns back, and adds*]

Oh, I've got to say it: you know, there's something downright cruel about sending our girls out into marriage this way.

I hope some of her girl friends have told her a thing or two. It's cruel, I know, but I couldn't bring myself to say anything. I went into it blind as a bat myself.

[*In half-amused exasperation*]

The whole world's wrong, that's what's the matter.

There they come.

[*She hurries to her place in the pew*

GEORGE *starts to come down the right aisle of the theatre, through the audience.*

Suddenly THREE MEMBERS *of his baseball team appear by the right proscenium pillar and start whistling and catcalling to him. They are dressed for the ball field.*]

THE BASEBALL PLAYERS: Eh, George, George! Hast – yaow! Look at him, fellas – he looks scared to death. Yaow! George, don't look so innocent, you old geezer. We know what you're thinking. Don't disgrace the team, big boy. Whoo-oo-oo.

STAGE MANAGER: All right! All right! That'll do. That's enough of that.

[*Smiling, he pushes them off the stage. They lean back to shout a few more catcalls.*]

There used to be an awful lot of that kind of thing at weddings in the old days – Rome, and later. We're more civilized now – so they say.

[*The choir starts singing 'Love Divine, All Love Excelling'.* GEORGE *has reached the stage. He stares at the congregation a moment, then takes a few steps of withdrawal, towards the right proscenium pillar. His mother, from the front row, seems to have felt his confusion. She leaves her seat and comes down the aisle quickly to him.*]

MRS GIBBS: George! George! What's the matter?

GEORGE: Ma, I don't want to grow old. Why's everybody pushing me so?

MRS GIBBS: Why, George . . . you wanted it.

GEORGE: No, Ma, listen to me –

MRS GIBBS: No, no, George – you're a man now.

GEORGE: Listen, Ma – for the last time I ask you. . . . All I want to do is to be a fella –

MRS GIBBS: George! If anyone should hear you! Now stop. Why, I'm ashamed of you!

GEORGE [*coming to himself and looking over the scene*]: What? Where's Emily?

MRS GIBBS [*relieved*]: George! You gave me such a turn.

GEORGE: Cheer up, Ma. I'm getting married.

MRS GIBBS: Let me catch me breath a minute.

GEORGE [*comforting her*]: Now, Ma, you save Thursday nights. Emily and I are coming over to dinner every Thursday night . . . you'll see. Ma, what are you crying for? Come on; we've got to get ready for this.

[MRS GIBBS, *mastering her emotion, fixes his tie and whispers to him.*

In the meantime, EMILY, *in white and wearing her wedding veil, has come through the audience and mounted on to the stage. She too draws back, frightened, when she sees the congregation in the church. The choir begins: 'Blessed Be the Tie That Binds'.*]

EMILY: I never felt so alone in my whole life. And George over there, looking so ...! I *hate* him. I wish I were dead. Papa! Papa!

MR WEBB [*leaving his seat in the pews and coming towards her anxiously*]: Emily! Emily! Now don't get upset. ...

EMILY: But, Papa – I don't want to get married. ...

MR WEBB: Sh – sh – Emily. Everything's all right.

EMILY: Why can't I stay for a while just as I am? Let's go away –

MR WEBB: No, no, Emily. Now stop and think a minute.

EMILY: Don't you remember that you used to say – all the time you used to say – all the time: that I was *your* girl! There must be lots of places we can go to. I'll work for you. I could keep house.

MR WEBB: Sh ... You mustn't think of such things. You're just nervous, Emily.
[*He turns and calls.*]
George! George! Will you come here a minute?
[*He leads her towards George.*]
Why you're marrying the best young fellow in the world. George is a fine fellow.

EMILY: But Papa –
[MRS GIBBS *returns unobtrusively to her seat.*
MR WEBB *has one arm around his daughter. He places his hand on George's shoulder.*]

MR WEBB: I'm giving away my daughter, George. Do you think you can take care of her?

GEORGE: Mr Webb, I want to ... I want to try. Emily, I'm going to do my best. I love you, Emily. I need you.

EMILY: Well, if you love me, help me. All I want is someone to love me.

GEORGE: I will, Emily. Emily, I'll try.

EMILY: And I mean for *ever*. Do you hear? For ever and ever.

[*They fall into each other's arms.*

The March from Lohengrin *is heard.*

The STAGE MANAGER, *as clergyman, stands on the box, up centre.*]

MR WEBB: Come, they're waiting for us. Now you know it'll be all right. Come, quick.

[GEORGE *slips away and takes his place beside the* STAGE MANAGER-CLERGYMAN.

EMILY *proceeds up the aisle on her father's arm.*]

STAGE MANAGER: Do you, George, take this woman, Emily, to be your wedded wife, to have . . .

[MRS SOAMES *has been sitting in the last row of the congregation.*

She now turns to her neighbours and speaks in a shrill voice.

Her chatter drowns out the rest of the clergyman's words.]

MRS SOAMES: Perfectly lovely wedding! Loveliest wedding I ever saw. Oh, I do love a good wedding, don't you? Doesn't she make a lovely bride?

GEORGE: I do.

STAGE MANAGER: Do you, Emily, take this man, George, to be your wedded husband . . .

[*Again his further words are covered by those of* MRS SOAMES.]

MRS SOAMES: Don't know *when* I've seen such a lovely wedding. But I always cry. Don't know why it is, but I always cry. I just like to see young people happy, don't you? Oh, I think it's lovely.

[*The ring.*

The kiss.

The stage is suddenly arrested into silent tableau.

The STAGE MANAGER, *his eyes on the distance, speaks as though to himself.*]

ACT TWO

STAGE MANAGER: I've married over two hundred couples in my day.

Do I believe in it?

I don't know.

M. ... marries N. ... millions of them.

The cottage, the go-cart, the Sunday-afternoon drives in the Ford, the first rheumatism, the grandchildren, the second rheumatism, the deathbed, the reading of the will –

[*He now looks at the audience for the first time, with a warm smile that removes any sense of cynicism from the next line.*]

Once in a thousand times it's interesting.

– Well, let's have Mendelssohn's 'Wedding March'!

[*The organ picks up the March.*

The BRIDE *and* GROOM *come down the aisle, radiant, but trying to be very dignified.*]

MRS SOAMES: Aren't they a lovely couple? Oh, I've never been to such a nice wedding. I'm sure they'll be happy. I always say: *happiness, that's the great thing! The important thing is to be happy.*

[*The* BRIDE *and* GROOM *reach the steps leading into the audience. A bright light is thrown upon them. They descend into the auditorium and run up the aisle joyously.*]

STAGE MANAGER: That's all the Second Act, folks. Ten minutes' intermission.

ACT THREE

During the intermission the audience has seen the STAGEHANDS *arranging the stage. On the right-hand side, a little right of the centre, ten or twelve ordinary chairs have been placed in three openly spaced rows facing the audience.*

These are graves in the cemetery.

Towards the end of the intermission the ACTORS *enter and take their places. The front row contains: towards the centre of the stage, an empty chair; then* MRS GIBBS; SIMON STIMSON.

The second row contains, among others, MRS SOAMES.

The third row has WALLY WEBB.

The dead do not turn their heads or their eyes to right or left, but they sit in a quiet without stiffness. When they speak their tone is matter-of-fact, without sentimentality, and, above all, without lugubriousness.

The STAGE MANAGER *takes his accustomed place and waits for the house lights to go down.*

STAGE MANAGER: This time nine years have gone by, friends – summer 1913.

Gradual changes in Grover's Corners. Horses are getting rarer.

Farmers coming into town in Fords.

Everybody locks their house doors now at night. Ain't been any burglars in town yet, but everybody's heard about 'em.

You'd be surprised, though – on the whole, things don't change much around here.

This is certainly an important part of Grover's Corners. It's on a hilltop – a windy hilltop – lots of sky, lots of clouds – often lots of sun and moon and stars.

You come up here, on a fine afternoon, and you can see range on range of hills – awful blue they are – up there by Lake Sunapee and Lake Winnipesaukee . . . and way up, if you've got a glass, you can see the White Mountains and Mt Washington – where North Conway and Conway is. And, of course, our favourite mountain, Mt Monadnock, 's right here – and all these towns that lie around it: Jaffrey, 'n East Jaffrey, 'n Peterborough, 'n Dublin; and [*then pointing down in the audience*] there, quite a ways down, is Grover's Corners.

Yes, beautiful spot up here. Mountain laurel and li-lacks. I often wonder why people like to be buried in Woodlawn and Brooklyn when they might pass the same time up here in New Hampshire.

Over there – [*pointing to stage left*] are the old stones – 1670, 1680. Strong-minded people that come a long way to be independent. Summer people walk around there laughing at the funny words on the tombstones . . . it don't do any harm. And genealogists come up from Boston – get paid by city people for looking up their ancestors. They want to make sure they're Daughters of the American Revolution and of the *Mayflower*. . . . Well, I guess that don't do any harm, either. Wherever you come near the human race, there's layers and layers of nonsense. . . .

Over there are some Civil War veterans. Iron flags on their graves . . . New Hampshire boys . . . had a notion that the Union ought to be kept together, though they'd never seen more than fifty miles of it themselves. All they knew was the name, friends – the United States of America. The United States of America. And they went and died about it.

This here is the part of the cemetery. Here's your friend Mrs Gibbs. 'N let me see – Here's Mr Stimson, organist at the Congregational Church. And Mrs Soames who enjoyed the wedding so – you remember? Oh, and a lot of others. And Editor Webb's boy, Wallace, whose appendix burst while he was on a Boy Scout trip to Crawford Notch.

Yes, an awful lot of sorrow has sort of quieted down up here. People just wild with grief have brought their relatives up to this hill. We all know how it is ... and then time ... and sunny days ... and rainy days ... 'n snow ... We're all glad they're in a beautiful place and we're coming up here ourselves when our fit's over.

Now there are some things we all know, but we don't take'm out and look at'm very often. We all know that *something* is eternal. And it ain't houses and it ain't names, and it ain't earth, and it ain't even the stars ... everybody knows in their bones that *something* is eternal, and that something has to do with human beings. All the greatest people ever lived have been telling us that for five thousand years and yet you'd be surprised how people are always losing hold of it. There's something way down deep that's eternal about every human being.

[*Pause.*]

You know as well as I do that the dead don't stay interested in us living people for very long. Gradually, gradually, they lose hold of the earth ... and the ambitions they had ... and the pleasures they had ... and the things they suffered ... and the people they loved.

They get weaned away from earth – that's the way I put it – weaned away.

And they stay here while the earth part of 'em burns away, burns out; and all that time they slowly get indifferent to what's goin' on in Grover's Corners.

They're waitin'. They're waitin' for something that they feel is comin'. Something important, and great. Aren't they waitin' for the eternal part in them to come out clear?

Some of the things they're going to say maybe'll hurt your feelings – but that's the way it is: mother'n daughter ... husband 'n wife ... enemy 'n enemy ... money 'n miser ... all those terribly important things kind of grow pale around here. And what's left when memory's gone, and your identity, Mrs Smith?

[*He looks at the audience a minute, then turns to the stage.*]

Well! There are some *living* people. There's Joe Stoddard, our undertaker, supervising a new-made grave. And here comes a Grover's Corners boy, that left town to go out West.

[JOB STODDARD *has hovered about in the background.* SAM CRAIG *enters left, wiping his forehead from the exertion. He carries an umbrella and strolls front.*]

SAM CRAIG: Good afternoon, Joe Stoddard.

JOB STODDARD: Good afternoon, good afternoon. Let me see now: do I know you?

SAM CRAIG: I'm Sam Craig.

JOB STODDARD: Gracious sakes' alive! Of all people! I should'a knowed you'd be back for the funeral. You've been away a long time, Sam.

SAM CRAIG: Yes, I've been away over twelve years. I'm in business out in Buffalo now, Joe. But I was in the East when I got news of my cousin's death, so I thought I'd combine things a little and come and see the old home. You look well.

JOB STODDARD: Yes, yes, can't complain. Very sad, our journey today, Samuel.

SAM CRAIG: Yes.

JOB STODDARD: Yes, yes. I always say I hate to supervise when a young person is taken. They'll be here in a few minutes now. I had to come here early today – my son's supervisin' at the home.

77

SAM CRAIG [*reading stones*]: Old Farmer McCarty, I used to do chores for him – after school. He had the lumbago.

JOE STODDARD: Yes, we brought Farmer McCarty here a number of years ago now.

SAM CRAIG [*staring at Mrs Gibbs's knees*]: Why, this is my Aunt Julia ... I'd forgotten that she'd ... of course, of course.

JOE STODDARD: Yes, Doc Gibbs lost his wife two-three years ago ... about this time. And today's another pretty bad blow for him, too.

MRS GIBBS [*to Simon Stimson in an even voice*]: That's my sister Carey's boy, Sam ... Sam Craig.

SIMON STIMSON: I'm always uncomfortable when *they're* around.

MRS GIBBS: Simon.

SAM CRAIG: Do they choose their own verses much, Joe?

JOE STODDARD: No ... not usual. Mostly the bereaved pick a verse.

SAM CRAIG: Doesn't sound like Aunt Julia. There aren't many of those Hersey sisters left now. Let me see: where are ... I wanted to look at my father's and mother's. ...

JOE STODDARD: Over there with Craigs. ... Avenue F.

SAM CRAIG [*reading Simon Stimson's epitaph*]: He was organist at church, wasn't he? – Hm, drank a lot, we used to say.

JOE STODDARD: Nobody was supposed to know about it. He'd seen a peck of trouble. [*Behind his hand*] Took his own life, y' know?

SAM CRAIG: Oh, did he?

JOE STODDARD: Hung himself in the attic. They tried to hush it up, but of course it got around. He chose his own epy-taph. You can see it there. It ain't a verse exactly.

SAM CRAIG: Why, it's just some notes of music – what is it?

JOE STODDARD: Oh, I wouldn't know. It was wrote up in the Boston papers at the time.

SAM CRAIG: Joe, what did she die of?

JOE STODDARD: Who?

SAM CRAIG: My cousin.

JOE STODDARD: Oh, didn't you know? Had some trouble bringin' a baby into the world. 'Twas her second, though. There's a little boy 'bout four years old.

SAM CRAIG [*opening his umbrella*]: The grave's going to be over there?

JOE STODDARD: Yes, there ain't much more room over here among the Gibbses, so they're opening up a whole new Gibbs section over by Avenue B. You'll excuse me now. I see they're comin'.

[*From left to centre, at the back of the stage, comes a procession.* FOUR MEN *carry a casket, invisible to us. All the rest are under umbrellas. One can vaguely see:* DR GIBBS, GEORGE, *the* WEBBS, *etc. They gather about a grave in the back centre of the stage, a little to the left of centre.*]

MRS SOAMES: Who is it, Julia?

MRS GIBBS [*without raising her eyes*]: My daughter-in-law, Emily Webb.

MRS SOAMES [*a little surprised, but no emotion*]: Well, I declare! The road up here must have been awful muddy. What did she die of, Julia?

MRS GIBBS: In childbirth.

MRS SOAMES: Childbirth.

[*Almost with a laugh*]

I'd forgotten all about that. My, wasn't life awful – [*with a sigh*] and wonderful.

SIMON STIMSON [*with a sideways glance*]: Wonderful, was it?

MRS GIBBS: Simon! Now, remember!

MRS SOAMES: I remember Emily's wedding. Wasn't it a

lovely wedding! And I remember her reading the class poem at Graduation Exercises. Emily was one of the brightest girls ever graduated from High School. I've heard Principal Wilkins say so time after time. I called on them at their new farm, just before I died. Perfectly beautiful farm.

A WOMAN FROM AMONG THE DEAD: It's on the same road we lived on.

A MAN AMONG THE DEAD: Yepp, right smart farm.

[*They subside. The group by the grave starts singing 'Blessed Be the Tie That Binds'.*]

A WOMAN AMONG THE DEAD: I always liked that hymn. I was hopin' they'd sing a hymn.

[*Pause. Suddenly* EMILY *appears from among the umbrellas. She is wearing a white dress. Her hair is down her back and tied by a white ribbon like a little girl. She comes slowly, gazingly wonderingly at the dead, a little dazed.*

She stops half-way and smiles faintly. After looking at the mourners for a moment, she walks slowly to the vacant chair beside Mrs Gibbs and sits down.]

EMILY [*to them all, quietly, smiling*]: Hello.

MRS SOAMES: Hello, Emily.

A MAN AMONG THE DEAD: Hello, M's Gibbs.

EMILY [*warmly*]: Hello, Mother Gibbs.

MRS GIBBS: Emily.

EMILY: Hello.

[*With surprise*]

It's raining.

[*Her eyes drift back to the funeral company.*]

MRS GIBBS: Yes ... They'll be gone soon, dear. Just rest yourself.

EMILY: It seems thousands and thousands of years since I ... Papa remembered that that was my favourite hymn.

Oh, I wish I'd been here a long time. I don't like being new here – How do you do, Mr Stimson?

SIMON STIMSON: How do you do, Emily?

[EMILY *continues to look about her with a wondering smile; as though to shut out from her mind the thought of the funeral company she starts speaking to Mrs Gibbs with a touch of nervousness.*]

EMILY: Mother Gibbs, George and I have made that farm into just the best place you ever saw. We thought of you all the time. We wanted to show you the new barn and a great long ce-ment drinking fountain for the stock. We bought that out of the money you left us.

MRS GIBBS: I did?

EMILY: Don't you remember, Mother Gibbs – the legacy you left us? Why, it was over three hundred and fifty dollars.

MRS GIBBS: Yes, yes, Emily.

EMILY: Well, there's a patent device on the drinking fountain so that it never overflows, Mother Gibbs, and it never sinks below a certain mark they have there. It's fine.

[*Her voice trails off and her eyes return to the funeral group.*]

It won't be the same to George without me, but it's a lovely farm.

[*Suddenly she looks directly at Mrs Gibbs.*]

Live people don't understand, do they?

MRS GIBBS: No, dear – not very much.

EMILY: They're sort of shut up in little boxes, aren't they? I feel as though I knew them last a thousand years ago. . . . My boy is spending the day at Mrs Carter's.

[*She sees Mr Carter among the dead.*]

Oh, Mr Carter, my little boy is spending the day at your house.

MR CARTER: Is he?

EMILY: Yes, he loves it there – Mother Gibbs, we have a Ford, too. Never gives any trouble. I don't drive, though. Mother Gibbs, when does this feeling go away? – Of being . . . one of *them*? How long does it . . .?

MRS GIBBS: Sh! dear. Just wait and be patient.

EMILY [*with a sigh*]: I know – Look, they're finished. They're going.

MRS GIBBS: Sh –

[*The umbrellas leave the stage.* DR GIBBS *has come over to his wife's grave and stands before it a moment.* EMILY *looks up at his face.* MRS GIBBS *does not raise her eyes.*]

EMILY: Look! Father Gibbs is bringing some of my flowers to you. He looks just like George, doesn't he? Oh, Mother Gibbs, I never realized before how troubled and how . . . how in the dark live persons are. Look at him. I loved him so. From morning till night, that's all they are – troubled.

[DR GIBBS *goes off.*]

THE DEAD: Little cooler than it was – Yes, that rain's cooled it off a little. Those north-east winds always do the same thing, don't they? If it isn't a rain, it's a three-day blow –

[*A patient calm falls on the stage. The* STAGE MANAGER *appears at his proscenium pillar, smoking.* EMILY *sits up abruptly with an idea.*]

EMILY: But, Mother Gibbs, one can go back; one can go back there again . . . into living. I feel it. I know it. Why just then for a moment I was thinking about . . . about the farm . . . and for a minute I *was* there, and my baby was on my lap as plain as day.

MRS GIBBS: Yes, of course you can.

EMILY: I can go back there and live all those days over again . . . why not?

MRS GIBBS: All I can say is, Emily, don't.

EMILY [*appealing urgently to the stage manager*]: But it's true, isn't it? I can go and live . . . back there . . . again.

STAGE MANAGER: Yes, some have tried – but they soon come back here.

MRS GIBBS: Don't do it, Emily.

MRS SOAMES: Emily, don't. It's not what you think it'd be.

EMILY: But I won't live over a sad day. I'll choose a happy one – I'll choose the day I first knew that I loved George. Why should that be painful?

[THE DEAD *are silent. Her question turns to the stage manager.*]

STAGE MANAGER: You not only live it; but you watch yourself living it.

EMILY: Yes?

STAGE MANAGER: And as you watch it, you see the thing that they – down there – never know. You see the future. You know what's going to happen afterwards.

EMILY: But is that – painful? Why?

MRS GIBBS: That's not the only reason why you shouldn't do it, Emily. When you've been here longer you'll see that our life here is to forget all that, and think only of what's ahead, and be ready for what's ahead. When you've been here longer you'll understand.

EMILY [*softly*]: But, Mother Gibbs, how can I *ever* forget that life? It's all I know. It's all I had.

MRS SOAMES: Oh, Emily. It isn't wise. Really, it isn't.

EMILY: But it's a thing I must know for myself. I'll choose a happy day, anyway.

MRS GIBBS: *No!* – At least, choose an unimportant day. Choose the least important day in your life. It will be important enough.

EMILY [*to herself*]: Then it can't be since I was married; or since the baby was born.

[*To the stage manager, eagerly*]

I can choose a birthday at least, can't I? – I choose my twelfth birthday.

STAGE MANAGER: All right. 11 February 1899. A Tuesday – Do you want any special time of day?

EMILY: Oh, I want the whole day.

STAGE MANAGER: We'll begin at dawn. You remember it had been snowing for several days; but it had stopped the night before, and they had begun clearing the roads. The sun's coming up.

EMILY [*with a cry; rising*]: There's Main Street . . . why, that's Mr Morgan's drugstore before he changed it! . . . And there's the livery stable.

[*The stage at no time in this act has been very dark; but now the left half of the stage gradually becomes very bright – the brightness of a crisp winter morning.*

EMILY *walks towards Main Street.*]

STAGE MANAGER: Yes, it's 1899. This is fourteen years ago.

EMILY: Oh, that's the town I knew as a little girl. And, *look*, there's the old white fence that used to be around our house. Oh, I'd forgotten that! Oh, I love it so! Are they inside?

STAGE MANAGER: Yes, your mother'll be coming downstairs in a minute to make breakfast.

EMILY [*softly*]: Will she?

STAGE MANAGER: And you remember: your father had been away for several days; he came back on the early-morning train.

EMILY: No . . . ?

STAGE MANAGER: He'd been back to his college to make a speech – in western New York, at Clinton.

EMILY: Look! There's Howie Newsome. There's our policeman. But he's *dead*; he *died*.

[*The voices of* HOWIE NEWSOME, CONSTABLE WARREN,

and JOE CROWELL, JR, *are heard at the left of the stage.*
EMILY *listens in delight.*]

HOWIE NEWSOME: Whoa, Bessie! – Bessie! 'Morning, Bill.

CONSTABLE WARREN: Morning, Howie.

HOWIE NEWSOME: You're up early.

CONSTABLE WARREN: Been rescuin' a party; darn near froze
   to death, down by Polish Town thar. Got drunk and lay
   out in the snowdrifts. Thought he was in bed when I
   shook'm.

EMILY: Why, there's Joe Crowell. . . .

JOE CROWELL: Good morning, Mr Warren. 'Morning,
   Howie.

[MRS WEBB *has appeared in her kitchen, but* EMILY *does not
   see her until she calls.*]

MRS WEBB: Chil-*dren!* Wally! Emily! . . . Time to get up.

EMILY: Mama, I'm here! Oh! how young Mama looks! I
   didn't know Mama was ever that young.

MRS WEBB: You can come and dress by the kitchen fire, if
   you like; but hurry.

[HOWIE NEWSOME *has entered along Main Street and brings
   the milk to Mrs Webb's door.*]

   Good morning, Mr Newsome. Whhhh – it's cold.

HOWIE NEWSOME: Ten below by my barn, Mrs Webb.

MRS WEBB: Think of it! Keep yourself wrapped up.

[*She takes her bottles in, shuddering.*]

EMILY [*with an effort*]: Mama, I can't find my blue hair ribbon
   anywhere.

MRS WEBB: Just open your eyes, dear, that's all. I laid it out
   for you special – on the dresser, there. If it were a snake it
   would bite you.

EMILY: Yes, yes . . .

[*She puts her hand on her heart.* MR WEBB *comes along Main
   Street, where he meets* CONSTABLE WARREN. *Their*

movements and voices are increasingly lively in the sharp air.]

MR WEBB: Good morning, Bill.

CONSTABLE WARREN: Good morning, Mr Webb. You're up early.

MR WEBB: Yes, just been back to my old college in New York State. Been any trouble here?

CONSTABLE WARREN: Well, I was called up this mornin' to rescue a Polish fella – darn near froze to death he was.

MR WEBB: We must get it in the paper.

CONSTABLE WARREN: 'Twan't much.

EMILY [*whispers*]: Papa.

[MR WEBB *shakes the snow off his feet and enters his house.* CONSTABLE WARREN *goes off, right.*]

MR WEBB: Good morning, Mother.

MRS WEBB: How did it go, Charles?

MR WEBB: Oh, fine, I guess. I told'm a few things – Everything all right here?

MRS WEBB: Yes – can't think of anything that's happened, special. Been right cold. Howie Newsome says it's ten below over to his barn.

MR WEBB: Yes, well, it's colder than that at Hamilton College. Students' ears are falling off. It ain't Christian – Paper have any mistakes in it?

MRS WEBB: None that I noticed. Coffee's ready when you want it.

[*He starts upstairs.*]

Charles! Don't forget; it's Emily's birthday. Did you remember to get her something?

MR WEBB [*patting his pocket*]: Yes, I've got something here.

[*Calling up the stairs*]

Where's my girl? Where's my birthday girl?

[*He goes off left.*]

MRS WEBB: Don't interrupt her now, Charles. You can see her at breakfast. She's slow enough as it is. Hurry up, children! It's seven o'clock. Now, I don't want to call you again.

EMILY [*softly, more in wonder than in grief*]: I can't bear it. They're so young and beautiful. Why did they ever have to get old? Mama, I'm here. I'm grown up. I love you all, everything – I can't look at everything hard enough.

[*She looks questioningly at the stage manager, saying or suggesting: 'Can I go in?' He nods briefly. She crosses to the inner door to the kitchen, left of her mother, and as though entering the room, speaks, suggesting the voice of a girl of twelve.*]

Good morning, Mama.

MRS WEBB [*crossing to embrace and kiss her; in her characteristic matter-of-fact manner*]: Well, now dear, a very happy birthday to my girl and many happy returns. There are some surprises waiting for you on the kitchen table.

EMILY: Oh, Mama, you *shouldn't* have.

[*She throws an anguished glance at the stage manager.*]

I can't – I can't.

MRS WEBB [*facing the audience, over her stove*]: But birthday or no birthday, I want you to eat your breakfast good and slow. I want you to grow up and be a good strong girl.

That in the blue paper is from your Aunt Carrie; and I reckon you can guess who brought the post-card album. I found it on the doorstep when I brought in the milk – George Gibbs ... must have come over in the cold pretty early ... right nice of him.

EMILY [*to herself*]: Oh, George! I'd forgotten that. ...

MRS WEBB: Chew that bacon good and slow. It'll help keep you warm on a cold day.

EMILY [*with mounting urgency*]: Oh, Mama, just look at me one minute as though you really saw me. Mama, fourteen years have gone by. I'm dead. You're a grandmother, Mama. I married George Gibbs, Mama. Wally's dead too. Mama, his appendix burst on a camping trip to North Conway. We felt just terrible about it – don't you remember? But, just for a moment now we're all together. Mama, just for a moment we're happy. *Let's look at one another.*

MRS WEBB: That in the yellow paper is something I found in the attic among your grandmother's things. You're old enough to wear it now, and I thought you'd like it.

EMILY: And this is from you. Why, Mama, it's just lovely and it's just what I wanted. It's beautiful!

[*She flings her arms around her mother's neck. Her* MOTHER *goes on with her cooking, but is pleased.*]

MRS WEBB: Well, I hoped you'd like it. Hunted all over. Your Aunt Norah couldn't find one in Concord, so I had to send all the way to Boston.

[*Laughing*]

Wally has something for you, too. He made it at manual-training class and he's very proud of it. Be sure you make a big fuss about it – Your father has a surprise for you, too; don't know what it is myself. Sh – here he comes.

MR WEBB [*off stage*]: Where's my girl? Where's my birthday girl?

EMILY [*in a loud voice to the stage manager*]: I can't. I can't go on. It goes so fast. We don't have time to look at one another.

[*She breaks down sobbing.*

The lights dim on the left half of the stage. MRS WEBB *disappears.*]

I didn't realize. So all that was going on and we never

noticed. Take me back – up the hill – to my grave. But first: Wait! One more look.

Good-bye, Good-bye, world. Good-bye, Grover's Corners ... Mama and Papa. Good-bye to clocks ticking ... and Mama's sunflowers. And food and coffee. And new-ironed dresses and hot baths ... and sleeping and waking up. Oh, earth, you're too wonderful for anybody to realize you.

[*She looks towards the stage manager and asks abruptly, through her tears*]

Do any human beings ever realize life while they live it? – every, every minute?

STAGE MANAGER: No.

[*Pause.*]

The saints and poets, maybe – they do some.

EMILY: I'm ready to go back.

[*She returns to her chair beside Mrs Gibbs.*

Pause.]

MRS GIBBS: Were you happy?

EMILY: No ... I should have listened to you. That's all human beings are! Just blind people.

MRS GIBBS: Look, it's clearing up. The stars are coming out.

EMILY: Oh, Mr Stimson, I should have listened to them.

SIMON STIMSON [*with mounting violence; bitingly*]: Yes, now you know. Now you know! That's what it was to be alive. To move about in a cloud of ignorance; to go up and down trampling on the feelings of those ... of those about you. To spend and waste time as though you had a million years. To be always at the mercy of one self-centred passion, or another. Now you know – that's the happy existence you wanted to go back to. Ignorance and blindness.

MRS GIBBS [*spiritedly*]: Simon Stimson, that ain't the whole truth and you know it. Emily, look at that star. I forget its name.

A MAN AMONG THE DEAD: My boy Joel was a sailor – knew 'em all. He'd set on the porch evenings and tell 'em all by name. Yes, sir, wonderful!

ANOTHER MAN AMONG THE DEAD: A star's mighty good company.

A WOMAN AMONG THE DEAD: Yes. Yes, 'tis.

SIMON STIMSON: Here's one of *them* coming.

THE DEAD: That's funny. 'Tain't no time for one of them to be here – Goodness sakes.

EMILY: Mother Gibbs, it's George.

MRS GIBBS: Sh, dear. Just rest yourself.

EMILY: It's George.

[GEORGE *enters from the left, and slowly comes towards them.*]

A MAN FROM AMONG THE DEAD: And my boy, Joel, who knew the stars – he used to say it took millions of years for that speck o' light to git to the earth. Don't seem like a body could believe it, but that's what he used to say – millions of years.

[GEORGE *sinks to his knees then falls full length at Emily's feet.*]

A WOMAN AMONG THE DEAD: Goodness! That ain't no way to behave!

MRS SOAMES: He ought to be home.

EMILY: Mother Gibbs?

MRS GIBBS: Yes, Emily?

EMILY: They don't understand, do they?

MRS GIBBS: No, dear. They don't understand.

[*The* STAGE MANAGER *appears at the right, one hand on a dark curtain which he slowly draws across the scene.*

In the distance a clock is heard striking the hour very faintly.]

STAGE MANAGER: Most everybody's asleep in Grover's

Corners. There are a few lights on: Shorty Hawkins, down at the depot, has just watched the Albany train go by. And at the livery stable somebody's setting up late and talking – Yes, it's clearing up. There are the stars – doing their old, old crisscross journeys in the sky. Scholars haven't settled the matter yet, but they seem to think there are no living beings up there. Just chalk ... or fire. Only this one is straining away. straining away all the time to make something of itself. The strain's so bad that every sixteen hours everybody lies down and gets a rest.

[*He winds his watch.*]

Hm ... Eleven o'clock in Grover's Corners – You get a good rest, too. Good night.

The Skin of Our Teeth

The first performance of *The Skin of Our Teeth* took place at the Shubert Theatre in New Haven, Connecticut, on 15 October 1942. It opened in New York at the Plymouth Theatre on 18 November. It was produced by Michael Myerberg and directed by Elia Kazan. Sabina was played by Tallulah Bankhead, Mr and Mrs Antrobus by Fredric March and Florence Eldridge, the Antrobus children by Montgomery Clift and Frances Heflin, the Fortune Teller by Florence Reed. The scenery was designed by Albert Johnson, the costumes by Mary Percy Schenck.

The London production opened at the Phoenix Theatre on 16 May 1945. It was presented by H. M. Tennent Ltd and directed by Sir Laurence Olivier. Sabina was played by Vivien Leigh, Mr and Mrs Antrobus by Cecil Parker (later by George Devine) and Joan Young (later by Esther Somers), the Antrobus children by Terry Morgan and Pamela Conroy, the Fortune Teller by Ena Burrill. The scenery and costumes were designed by Roger Furse. On a tour of Australia and New Zealand in 1948, the role of Mr Antrobus was played by Sir Laurence Olivier.

In a revival produced by the American National Theatre and Academy for presentation in Paris in June 1955 as a part of the Festival 'Salut à la France', and later presented in a number of cities in the United States, Sabina was played by Mary Martin, Mr and Mrs Antrobus by George Abbott and Helen Hayes, and the Fortune Teller by Florence Reed. The play was directed by Alan Schneider.

CAST

(in the order of their appearance)

ANNOUNCER	MISS M. MUSE
SABINA	USHER
MR FITZPATRICK	USHER
MRS ANTROBUS	GIRL } DRUM MAJORETTES
DINOSAUR	GIRL }
MAMMOTH	FORTUNE TELLER
TELEGRAPH BOY	CHAIR PUSHER
HENRY	CHAIR PUSHER
GLADYS	CONVEENERS
MR ANTROBUS	BROADCAST OFFICIAL
DOCTOR	DEFEATED CANDIDATE
PROFESSOR	MR TREMAYNE
JUDGE	HESTER
HOMER	IVY
MISS E. MUSE	FRED BAILEY
MISS T. MUSE	

Act One Home, Excelsior, New Jersey.

Act Two Atlantic City Boardwalk.

Act Three Home, Excelsior, New Jersey.

ACT ONE

A projection screen in the middle of the curtain. The first lantern slide: the name of the theatre, and the words: NEWS EVENTS OF THE WORLD. *An* ANNOUNCER'S *voice is heard.*

ANNOUNCER: The management takes pleasure in bringing to you – The News Events of the World:

[*Slide of the sun appearing above the horizon*]

Freeport. Long Island.

The sun rose this morning at 6.32 a.m. This gratifying event was first reported by Mrs Dorothy Stetson, of Freeport, Long Island, who promptly telephoned the Mayor.

The Society for Affirming the End of the World at once went into a special session and postponed the arrival of that event for TWENTY-FOUR HOURS.

All honour to Mrs Stetson for her public spirit.

New York City:

[*Slide of the front doors of the theatre in which this play is playing; three cleaning women with mops and pails*]

The X Theatre. During the daily cleaning of this theatre a number of lost objects were collected as usual by Mesdames Simpson, Pateslewski, and Moriarty.

Among these objects found today was a wedding ring, inscribed: To Eva from Adam Genesis II: 18. The ring will be restored to the owner or owners, if their credentials are satisfactory.

Tippehatchee, Vermont:

[*Slide representing a glacier*]

The unprecedented cold weather of this summer has produced a condition that has not yet been satisfactorily explained. There is a report that a wall of ice is moving

97

southward across these counties. The disruption of communications by the cold wave now crossing the country has rendered exact information difficult, but little credence is given to the rumour that the ice had pushed the Cathedral of Montreal as far as St Albans, Vermont.

For further information see your daily papers.

Excelsior, New Jersey:

[*Slide of a modest suburban home*]

The home of Mr George Antrobus, the inventor of the wheel. The discovery of the wheel, following so closely on the discovery of the lever, has centred the attention of the country on Mr Antrobus of this attractive suburban residence district. This is his home, a commodious seven-room house, conveniently situated near a public school, a Methodist church, and a firehouse; it is right handy to an A. and P.

[*Slide of Mr Antrobus on his front steps, smiling and lifting his straw hat. He holds a wheel.*]

Mr Antrobus, himself. He comes of very old stock and has made his way up from next to nothing.

It is reported that he was once a gardener, but left that situation under circumstances that have been variously reported.

Mr Antrobus is a veteran of foreign wars, and bears a number of scars, front and back.

[*Slide of Mrs Antrobus, holding some roses*]

This is Mrs Antrobus, the charming and gracious president of the Excelsior Mothers' Club.

Mrs Antrobus is an excellent needlewoman; it is she who invented the apron on which so many interesting changes have been rung since.

[*Slide of the family and Sabina*]

Here we see the Antrobuses with their two children,

ACT ONE

Henry and Gladys, and friend. The friend in the rear is Lily Sabina, the maid.

I know we all want to congratulate this typical American family on its enterprise. We all wish Mr Antrobus a successful future. Now the management takes you to the interior of this home for a brief visit.

[*Curtain rises. Living-room of a commuter's home.* SABINA — *straw-blonde, over-rouged — is standing by the window back centre, a feather duster under her elbow*.]

SABINA: Oh, oh, oh! Six o'clock and the master not home yet.

Pray God nothing serious has happened to him crossing the Hudson River. If anything happened to him, we would certainly be inconsolable and have to move into a less desirable residence district.

The fact is I don't know what'll become of us. Here it is the middle of August and the coldest day of the year. It's simply freezing; the dogs are sticking to the sidewalks; can nobody explain that? No. But I'm not surprised. The whole world's at sixes and sevens, and why the house hasn't fallen down about our ears long ago is a miracle to me.

[*A fragment of the right wall leans precariously over the stage.* SABINA *looks at it nervously and it slowly rights itself*.]

Every night this same anxiety as to whether the master will get home safely: whether he'll bring home anything to eat. In the midst of life we are in the midst of death, a truer word was never said.

[*The fragment of scenery flies up into the lofts.* SABINA *is struck dumb with surprise, shrugs her shoulders, and starts dusting Mr Antrobus's chair, including the under side*.]

Of course, Mr Antrobus is a very fine man, an excellent husband and father, a pillar of the church, and has all the best interests of the community at heart. Of course,

99

every muscle goes tight every time he passes a policeman; but what I think is that there are certain charges that ought not to be made, and I think I may add, ought not to be allowed to be made; we're all human; who isn't?

[*She dusts Mrs Antrobus's chair.*]

Mrs Antrobus is as fine a woman as you could hope to see. She lives only for her children; and if it would be any benefit to her children she'd see the rest of us stretched out dead at her feet without turning a hair – that's the truth. If you want to know anything more about Mrs Antrobus, just go and look at a tigress, and look hard.

As to the children –

Well, Henry Antrobus is a real, clean-cut American boy. He'll graduate from High School one of these days, if they make the alphabet any easier – Henry, when he has a stone in his hand, has a perfect aim; he can hit anything from a bird to an older brother – Oh! I didn't mean to say that! – but it certainly was an unfortunate accident, and it was very hard getting the police out of the house.

Mr and Mrs Antrobus's daughter is named Gladys. She'll make some good man a good wife some day, if he'll just come down off the movie screen and ask her.

So here we are!

We've managed to survive for some time now, catch as catch can, the fat and the lean, and if the dinosaurs don't trample us to death, and if the grasshoppers don't eat up our garden, we'll all live to see better days, knock on wood.

Each new child that's born to the Antrobuses seems to them to be sufficient reason for the whole universe's being set in motion; and each new child that dies seems to them to have been spared a whole world of sorrow, and what the end of it will be is still very much an open question.

We've rattled along, hot and cold, for some time now –

[*A portion of the wall above the door, right, flies up into the air and disappears.*]

– and my advice to you is not to inquire into why or whither, but just enjoy your ice-cream while it's on your plate – that's my philosophy.

Don't forget that a few years ago we came through the depression by the skin of our teeth! One more tight squeeze like that and where will we be?

[*This is a cue line.* SABINA *looks angrily at the kitchen door and repeats*]

... we came through the depression by the skin of our teeth; one more tight squeeze like that and where will we be?

[*Flustered, she looks through the opening in the right wall; then goes to the window and reopens the act.*]

Oh, oh, oh! Six o'clock and the master not home yet. Pray God nothing has happened to him crossing the Hudson. Here it is the middle of August and the coldest day of the year. It's simply freezing; the dogs are sticking. One more tight squeeze like that and where will we be?

VOICE [*off stage*]: Make up something! Invent something!

SABINA: Well ... uh ... this certainly is a fine American home ... and – uh ... everybody's very happy ... and – uh ... [*She suddenly flings pretence to the winds and coming downstage says with indignation*] I can't invent any words for this play, and I'm glad I can't. I hate this play and every word in it.

As for me, I don't understand a single word of it, anyway – all about the troubles the human race has gone through, there's a subject for you.

Besides the author hasn't made up his silly mind as to whether we're all living back in caves or in New Jersey today, and that's the way it is all the way through.

Oh – why can't we have plays like we used to have – *Peg o' My Heart*, and *Smilin' Thru*, and *The Bat*, good entertainment with a message you can take home with you?

I took this hateful job because I had to. For two years I've sat up in my room living on a sandwich and a cup of tea, waiting for better times in the theatre. And look at me now: I – I who've played *Rain* and *The Barretts of Wimpole Street* and *First Lady* – God in Heaven!

[*The* STAGE MANAGER *puts his head out from the hole in the scenery.*]

MR FITZPATRICK: Miss Somerset!! Miss Somerset!

SABINA: Oh! Anyway! – nothing matters! It'll all be the same in a hundred years. [*Loudly*] We came through the depression by the skin of our teeth – that's true! – one more tight squeeze like that and where will we be?

[*Enter* MRS ANTROBUS, *a mother.*]

MRS ANTROBUS: Sabina, you've let the fire go out.

SABINA [*in a lather*]: One-thing-and-another; don't-know-whether-my-wits-are-upside-or-down; might-as-well-be-dead-as-alive-in-a-house-all-sixes-and-sevens. . . .

MRS ANTROBUS: You've let the fire go out. Here it is the coldest day of the year right in the middle of August, and you've let the fire go out.

SABINA: Mrs Antrobus, I'd like to give my two weeks' notice, Mrs Antrobus. A girl like I can get a situation in a home where they're rich enough to have a fire in every room, Mrs Antrobus, and a girl don't have to carry the responsibility of the whole house on her two shoulders. And a home without children, Mrs Antrobus, because children are a thing only a parent can stand, and a truer word was never said; and a home, Mrs Antrobus, where the master of the house don't pinch decent, self-respecting girls when he meets them in a dark corridor. I mention no names and make no charges. So you have my notice, Mrs Antrobus. I hope that's perfectly clear.

MRS ANTROBUS: You've let the fire go out! – Have you milked the mammoth?

SABINA: I don't understand a word of this play – Yes, I've milked the mammoth.

MRS ANTROBUS: Until Mr Antrobus comes home we have no food and we have no fire. You'd better go over to the neighbours and borrow some fire.

SABINA: Mrs Antrobus! I can't! I'd die on the way, you know I would. It's worse than January. The dogs are sticking to the sidewalks. I'd die.

MRS ANTROBUS: Very well, I'll go.

SABINA [even more distraught, coming forward and sinking on her knees]: You'd never come back alive; we'd all perish; if you weren't here, we'd just perish. How do we know Mr Antrobus'll be back? We don't know. If you go out, I'll just kill myself.

MRS ANTROBUS: Get up, Sabina.

SABINA: Every night it's the same thing. Will he come back safe, or won't he? Will we starve to death, or freeze to death, or boil to death or will we be killed by burglars? I don't know why we go on living. I don't know why we go on living at all. It's easier being dead. [She flings her arms on the table and buries her head in them. In each of the succeeding speeches she flings her head up – and sometimes her hands – then quickly buries her head again.]

MRS ANTROBUS: The same thing! Always throwing up the sponge, Sabina. Always announcing your own death. But give you a new hat – or a plate of ice-cream – or a ticket to the movies, and you want to live for ever.

SABINA: You don't care whether we live or die; all you care

about is those children. If it would be any benefit to them you'd be glad to see us all stretched out dead.

MRS ANTROBUS: Well, maybe I would.

SABINA: And what do they care about? Themselves – that's all they care about. [*Shrilly*] They make fun of you behind your back. Don't tell me: they're ashamed of you. Half the time, they pretend they're someone else's children. Little thanks you get from them.

MRS ANTROBUS: I'm not asking for any thanks.

SABINA: And Mr Antrobus – you don't understand *him*. All that work he does – trying to discover the alphabet and the multiplication table. Whenever he tries to learn anything you fight against it.

MRS ANTROBUS: Oh, Sabina, I know you.

When Mr Antrobus raped you home from your Sabine hills, he did it to insult me.

He did it for your pretty face, and to insult me.

You were the new wife, weren't you?

For a year or two you lay on your bed all day and polished the nails on your hands and feet.

You made puff-balls of the combings of your hair and you blew them up to the ceiling.

And I washed your underclothes and I made you chicken broths.

I bore children and between my very groans I stirred the cream that you'd put on your face.

But I knew you wouldn't last.

You didn't last.

SABINA: But it was I who encouraged Mr Antrobus to make the alphabet. I'm sorry to say it, Mrs Antrobus, but you're not a beautiful woman, and you can never know what a man could do if he tried. It's girls like I who inspire the multiplication table.

I'm sorry to say it, but you're not a beautiful woman, Mrs Antrobus, and that's the God's truth.

MRS ANTROBUS: And you didn't last – you sank to the kitchen. And what do you do there? *You let the fire go out!* No wonder to you it seems easier being dead.

Reading and writing and counting on your fingers is all very well in their way – but I keep the home going. – There's that dinosaur on the front lawn again – Shoo! Go away. Go away.

[*The baby* DINOSAUR *puts his head in the window.*]

DINOSAUR: It's cold.

MRS ANTROBUS: You go around to the back of the house where you belong.

DINOSAUR: It's cold.

[*The* DINOSAUR *disappears.* MRS ANTROBUS *goes calmly out.*

SABINA *slowly raises her head and speaks to the audience. The central portion of the centre wall rises, pauses, and disappears into the loft.*]

SABINA: Now that you audience are listening to this, too, I understand it a little better.

I wish eleven o'clock were here; I don't want to be dragged through this whole play again.

[*The* TELEGRAPH BOY *is seen entering along the back wall of the stage from the right. She catches sight of him and calls*]

Mrs Antrobus! Mrs Antrobus! Help! There's a strange man coming to the house. He's coming up the walk, help!

[*Enter* MRS ANTROBUS *in alarm, but efficient.*]

MRS ANTROBUS: Help me quick!

[*They barricade the door by piling the furniture against it.*]

Who is it? What do you want?

TELEGRAPH BOY: A telegram for Mrs Antrobus from Mr Antrobus in the city.

SABINA: Are you sure, are you sure! Maybe it's just a trap!

MRS ANTROBUS: I know his voice, Sabina. We can open the door.

[*Enter the* TELEGRAPH BOY, *twelve years old, in uniform. The* DINOSAUR *and* MAMMOTH *slip by him into the room and settle down front right.*]

I'm sorry we kept you waiting. We have to be careful, you know. [*To the animals*] Hm! ... Will you be quiet?

[*They nod.*]

Have you had your supper?

[*They nod.*]

Are you *ready* to come in?

[*They nod.*]

Young man, have you any fire with you? Then light the grate, will you?

[*He nods, produces something like a briquet; and kneels by the imagined fireplace, footlights centre. Pause.*]

What are people saying about this cold weather?

[*He makes a doubtful shrug with his shoulders.*]

Sabina, take this stick and go and light the stove.

SABINA: Like I told you, Mrs Antrobus; two weeks. That's the law. I hope that's perfectly clear. [*Exit.*]

MRS ANTROBUS: What about this cold weather?

TELEGRAPH BOY [*lowered eyes*]: Of course, I don't know anything ... but they say there's a wall of ice moving down from the North, that's what they say. We can't get Boston by telegraph, and they're burning pianos in Hartford. ... It moves everything in front of it, churches and post offices and city halls.

I live in Brooklyn myself.

MRS ANTROBUS: What are people doing about it?

TELEGRAPH BOY: Well ... uh ... Talking mostly.

Or just what you'd do a day in February.

There are some that are trying to go South and the roads are crowded; but you can't take old people and children very far in a cold like this.

MRS ANTROBUS: What's this telegram you have for me?

TELEGRAPH BOY [*fingertips to his forehead*]: If you just wait a minute; I've got to remember it.

[*The* ANIMALS *have left their corner and are nosing him. Presently they take places on either side of him, leaning against his hips, like heraldic beasts.*]

This telegram was flashed from Murray Hill to University Heights! And then by puffs of smoke from University Heights to Staten Island.

And then by lantern from Staten Island to Plainfield, New Jersey. What hath God wrought! [*He clears his throat.*] 'To Mrs Antrobus, Excelsior, New Jersey: My dear wife, will be an hour late. Busy day at the office. Don't worry the children about the cold just keep them warm burn everything except Shakespeare.'

[*Pause.*]

MRS ANTROBUS: Men! – He knows I'd burn ten Shakespeares to prevent a child of mine from having one cold in the head. What does it say next?

[*Enter* SABINA.]

TELEGRAPH BOY: 'Have made great discoveries today have separated em from en.'

SABINA: I know what that is, that's the alphabet, yes it is. Mr Antrobus is just the cleverest man. Why, when the alphabet's finished, we'll be able to tell the future and everything.

TELEGRAPH BOY: Then listen to this: 'Ten tens make a hundred semi-colon consequences far-reaching.' [*Watches for effect.*]

MRS ANTROBUS: The earth's turning to ice, and all he can do is to make up new numbers.

TELEGRAPH BOY: Well, Mrs Antrobus, like the head man at our office said: a few more discoveries like that and we'll be worth freezing.

MRS ANTROBUS: What does he say next?

TELEGRAPH BOY: I ... I can't do this last part very well. [*He clears his throat and sings.*] 'Happy w'dding ann'vers'ry to you, Happy ann'vers'ry to you –'

[*The* ANIMALS *begin to howl soulfully;* SABINA *screams with pleasure.*]

MRS ANTROBUS: Dolly! Frederick! Be quiet.

TELEGRAPH BOY [*above the din*]: 'Happy w'dding ann'-vers'ry, dear Eva; happy w'dding ann'vers'ry to you.'

MRS ANTROBUS: Is that in the telegram? Are they singing telegrams now?

[*He nods.*]

The earth's getting so silly no wonder the sun turns cold.

SABINA: Mrs Antrobus, I want to take back the notice I gave you. Mrs Antrobus, I don't want to leave a house that gets such interesting telegrams and I'm sorry for anything I said. I really am.

MRS ANTROBUS: Young man, I'd like to give you something for all this trouble; Mr Antrobus isn't home yet and I have no money and no food in the house –

TELEGRAPH BOY: Mrs Antrobus ... I don't like to ... appear to ... ask for anything, but ...

MRS ANTROBUS: What is it you'd like?

TELEGRAPH BOY: Do you happen to have an old needle you could spare? My wife just sits home all day thinking about needles.

SABINA [*shrilly*]: We only got two in the house. Mrs Antrobus, you know we only got two in the house.

MRS ANTROBUS [*after looking at Sabina taking a needle from her collar*]: Why yes, I can spare this.

TELEGRAPH BOY [*lowered eyes*]: Thank you, Mrs Antrobus. Mrs Antrobus, can I ask you something else? I have two sons of my own; if the cold gets worse, what should I do?

SABINA: I think we'll all perish, that's what I think. Cold like this in August is just the end of the whole world.

[*Silence.*]

MRS ANTROBUS: I don't know. After all, what does one do about anything? Just keep as warm as you can. And don't let your wife and children see that you're worried.

TELEGRAPH BOY: Yes.... Thank you, Mrs Antrobus. Well, I'd better be going. – Oh, I forgot! There's one more sentence in the telegram. 'Three cheers have invented the wheel.'

MRS ANTROBUS: A wheel? What's a wheel?

TELEGRAPH BOY: I don't know: That's what it said. The sign for it is like this. Well, good-bye.

[*The women see him to the door, with good-byes and injunctions to keep warm.*]

SABINA [*apron to her eyes, wailing*]: Mrs Antrobus, it looks to me like all the nice men in the world are already married; I don't know why that is.

[*Exit.*]

MRS ANTROBUS [*thoughtful; to the animals*]: Do you ever remember hearing tell of any cold like this in August?

[*The ANIMALS shake their heads.*]

From your grandmothers or anyone?

[*They shake their heads.*]

Have you any suggestions?

[*They shake their heads. She pulls her shawl around, goes to the front door and opening it an inch calls*]

HENRY. GLADYS. CHILDREN. Come right in and get warm. No, no, when mama says a thing she means it.

Henry! HENRY. Put down that stone. You know what happened last time.

[*Shriek*]

HENRY! Put down that stone!

Gladys! Put down your dress! Try and be a lady.

[*The* CHILDREN *bound in and dash to the fire. They take off their winter things and leave them in heaps on the floor.*]

GLADYS: Mama, I'm hungry. Mama, why is it so cold?

HENRY [*at the same time*]: Mama, why doesn't it snow? Mama, when's supper ready? Maybe it'll snow and we can make snowballs.

GLADYS: Mama, it's so cold that in one more minute I just couldn't of stood it.

MRS ANTROBUS: Settle down, both of you, I want to talk to you.

[*She draws up a hassock and sits front centre over the orchestra pit before the imaginary fire. The* CHILDREN *stretch out on the floor, leaning against her lap. Tableau by Raphael. The* ANIMALS *edge up and complete the triangle.*]

It's just a cold spell of some kind. Now listen to what I'm saying:

When your father comes home I want you to be extra quiet. He's had a hard day at the office and I don't know but what he may have one of his moods.

I just got a telegram from him very happy and excited, and you know what that means. Your father's temper's uneven; I guess you know that.

[*Shriek*]

Henry! Henry!

Why – why can't you remember to keep your hair down over your forehead? You must keep that scar covered up.

Don't you know that when your father sees it he loses all control over himself? He goes crazy. He wants to die.

[*After a moment's despair she collects herself decisively, wets the hem of her apron in her mouth, and starts polishing his forehead vigorously.*]

Lift up your head. Stop squirming. Blessed me, sometimes I think that it's going away – and then there it is: just as red as ever.

HENRY: Mama, today at school two teachers forgot and called me by my old name. They forgot, Mama. You'd better write another letter to the principal, so that he'll tell them I've changed my name. Right out in class they called me: Cain.

MRS ANTROBUS [*putting her hand on his mouth, too late; hoarsely*]: Don't say it. [*Polishing feverishly*] If you're good they'll forget it. Henry, you didn't hit anyone ... today, did you?

HENRY: Oh ... no-o!

MRS ANTROBUS [*still working, not looking at Gladys*]: And, Gladys, I want you to be especially nice to your father tonight. You know what he calls you when you're good – his little angel, his little star. Keep your dress down like a little lady. And keep your voice nice and low. Gladys Antrobus!! What's that red stuff you have on your face? [*Slaps her.*] You're a filthy detestable child! [*Rises in real, though temporary, repudiation and despair.*] Get away from me, both of you! I wish I'd never seen sight or sound of you. Let the cold come! I can't stand it. I don't want to go on. [*She walks away.*]

GLADYS [*weeping*]: All the girls at school do, Mama.

MRS ANTROBUS [*shrieking*]: I'm through with you, that's all! Sabina! Sabina! Don't you know your father'd go crazy if he saw that paint on your face? Don't you know your father thinks you're perfect? Don't you know he couldn't live if he didn't think you were perfect? – Sabina!

[*Enter* SABINA.]

SABINA: Yes, Mrs Antrobus!

MRS ANTROBUS: Take this girl out into the kitchen and wash her face with the scrubbing brush.

MR ANTROBUS [*outside, roaring*]: 'I've been working on the railroad, all the live-long day . . . etc.'

[*The* ANIMALS *start running around in circles, bellowing.* SABINA *rushes to the window.*]

MRS ANTROBUS: Sabina, what's that noise outside?

SABINA: Oh, it's a drunken tramp. It's a giant, Mrs Antrobus. We'll all be killed in our beds, I know it!

MRS ANTROBUS: Help me quick. Quick everybody.

[*Again they stack all the furniture against the door.* MR ANTROBUS *pounds and bellows.*]

Who is it? What do you want? – Sabina, have you any boiling water ready? – Who is it?

MR ANTROBUS: Broken-down camel of a pig's snout, open this door.

MRS ANTROBUS: God be praised! It's your father – Just a minute, George! – Sabina, clear the door, quick. Gladys, come here while I clean your nasty face!

MR ANTROBUS: She-bitch of a goat's gizzard, I'll break every bone in your body. Let me in or I'll tear the whole house down.

MRS ANTROBUS: Just a minute, George, something's the matter with the lock.

MR ANTROBUS: Open the door or I'll tear your livers out. I'll smash your brains on the ceiling, and Devil take the hindmost.

MRS ANTROBUS: Now, you can open the door, Sabina. I'm ready.

ACT ONE

[*The door is flung open. Silence.* MR ANTROBUS – *face of a Keystone Comedy Cop – stands there in fur cap and blanket. His arms are full of parcels, including a large stone wheel with a centre in it. One hand carries a railroad man's lantern. Suddenly he bursts into joyous roar.*]

MR ANTROBUS: Well, how's the whole crooked family?

[*Relief. Laughter. Tears. Jumping up and down.* ANIMALS *cavorting.* ANTROBUS *throws the parcels on the ground. Hurls his cap and blanket after them. Heroic embraces. Mêlée of humans and animals, Sabina included.*]

I'll be scalded and tarred if a man can't get a little welcome when he comes home. Well, Maggie, you old gunny-sack, how's the broken-down old weather hen? – Sabina, old fishbait, old skunkpot – And the children – how've the little smellers been?

GLADYS: Papa, Papa, Papa, Papa, Papa.

MR ANTROBUS: How've they been, Maggie?

MRS ANTROBUS: Well, I must say, they've been as good as gold. I haven't had to raise my voice once. I don't know what's the matter with them.

ANTROBUS [*kneeling before Gladys*]: Papa's little weasel, eh? – Sabina, there's some food for you – Papa's little gopher?

GLADYS [*her arm around his neck*]: Papa, you're always teasing me.

ANTROBUS: And Henry? Nothing rash today, I hope. Nothing rash?

HENRY: No, Papa.

ANTROBUS [*roaring*]: Well that's good, that's good – I'll bet Sabina let the fire go out.

SABINA: Mr Antrobus, I've given my notice. I'm leaving two weeks from today. I'm sorry, but I'm leaving.

ANTROBUS [*roar*]: Well, if you leave now you'll freeze to death, so go and cook the dinner.

SABINA: Two weeks, that's the law. [*Exit.*]

ANTROBUS: Did you get my telegram?

MRS ANTROBUS: Yes. – What's a wheel?

[*He indicates the wheel with a glance.* HENRY *is rolling it around the floor. Rapid, hoarse interchange;* MRS ANTROBUS: 'What does this cold weather mean? It's below freezing.' ANTROBUS: 'Not before the children!' MRS ANTROBUS: 'Shouldn't we do something about it? – start off, move?' ANTROBUS: 'Not before the children ! ! !' He gives Henry à sharp slap.*]

HENRY: Papa, you hit me!

ANTROBUS: Well, remember it. That's to make you remember today. Today. The day the alphabet's finished; and the day that we *saw* the hundred – the hundred, the hundred, the hundred, the hundred, the hundred – there's no end to 'em.

I've had a day at the office!

Take a look at that wheel, Maggie – when I've got that to rights: you'll see a sight.

There's a reward there for all the walking you've done.

MRS ANTROBUS: How do you mean?

ANTROBUS [*on the hassock looking into the fire; with awe*]: Maggie, we've reached the top of the wave. There's not much more to be done. We're there!

MRS ANTROBUS [*cutting across his mood sharply*]: And the ice?

ANTROBUS: The ice!

HENRY [*playing with the wheel*]: Papa, you could put a chair on this.

ANTROBUS [*broodingly*]: Ye-e-s, any booby can fool with it now – but I thought of it first.

MRS ANTROBUS: Children, go out in the kitchen. I want to talk to your father alone.

[*The* CHILDREN *go out.* ANTROBUS *has moved to his chair*

up left. He takes the goldfish bowl on his lap; pulls the canary cage down to the level of his face. Both the ANIMALS *put their paws up on the arm of his chair.* MRS ANTROBUS *faces him across the room, like a judge.*]

MRS ANTROBUS: Well?

ANTROBUS [*shortly*]: It's cold – How things been, eh ? Keck, keck, keck – And you, Maggie?

MRS ANTROBUS: I know it's cold.

ANTROBUS [*to the canary*]: No spilling of sunflower seed, eh? No singing after lights-out, y'know what I mean?

MRS ANTROBUS: You can try and prevent us freezing to death, can't you? You can do something? We can start moving. Or we can go on the animals' backs?

ANTROBUS: The best thing about animals is that they don't talk much.

MAMMOTH: It's cold.

ANTROBUS: Eh, eh, eh! Watch that! –

– By midnight we'd turn to ice. The roads are full of people now who can scarcely lift a foot from the ground. The grass out in front is like iron – which reminds me, I have another needle for you – The people up north – where are they?

Frozen ... crushed. ...

MRS ANTROBUS: Is that what's going to happen to us? – Will you answer me?

ANTROBUS: I don't know. I don't know anything. Some say that the ice is going slower. Some say that it's stopped. The sun's growing cold. What can I do about that. Nothing we can do but burn everything in the house, and the fence-posts and the barn. Keep the fire going. When we have no more fire, we die.

MRS ANTROBUS: Well, why didn't you say so in the first place?

[MRS ANTROBUS *is about to march off when she catches sight of two Refugees, men who have appeared against the back wall of the theatre and who are soon joined by others.*]

REFUGEES: Mr Antrobus! Mr Antrobus! Mr An-nn-tro-bus!

MRS ANTROBUS: Who's that? Who's that calling you?

ANTROBUS [*clearing his throat guiltily*]: Hm – let me see.

[*Two* REFUGEES *come up to the window.*]

REFUGEE: Could we warm our hands for a moment, Mr Antrobus. It's very cold, Mr Antrobus.

ANOTHER REFUGEE: Mr Antrobus, I wonder if you have a piece of bread or something that you could spare.

[*Silence. They wait humbly.* MRS ANTROBUS *stands rooted to the spot. Suddenly a knock at the door, then another hand knocking in short rapid blows.*]

MRS ANTROBUS: Who are these people? Why, they're all over the front yard. What have they come *here* for?

[*Enter* SABINA.]

SABINA: Mrs Antrobus! There are some tramps knocking at the back door.

MRS ANTROBUS: George, tell these people to go away. Tell them to move right along. I'll go and send them away from the back door. Sabina, come with me. [*She goes out energetically.*]

ANTROBUS: Sabina! Stay here! I have something to say to you.

[*He goes to the door and opens it a crack and talks through it.*]
Ladies and gentlemen! I'll have to ask you to wait a few minutes longer. It'll be all right ... while you're waiting you might each one pull up a stake of the fence. We'll need them all for the fireplace. There'll be coffee and sandwiches in a moment.

[SABINA *looks out door over his shoulder and suddenly extends her arm pointing, with a scream.*]

116

SABINA: Mr Antrobus, what's that? ? – that big white thing? Mr Antrobus, it's ICE. It's ICE! !

ANTROBUS: Sabina, I want you to go in the kitchen and make a lot of coffee. Make a whole pail full.

SABINA: Pail full!!

ANTROBUS [*with gesture*]: And sandwiches ... piles of them ... like this.

SABINA: Mr An ... !!

[*Suddenly she drops the play, and says in her own person as Miss Somerset, with surprise.*]

Oh, *I* see what this part of the play means now! This means refugees.

[*She starts to cross to the proscenium.*]

Oh, I don't like it. I don't like it.

[*She leans against the proscenium and bursts into tears.*]

ANTROBUS: Miss Somerset!

VOICE OF STAGE MANAGER: Miss Somerset!

SABINA [*energetically, to the audience*]: Ladies and gentlemen! Don't take this play serious. The world's not coming to an end. You know it's not. People exaggerate! Most people really have enough to eat and a roof over their heads. Nobody actually starves – you can always eat grass or something. That ice business – why, it was a long, long time ago. Besides they were only savages. Savages don't love their families – not like we do.

ANTROBUS *and* STAGE MANAGER: Miss Somerset!!

[*There is renewed knocking at the door.*]

SABINA: All right. I'll say the lines, but I won't think about the play.

[*Enter* MRS ANTROBUS.]

SABINA [*parting thrust at the audience*]: And I advise you not to. think about the play, either.

[*Exit* SABINA.]

MRS ANTROBUS: George, these tramps say that you asked them to come to the house. What does this mean?

[*Knocking at the door*]

ANTROBUS: Just ... uh. ... There are a few friends, Maggie, I met on the road. Real nice, real useful people. ...

MRS ANTROBUS [*back to the door*]: Now, don't you ask them in!

George Antrobus, not another soul comes in here over my dead body.

ANTROBUS: Maggie, there's a doctor there. Never hurts to have a good doctor in the house. We've lost a peck of children, one way and another. You can never tell when a child's throat will get stopped up. What you and I have seen – !!! [*He puts his fingers on his throat, and imitates diphtheria.*]

MRS ANTROBUS: Well, just one person then, the Doctor. The others can go right along the road.

ANTROBUS: Maggie, there's an old man, particular friend of mine –

MRS ANTROBUS: I won't listen to you –

ANTROBUS: It was he that really started off the A.B.Cs.

MRS ANTROBUS: I don't care if he perishes. We can do without reading or writing. We can't do without food.

ANTROBUS: Then let the ice come!! Drink your coffee!! I don't want any coffee if I can't drink it with some good people.

MRS ANTROBUS: Stop shouting. Who else is there trying to push us off the cliff?

ANTROBUS: Well, there's the man ... who makes all the laws. Judge Moses!

MRS ANTROBUS: Judges can't help us now.

ANTROBUS: And if the ice melts? ... and if we pull through?

Have you and I been able to bring up Henry? What have we done?

MRS ANTROBUS: Who are those old women?

ANTROBUS [*coughs*]: Up in town there are nine sisters. There are three or four of them here. They're sort of music teachers ... and one of them recites and one of them –

MRS ANTROBUS: That's the end. A singing troupe! Well, take your choice, live or die. Starve your own children before your face.

ANTROBUS [*gently*]: These people don't take much. They're used to starving. They'll sleep on the floor.

Besides, Maggie, listen: no listen:

Who've we got in the house, but Sabina? Sabina's always afraid the worst will happen. Whose spirits can she keep up? Maggie, these people never give up. They think they'll live and work for ever.

MRS ANTROBUS [*walks slowly to the middle of the room*]: All right, let them in. Let them in. You're master here. [*Softly*] – But these animals must go. Enough's enough. They'll soon be big enough to push the walls down, anyway. Take them away.

ANTROBUS [*sadly*]: All right. The dinosaur and mammoth! – Come on, baby, come on Frederick. Come for a walk. That's a good little fellow.

DINOSAUR: It's cold.

ANTROBUS: Yes, nice cold fresh air. Bracing.

[*He holds the door open and the* ANIMALS *go out. He beckons to his friends. The* REFUGEES *are typical elderly out-of-works from the streets of New York today.* JUDGE MOSES *wears a skull cap.* HOMER *is a blind beggar with a guitar. The seedy crowd shuffles in and waits humbly and expectantly.* ANTROBUS *introduces them to his wife who bows to each with a stately bend of her head.*]

Make yourself at home, Maggie, this is the doctor ... m ... Coffee'll be here in a minute. ... Professor, this is my wife. ... And: ... Judge ... Maggie, you know the Judge.

[*An old blind man with a guitar*]

Maggie, you know ... you know Homer? – Come right in, Judge. –

Miss Muse – are some of your sisters here? Come right in. ... Miss E. Muse, Miss T. Muse, Miss M. Muse.

MRS ANTROBUS: Pleased to meet you.

Just ... make yourself comfortable. Supper'll be ready in a minute.

[*She goes out, abruptly.*]

ANTROBUS: Make yourself at home, friends. I'll be right back.

[*He goes out.*

The REFUGEES *stare about them in awe. Presently several voices start whispering 'Homer! Homer!' All take it up.* HOMER *strikes a chord or two on his guitar, then starts to speak.*]

HOMER: Μῆνιν ἄειδε, θεά, Πηληϊάδεω Ἀχιλῆος,
οὐλομένην, ἣ μυρί' Ἀχαιοῖς ἄλγε' ἔθηκεν,
πολλὰς δ' ἰφθίμους ψυχὰς –

[HOMER'S *face shows he is lost in thought and memory and the words die away on his lips. The* REFUGEES *likewise nod in dreamy recollection. Soon the whisper 'Moses, Moses!' goes around. An aged Jew parts his beard and recites dramatically.*]

MOSES: בְּרֵאשִׁית בָּרָא אֱלֹהִים אֵת הַשָּׁמַיִם וְאֵת הָאָרֶץ: וְהָאָרֶץ הָיְתָה תֹהוּ
וָבֹהוּ וְחֹשֶׁךְ עַל־פְּנֵי תְהוֹם וְרוּחַ אֱלֹהִים מְרַחֶפֶת עַל־פְּנֵי הַמָּיִם:

[*The same dying away of the words takes place, and on the part of the* REFUGEES *the same retreat into recollection. Some of them murmur, 'Yes, yes.'*

The mood is broken by the abrupt entrance of MR *and* MRS ANTROBUS *and* SABINA *bearing platters of sandwiches and a pail of coffee.* SABINA *stops and stares at the guests.*

Sabina, MR ANTROBUS: pass the sandwiches.

SABINA: I thought I was working in a respectable house that had respectable guests. I'm giving my notice, Mr Antrobus: two weeks, that's the law.

MR ANTROBUS: Sabina! Pass the sandwiches.

SABINA: Two weeks, that's the law.

MR ANTROBUS: There's the law. That's Moses.

SABINA [stares]: The Ten Commandments – FAUGH!! – [To audience] That's the worst line I've ever had to say on any stage.

ANTROBUS: I think the best thing to do is just not to stand on ceremony, but pass the sandwiches around from left to right – Judge, help yourself to one of these.

MRS ANTROBUS: The roads are crowded, I hear?

THE GUESTS [all talking at once]: Oh, ma'am, you can't imagine. . . . You can hardly put one foot before you . . . people are trampling one another.

[Sudden silence]

MRS ANTROBUS: Well, you know what I think it is – I think it's sun-spots!

THE GUESTS [discreet hubbub]: Oh, you're right, Mrs Antrobus . . . that's what it is. . . . That's what I was saying the other day.

[Sudden silence]

ANTROBUS: Well, I don't believe the whole world's going to turn to ice.

[All eyes are fixed on him, waiting.]

I can't believe it. Judge! Have we worked for nothing? Professor! Have we just failed in the whole thing?

MRS ANTROBUS: It is certainly very strange – well fortunately on both sides of the family we come of very hearty stock – Doctor, I want you to meet my children. They're eating their supper now. And of course I want them to meet you.

MISS M. MUSE: How many children have you, Mrs Antrobus?

MRS ANTROBUS: I have two – a boy and a girl.

THE JUDGE [*softly*]: I understood you had two sons, Mrs Antrobus.

[MRS ANTROBUS *rises in blind suffering; she walks towards the footlights.*]

MRS ANTROBUS [*in a low voice*]: Abel, Abel, my son, my son, Abel, my son, Abel, Abel, my son.

[*The* REFUGEES *move with few steps towards her as though in comfort, murmuring words in Greek, Hebrew, German, et cetera.*

A piercing shriek from the kitchen – SABINA'S *voice. All heads turn.*]

ANTROBUS: What's that?

[SABINA *enters, bursting with indignation, pulling on her gloves.*]

SABINA: Mr Antrobus – that son of yours, that boy Henry Antrobus – I don't stay in this house another moment! – He's not fit to live among respectable folks and that's a fact.

MRS ANTROBUS: Don't say another word, Sabina. I'll be right back.

[*Without waiting for an answer she goes past her into the kitchen.*]

SABINA: Mr Antrobus, Henry has thrown a stone again and if he hasn't killed the boy that lives next door, I'm very much mistaken. He finished his supper and went out to play; and I heard such a fight; and then I saw it. I saw it with my own eyes. And it looked to me like stark murder.

[MRS ANTROBUS *appears at the kitchen door, shielding* HENRY *who follows her. When she steps aside, we see on Henry's forehead a large ochre and scarlet scar in the shape of a* C. MR ANTROBUS *starts towards him. A pause.* HENRY *is heard saying under his breath*]

HENRY: He was going to take the wheel away from me. He started to throw a stone at me first.

MRS ANTROBUS: George, it was just a boyish impulse. Remember how young he is. [*Louder, in a urgent wail*] George, he's only four thousand years old.

SABINA: And everything was going along so nicely!
[*Silence.* ANTROBUS *goes back to the fireplace.*]

ANTROBUS: Put out the fire! Put out all the fires. [*Violently*] No wonder the sun grows cold. [*He starts stamping on the fireplace.*]

MRS ANTROBUS: Doctor! Judge! Help me! – George, have you lost your mind?

ANTROBUS: There is no mind. We'll not try to live. [*To the guests*] Give it up. Give up trying.
[MRS ANTROBUS *seizes him.*]

SABINA: Mr Antrobus! I'm downright ashamed of you.

MRS ANTROBUS: George, have some more coffee – Gladys! Where's Gladys gone?
[GLADYS *steps in, frightened.*]

GLADYS: Here I am, mama.

MRS ANTROBUS: Go upstairs and bring your father's slippers. How could you forget a thing like that, when you know how tired he is?
[ANTROBUS *sits in his chair. He covers his face with his hands.* MRS ANTROBUS *turns to the Refugees.*]
Can't some of you sing? It's your business in life to sing, isn't it? Sabina!
[*Several of the women clear their throats tentatively, and with frightened faces gather around Homer's guitar. He establishes a few chords. Almost inaudibly they start singing, led by* SABINA, *'Jingle Bells'.* MRS ANTROBUS *continues to* ANTROBUS *in a low voice, while taking off his shoes.*]

George, remember all the other times. When the volcanoes came right up in the front yard.

And the time the grasshoppers ate every single leaf and blade of grass, and all the grain and spinach you'd grown with your own hands. And the summer there were earthquakes every night.

ANTROBUS: Henry! Henry! [*Puts his hand on his forehead.*] Myself. All of us, we're covered with blood.

MRS ANTROBUS: Then remember all the times you were pleased with him and when you were proud of yourself. – Henry! Henry! Come here and recite to your father the multiplication table that you do so nicely.

[HENRY *kneels on one knee beside his father and starts whispering the multiplication table.*]

HENRY [*finally*]: Two times six is twelve; three times six is eighteen – I don't think I know the sixes.

[*Enter* GLADYS *with the slippers.* MRS ANTROBUS *makes stern gestures to her: Go in there and do your best. The* GUESTS *are now singing 'Tenting Tonight'.*]

GLADYS [*putting slippers on his feet*]: Papa . . . papa . . . I was very good in school today. Miss Conover said right out in class that if all the girls had as good manners as Gladys Antrobus, that the world would be a very different place to live in.

MRS ANTROBUS: You recited a piece at assembly, didn't you? Recite it to your father.

GLADYS: Papa, do you want to hear what I recited in class?

[*Fierce directional glance from her mother*]

'THE STAR' by Henry Wadsworth LONGFELLOW.

MRS ANTROBUS: Wait!!! The fire's going out. There isn't enough wood! Henry go upstairs and bring down the chairs and start breaking up the beds.

[*Exit* HENRY. *The singers return to 'Jingle Bells', still very softly.*]

GLADYS: Look, Papa, here's my report card. Lookit. Conduct A! Look, Papa. Papa, do you want to hear the Star, by Henry Wadsworth Longfellow? Papa, you're not mad at me, are you? – I know it'll get warmer. Soon it'll be just like spring, and we can go to a picnic at the Hibernian Picnic Grounds like you always like to do, don't you remember? Papa, just look at me once.

[*Enter* HENRY *with some chairs.*]

ANTROBUS: You recited in assembly, did you?

[*She nods eagerly.*]

You didn't forget it?

GLADYS: No!!! I was perfect.

[*Pause. Then* ANTROBUS *rises, goes to the front door, and opens it. The* REFUGEES *draw back timidly; the song stops; he peers out of the door, then closes it.*]

ANTROBUS [*with decision, suddenly*]: Build up the fire. It's cold. Build up the fire. We'll do what we can. Sabina, get some more wood. Come around the fire, everybody. At least the young ones may pull through. Henry, have you eaten something?

HENRY: Yes, papa.

ANTROBUS: Gladys, have you had some supper?

GLADYS: I ate in the kitchen, papa.

ANTROBUS: If you do come through this – what'll you be able to do? What do you know? Henry, did you take a good look at that wheel?

HENRY: Yes, papa.

ANTROBUS [*sitting down in his chair*]: Six times two are –

HENRY: – twelve; six times three are eighteen; six times four are – Papa, it's hot and cold. It makes my head all funny. It makes me sleepy.

ANTROBUS [*gives him a cuff*]: Wake up. I don't care if your head is sleepy. Six times four are twenty-four. Six times five are –

HENRY: Thirty. Papa!

ANTROBUS: Maggie, put something into Gladys's head on the chance she can use it.

MRS ANTROBUS: What do you mean, George?

ANTROBUS: Six times six are thirty-six.

Teach her the beginning of the Bible.

GLADYS: But, Mama, it's so cold and close.

[HENRY *has all but drowsed off. His father slaps him sharply and the lesson goes on.*]

MRS ANTROBUS: 'In the beginning God created the heavens and the earth; and the earth was waste and void; and the darkness was upon the face of the deep – '

[*The singing starts up again louder.* SABINA *has returned with wood.*]

SABINA [*after placing wood on the fireplace comes down to the footlights and addresses the audience*]: Will you please start handing up your chairs? We'll need everything for this fire. Save the human race. – Ushers, will you pass the chairs up here? Thank you.

HENRY: Six times nine are fifty-four; six times ten are sixty.

[*In the back of the auditorium the sound of chairs being ripped up can be heard.* USHERS *rush down the aisles with chairs and hand them over.*]

GLADYS: 'And God called the light Day and the darkness he called Night.'

SABINA: Pass up your chairs, everybody. Save the human race.

CURTAIN

ACT TWO

Towards the end of the intermission, though with the houselights
still up, lantern slide projections begin to appear on the curtain.
Timetables for trains leaving Pennsylvania Station for Atlantic
City. Advertisements of Atlantic City hotels, drugstores, churches,
rug merchants, fortune tellers, Bingo parlours.

When the houselights go down, the voice of an ANNOUNCER *is*
heard.

ANNOUNCER: The Management now brings you the News
Events of the World. Atlantic City, New Jersey.

[*Projection of a chrome postcard of the waterfront, trimmed in*
mica with the legend: FUN AT THE BEACH]

This great convention city is playing host this week to
the anniversary convocation of that great fraternal order –
the Ancient and Honourable Order of Mammals, Sub-
division Humans. This great fraternal, militant and burial
society is celebrating on the Boardwalk, ladies and gentlemen, its six hundred thousandth Annual Convention.

It has just elected its president for the ensuing term,

[*Projection of Mr and Mrs Antrobus posed as they will be*
shown a few moments later]

Mr George Antrobus of Excelsior, New Jersey. We
show you President Antrobus and his gracious and charming
wife, every inch a mammal. Mr Antrobus has had a long
and chequered career. Credit has been paid to him for many
useful enterprises including the introduction of the lever,
of the wheel and the brewing of beer. Credit has been also
extended to President Antrobus's gracious and charming
wife for many practical suggestions, including the hem, the
gore, and the gusset; and the novelty of the year – frying

in oil. Before we show you Mr Antrobus accepting the nomination, we have an important announcement to make. As many of you know, this great celebration of the Order of the Mammals has received delegations from the other rival Orders – or shall we say: esteemed concurrent Orders: the WINGS, the FINS, the SHELLS, and so on. These Orders are holding their conventions also, in various parts of the world, and have sent representatives to our own, two of a kind.

Later in the day we will show you President Antrobus broadcasting his words of greeting and congratulation to the collected assemblies of the whole natural world.

Ladies and Gentlemen! We give you President Antrobus!
[*The screen becomes a transparency.* MR ANTROBUS *stands beside a pedestal;* MRS ANTROBUS *is seated wearing a corsage of orchids.* ANTROBUS *wears an untidy Prince Albert; spats; from a red rosette in his buttonhole hangs a fine long purple ribbon of honour. He wears a gay lodge hat – something between a fez and a legionnaire's cap.*]

ANTROBUS: Fellow-mammals, fellow-vertebrates, fellow-humans, I thank you. Little did my dear parents think – when they told me to stand on my own feet – that I'd arrive at this place.

My friends, we have come a long way.

During this week of happy celebration it is perhaps not fitting that we dwell on some of the difficult times we have been through. The dinosaur is extinct –
[*Applause*]
– the ice has retreated; and the common cold is being pursued by every means within our power.
[MRS ANTROBUS *sneezes, laughs prettily, and murmurs: 'I beg your pardon.'*]

In our memorial service yesterday we did honour to all

our friends and relatives who are no longer with us, by reason of cold, earthquakes, plagues and ... and ... [*Coughs*] differences of opinion.

As our Bishop so ably said ... uh ... so ably said. ...

MRS ANTROBUS [*closed lips*]: Gone, but not forgotten.

ANTROBUS: 'They are gone, but not forgotten.'

I think I can say, I think I can prophesy with complete ... uh ... with complete. ...

MRS ANTROBUS: Confidence.

ANTROBUS: Thank you my dear – with complete lack of confidence, that a new day of security is about to dawn. The watchword of the closing year was: Work. I give you the watchword for the future: Enjoy Yourselves.

MRS ANTROBUS: George, sit down!

ANTROBUS: Before I close, however, I wish to answer one of those unjust and malicious accusations that were brought against me during this last electoral campaign.

Ladies and gentlemen, the charge was made that at various points in my career I leaned towards joining some of the rival orders – that's a lie.

As I told reporters of the *Atlantic City Herald*, I do not deny that a few months before my birth I hesitated between ... uh ... between pinfeathers and gill-breathing – and so did many of us here – but for the last million years I have been viviparous, hairy, and diaphragmatic.

[*Applause. Cries of 'Good old Antrobus', 'The Prince chap!' 'Georgie', etc.*]

ANNOUNCER: Thank you. Thank you very much, Mr Antrobus. Now I know that our visitors will wish to hear a word from that gracious and charming mammal, Mrs Antrobus, wife and mother – Mrs Antrobus!

[MRS ANTROBUS *rises, lays her programme on her chair, and bows.*]

MRS ANTROBUS: Dear friends, I don't really think I should say anything. After all, it was my husband who was elected and not I.

Perhaps, as president of the Women's Auxiliary Bed and Board Society – I had some notes here, oh, yes, here they are · – I should give a short report from some of our committees that have been meeting in this beautiful city.

Perhaps it may interest you to know that it has at last been decided that the tomato is edible. Can you all hear me? The tomato *is* edible.

A delegate from across the sea reports that the thread woven by a silkworm gives a cloth . . . I have a sample of it here . . . can you see it? smooth, elastic. I should say that it's rather attractive – though personally I prefer less shiny surfaces. Should the windows of a sleeping apartment be open or shut? I know all mothers will follow our debates on this matter with close interest. I am sorry to say that the most expert authorities have not yet decided. It does seem to me that the night air would be bound to be unhealthy for our children, but there are many distinguished authorities on both sides. Well, I could go on talking for ever – as Shakespeare says: a woman's work is seldom done; but I think I'd better join my husband in saying thank you, and sit down. Thank you.

[*She sits down.*]

ANNOUNCER: Oh, Mrs Antrobus!

MRS ANTROBUS: Yes?

ANNOUNCER: We understand that you are about to celebrate a wedding anniversary. I know our listeners would like to extend their felicitations and hear a few words from you on that subject.

MRS ANTROBUS: I have been asked by this kind gentleman

... yes, my friends, this Spring Mr Antrobus and I will be celebrating our five thousandth wedding anniversary.

I don't know if I speak for my husband, but I can say that, as for me, I regret every moment of it.

[*Laughter of confusion*]

I beg your pardon. What I *mean* to say is that I do not regret one moment of it. I hope none of you catch my cold. We have two children. We've always had two children, though it hasn't always been the same two. But as I say, we have two fine children, and we're very grateful for that. Yes, Mr Antrobus and I have been married five thousand years. Each wedding anniversary reminds me of the times when there were no weddings. We had to crusade for marriage. Perhaps there are some women within the sound of my voice who remember that crusade and those struggles; we fought for it, didn't we? We chained ourselves to lamp-posts and we made disturbances in the Senate – anyway, at last we women got the ring. A few men helped us, but I must say that most men blocked our way at every step: they said we were unfeminine.

I only bring up these unpleasant memories, because I see some signs of backsliding from that great victory.

Oh, my fellow mammals, keep hold of that.

My husband says that the watchword for the year is Enjoy Yourselves. I think that's very open to misunderstanding. My watchword for the year is: Save the Family. It's held together for over five thousand years: Save it! Thank you.

ANNOUNCER: Thank you, Mrs Antrobus.

[*The transparency disappears.*]

We had hoped to show you the Beauty Contest that took place here today.

President Antrobus, an experienced judge of pretty girls,

gave the title of Miss Atlantic City 1942 to Miss Lily-Sabina Fairweather, charming hostess of our Boardwalk Bingo Parlour.

Unfortunately, however, our time is up, and I must take you to some views of the Convention City and conveeners – enjoying themselves.

[A burst of music; the curtain rises.

The Boardwalk. The audience is sitting in the ocean. A hand-rail of scarlet cord stretches across the front of the stage. A ramp – also with scarlet handrail – descends to the right corner of the orchestra pit where a great scarlet beach umbrella or a cabana stands. Front and right stage left are benches facing the sea; attached to each bench is a street-lamp.

The only scenery is two cardboard cut-outs six feet high, re-presenting shops at the back of the stage. Reading from left to right they are: SALT WATER TAFFY: FORTUNE TELLER; *then the blank space;* BINGO PARLOUR; TURKISH BATH. *They have practical doors, that of the Fortune Teller's being hung with bright gipsy curtains.*

By the left proscenium and rising from the orchestra pit is the weather signal; it is like the mast of a ship with cross bars. From time to time black discs are hung on it to indicate the storm and hurricane warnings. Three roller-chairs, pushed by melancholy NEGROES, *file by empty. Throughout the act they traverse the stage in both directions.*

From time to time, CONVEENERS, *dressed like Mr Antrobus, cross the stage. Some walk sedately by; others engage in inane horseplay. The old gipsy* FORTUNE TELLER *is seated at the door of her shop, smoking a corncob pipe.*

From the Bingo Parlour comes the voice of the CALLER.]

BINGO CALLER: A – nine; A – nine. C – twenty-six; C – twenty-six.

A – four; A – four. B – twelve.

CHORUS [*back-stage*]: Bingo!!!

[*The front of the Bingo Parlour shudders, rises a few feet in the air and returns to the ground trembling.*]

FORTUNE TELLER [*mechanically, to the unconscious back of a passer-by, pointing with her pipe*]: Bright's disease! Your partner's deceiving you in that Kansas City deal. You'll have six grandchildren. Avoid high places.

[*She rises and shouts after another.*]

Cirrhosis of the liver!

[SABINA *appears at the door of the Bingo Parlour. She hugs about her a blue raincoat that almost conceals her red bathing suit. She tries to catch the Fortune Teller's attention.*]

SABINA: Ssssst! Esmeralda! Sssst!

FORTUNE TELLER: Keck!

SABINA: Has President Antrobus come along yet?

FORTUNE TELLER: No, no, no. Get back there. Hide yourself.

SABINA: I'm afraid I'll miss him. Oh, Esmeralda, if I fail in this, I'll die; I know I'll die. President Antrobus!!! And I'll be his wife! If it's the last thing I'll do, I'll be Mrs George Antrobus. – Esmeralda, tell me my future.

FORTUNE TELLER: Keck!

SABINA: All right, I'll tell *you* my future. [*Laughing dreamily and tracing it out with one finger on the palm of her hand*] I've won the Beauty Contest in Atlantic City – well, I'll win the Beauty Contest of the whole world. I'll take President Antrobus away from that wife of his. Then I'll take every man away from his wife. I'll turn the whole world upside down.

FORTUNE TELLER: Keck!

SABINA: When all those husbands just think about me they'll get dizzy. They'll faint in the streets. They'll have to lean against lamp-posts. – Esmeralda, who was Helen of Troy?

FORTUNE TELLER [*furiously*]: Shut your foolish mouth. When Mr Antrobus comes along you can see what you can do. Until then – go away.

[SABINA *laughs. As she returns to the door of her Bingo Parlour a group of* CONVEENERS *rush over and smother her with attentions:* 'Oh, Miss Lily, you know me. You've known me for years.']

SABINA: Go away, boys, go away. I'm after bigger fry than you are – Why, Mr Simpson!! How *dare* you!! I expect that even you nobodies must have girls to amuse you; but where you find them and what you do with them, is of absolutely no interest to me.

[*Exit. The* CONVEENERS *squeal with pleasure and stumble after her.*

The FORTUNE TELLER *rises, puts her pipe down on the stool, unfurls her voluminous skirts, gives a sharp wrench to her bodice, and strolls towards the audience, swinging her hips like a young woman.*]

FORTUNE TELLER: I tell the future. Keck. Nothing easier. Everybody's future is in their face. Nothing easier.

But who can tell your past – eh? Nobody!

Your youth – where did it go? It slipped away while you weren't looking. While you were asleep. While you were drunk? Puh! You're like our friends, Mr and Mrs Antrobus; you lie awake nights trying to know your past. What did it mean? What was it trying to say to you?

Think! Think! Split your heads. I can't tell the past and neither can you. If anybody tries to tell you the past, take my word for it, they're charlatans! Charlatans! But I can tell the future. [*She suddenly barks at a passing chair-pusher.*] Apoplexy! [*She returns to the audience.*] Nobody listens –

Keck! I see a face among you now – I won't embarrass him by pointing him out, but, listen, it may be you: Next year the watchsprings inside you will crumble up. Death by regret – Type Y. It's in the corners of your mouth. You'll decide that you should have lived for pleasure, but that you missed it. Death by regret – Type Y. . . . Avoid mirrors. You'll try to be angry – but no! – no anger. [*Far forward, confidentially*] And now what's the immediate future of our friends, the Antrobuses? Oh, you've seen it as well as I have, keck – that dizziness of the head; that Great Man dizziness? The inventor of beer and gunpowder. The sudden fits of temper and then the long stretches of inertia? 'I'm a sultan; let my slave-girls fan me?'

You know as well as I what's coming. Rain. Rain. Rain in floods. The deluge. But first you'll see shameful things – shameful things. Some of you will be saying: 'Let him drown. He's not worth saving. Give the whole thing up.' I can see it in your faces. But you're wrong. Keep your doubts and despairs to yourselves.

Again there'll be the narrow escape. The survival of a handful. From destruction – total destruction. [*She points sweeping with her hand to the stage.*] Even of the animals, a few will be saved: two of a kind, male and female, two of a kind.

[*The heads of* CONVEENERS *appear about the stage and in the orchestra pit, jeering at her.*]

CONVEENERS: Charlatan! Madam Kill-joy! Mrs Jeremiah! Charlatan!

FORTUNE TELLER: And *you*! Mark my words before it's too late. Where'll you be?

CONVEENERS: The croaking raven. Old dust and ashes. Rags, bottles, sacks.

FORTUNE TELLER: Yes, stick out your tongues. You can't

stick your tongues out far enough to lick the death-sweat from your foreheads. It's too late to work now – bail out the flood with your soup spoons. You've had your chance and you've lost.

CONVEENERS: Enjoy yourselves!!!

[*They disappear. The* FORTUNE TELLER *looks off left and puts her finger on her lip.*]

FORTUNE TELLER: They're coming – the Antrobuses. Keck. Your hope. Your despair. Your selves.

[*Enter from the left,* MR *and* MRS ANTROBUS *and* GLADYS]

MRS ANTROBUS: Gladys Antrobus, stick your stummick in.

GLADYS: But it's easier this way.

MRS ANTROBUS: Well, it's too bad the new president has such a clumsy daughter, that's all I can say. Try and be a lady.

FORTUNE TELLER: Aijah! That's been said a hundred billion times.

MRS ANTROBUS: Goodness! Where's Henry? He was here just a minute ago. Henry!

[*Sudden violent stir. A roller-chair appears from the left. About it are dancing in great excitement* HENRY *and a* NEGRO CHAIR-PUSHER.]

HENRY [*slingshot in hand*]: I'll put your eye out. I'll make you yell, like you never yelled before.

NEGRO [*at the same time*]: Now, I warns you. I warns you. If you make me mad, you'll get hurt.

ANTROBUS: Henry! What is this? Put down that slingshot.

MRS ANTROBUS [*at the same time*]: Henry! HENRY! Behave yourself.

FORTUNE TELLER: That's right, young man. There are too many people in the world as it is. Everybody's in the way, except one's self.

HENRY: All I wanted to do was – have some fun.

NEGRO: Nobody can't touch my chair, nobody, without I allow 'em to. You get clean away from me and you get away fast.

[*He pushes his chair off, muttering.*]

ANTROBUS: What were you doing, Henry?

HENRY: Everybody's always getting mad. Everybody's always trying to push you around. I'll make him sorry for this; I'll make him sorry.

ANTROBUS: Give me that slingshot.

HENRY: I won't. I'm sorry I came to this place. I wish I weren't here. I wish I weren't anywhere.

MRS ANTROBUS: Now, Henry, don't get so excited about nothing. I declare I don't know what we're going to do with you. Put your slingshot in your pocket, and don't try to take hold of things that don't belong to you.

ANTROBUS: After this you can stay home. I wash my hands of you.

MRS ANTROBUS: Come now, let's forget all about it. Everybody take a good breath of that sea air and calm down.

[*A passing* CONVEENER *bows to Antrobus who nods to him.*]

Who was that you spoke to, George?

ANTROBUS: Nobody, Maggie. Just the candidate who ran against me in the election.

MRS ANTROBUS: The man who ran against you in the election!!

[*She turns and waves her umbrella after the disappearing Conveener.*]

My husband didn't speak to you and he never will speak to you.

ANTROBUS: Now, Maggie.

MRS ANTROBUS: After those lies you told about him in your speeches!

Lies, that's what they were.

GLADYS *and* HENRY: Mama, everybody's looking at you. Everybody's laughing at you.

MRS ANTROBUS: If you must know, my husband's a SAINT, a downright SAINT, and you're not fit to speak to him on the street.

ANTROBUS: Now, Maggie, now, Maggie, that's enough of that.

MRS ANTROBUS: George Antrobus, you're a perfect worm. If you won't stand up for yourself, I will.

GLADYS: Mama, you just act awful in public.

MRS ANTROBUS [*laughing*]: Well, I must say I enjoyed it. I feel better. Wish his wife had been there to hear it. Children, what do you want to do?

GLADYS: Papa, can we ride in one of those chairs? Mama, I want to ride in one of those chairs.

MRS ANTROBUS: No, sir. If you're tired you just sit where you are. We have no money to spend on foolishness.

ANTROBUS: I guess we have money enough for a thing like that. It's one of the things you do at Atlantic City.

MRS ANTROBUS: Oh, we have? I tell you it's a miracle my children have shoes to stand up in. I didn't think I'd ever live to see them pushed around in chairs.

ANTROBUS: We're on vacation, aren't we? We have a right to some treats, I guess. Maggie, some day you're going to drive me crazy.

MRS ANTROBUS: All right, go. I'll just sit here and laugh at you. And you can give me a dollar right in my hand. Mark my words, a rainy day is coming. There's a rainy day ahead of us. I feel it in my bones. Go on, throw your money around. I can starve. I've starved before. I know how.

CONVEENER [*puts his head through Turkish Bath window, and*

says with raised eyebrows]: Hello, George, How are ya? I see where you brought the WHOLE family along.

MRS ANTROBUS: And what do you mean by that?

[CONVEENER *withdraws head and closes window.*]

ANTROBUS: Maggie, I tell you there's a limit to what I can stand. God's Heaven, haven't I worked *enough*? Don't I get *any* vacation? Can't I even give my children so much as a ride in a roller-chair?

MRS ANTROBUS [*putting out her hand for raindrops*]: Anyway, it's going to rain very soon and you have your broadcast to make.

ANTROBUS: Now, Maggie, I warn you. A man can stand a family only just so long. I'm warning you.

[*Enter* SABINA *from the Bingo Parlour. She wears a flounced red silk bathing suit, 1905. Red stockings, shoes, parasol. She bows demurely to Antrobus and starts down the ramp.* ANTROBUS *and the* CHILDREN *stare at her.* ANTROBUS *bows gallantly.*]

MRS ANTROBUS: Why, George Antrobus, how can you say such a thing! You have the best family in the world.

ANTROBUS: Good morning, Miss Fairweather.

[SABINA *finally disappears behind the beach umbrella or in a cabana in the orchestra pit.*]

MRS ANTROBUS: Who on earth was that you spoke to, George?

ANTROBUS [*complacent; mock-modest*]: Hm ... m ... just a ... solambaka keray.

MRS ANTROBUS: What? I can't understand you.

GLADYS: Mama, wasn't she beautiful?

HENRY: Papa, introduce her to me.

MRS ANTROBUS: Children, will you be quiet while I ask your father a simple question? – Who did you say it was, George?

ANTROBUS: Why-uh . . . a friend of mine. Very nice refined girl.

MRS ANTROBUS: I'm waiting.

ANTROBUS: Maggie that's the girl I gave the prize to in the beauty contest – that's Miss Atlantic City 1942.

MRS ANTROBUS: Hm! She looked like Sabina to me.

HENRY [at the railing]: Mama, the life-guard knows her, too. Mama, he knows her well.

ANTROBUS: Henry, come here. – She's a very nice girl in every way and the sole support of her aged mother.

MRS ANTROBUS: So was Sabina, so was Sabina; and it took a wall of ice to open your eyes about Sabina – Henry, come over and sit down on this bench.

ANTROBUS: She's a very different matter from Sabina. Miss Fairweather is a college graduate, Phi Beta Kappa.

MRS ANTROBUS: Henry, you sit here by mama. Gladys –

ANTROBUS [sitting]: Reduced circumstances have required her taking a position as hostess in a Bingo Parlour; but there isn't a girl with higher principles in the country.

MRS ANTROBUS: Well, let's not talk about it – Henry, I haven't seen a whale yet.

ANTROBUS: She speaks seven languages and has more culture in her little finger than you've acquired in a lifetime.

MRS ANTROBUS [assumed amiability]: All right, all right, George. I'm glad to know there are such superior girls in the Bingo Parlours – Henry, what's that? [Pointing at the storm signal, which has one black disc]

HENRY: What is it, Papa?

ANTROBUS: What? Oh, that's the storm signal. One of those black discs means bad weather, two means storm; three means hurricane; and four means the end of the world.

[As they watch it a second black disc rolls into place.]

MRS ANTROBUS: Goodness! I'm going this very minute to buy you all some raincoats.

GLADYS [*putting her cheek against her father's shoulder*]: Mama, don't go yet. I like sitting this way. And the ocean coming in and coming in. Papa, don't you like it?

MRS ANTROBUS: Well, there's only one thing I lack to make me a perfectly happy woman: I'd like to see a whale.

HENRY: Mama, we saw two. Right out there. They're delegates to the convention. I'll find you one.

GLADYS: Papa, ask me something. Ask me a question.

ANTROBUS: Well . . . how big's the ocean?

GLADYS: Papa, you're teasing me. It's-three-hundred and sixty million square-miles-and-it-covers-three-fourths-of-the-earth's-surface-and-its-deepest-place-is-five-and-a-half miles-deep-and-its-average-depth-is-twelve-thousand-feet. No, Papa, ask me something hard, real hard.

MRS ANTROBUS [*rising*]: Now I'm going off to buy those raincoats. I think that bad weather's going to get worse and worse. I hope it doesn't come before your broadcast. I should think we have about an hour or so.

HENRY: I hope it comes and zzzzzz everything before it. I hope it –

MRS ANTROBUS: Henry! – George, I think . . . maybe, it's one of those storms that are just as bad on land as on the sea. When you're just as safe and safer in a good stout boat.

HENRY: There's a boat out at the end of the pier.

MRS ANTROBUS: Well, keep your eye on it. George, you shut your eyes and get a good rest before the broadcast.

ANTROBUS: Thundering Judas, do I have to be told when to open and shut my eyes? Go and buy your raincoats.

MRS ANTROBUS: Now, children, you have ten minutes to

walk around. Ten minutes. And, Henry: control yourself. Gladys, stick by your brother and don't get lost.

[*They run off.*]

MRS ANTROBUS: Will you be all right, George?

[CONVEENERS *suddenly stick their heads out of the Bingo
Parlour and Salt Water Taffy store, and voices rise from the
orchestra pit.*]

CONVEENERS: George. Geo-r-r-rge! George! Leave the old
hencoop at home, George. Do-mes-ticated Georgie!

MRS ANTROBUS [*shaking her umbrella*]: Low common oafs!
That's what they are. Guess a man has a right to bring his
wife to a convention, if he wants to. [*She starts off.*] What's
the matter with a family, I'd like to know. What else have
they got to offer?

[*Exit.* ANTROBUS *has closed his eyes. The* FORTUNE TEL-
LER *comes out of her shop and goes over to the left proscenium.
She leans against it watching Sabina quizzically.*]

FORTUNE TELLER: Heh! Here she comes!

SABINA [*loud whisper*]: What's he doing?

FORTUNE TELLER: Oh, he's ready for you. Bite your lips,
dear, take a long breath and come on up.

SABINA: I'm nervous. My whole future depends on this. I'm
nervous.

FORTUNE TELLER: Don't be a fool. What more could you
want? He's forty-five. His head's a little dizzy. He's just
been elected president. He's never known any other woman
than his wife. Whenever he looks at her he realizes that she
knows every foolish thing he's ever done.

SABINA [*still whispering*]: I don't know why it is, but every
time I start one of these I'm nervous.

[*The* FORTUNE TELLER *stands in the centre of the stage
watching.*]

FORTUNE TELLER: You make me tired.

SABINA: First tell me my fortune.

[*The* FORTUNE TELLER *laughs dryly and makes the gesture of brushing away a nonsensical question.* SABINA *coughs.*]

Oh, Mr Antrobus – dare I speak to you for a moment?

ANTROBUS: What? – Oh, certainly, certainly, Miss Fairweather.

SABINA: Mr Antrobus . . . I've been so unhappy. I've wanted . . . I've wanted to make sure that you don't think I'm the kind of girl who goes out for beauty contests.

FORTUNE TELLER: That's the way!

ANTROBUS: Oh, I understand. I understand perfectly.

FORTUNE TELLER: Give it a little more. Lean on it.

SABINA: I knew you would. My mother said to me this morning: Lily, she said, that fine Mr Antrobus gave you the prize because he saw at once that you weren't the kind of girl who'd go in for a thing like that. But, honestly, Mr Antrobus, in this world, honestly, a good girl doesn't know where to turn.

FORTUNE TELLER: Now you've gone too far.

ANTROBUS: My dear Miss Fairweather!

SABINA: You wouldn't know how hard it is. With that lovely wife and daughter you have. Oh, I think Mrs Antrobus is the finest woman I ever saw. I wish I were like her.

ANTROBUS: There, there. There's . . . uh . . . room for all kinds of people in the world, Miss Fairweather.

SABINA: How wonderful of you to say that. How generous! – Mr Antrobus, have you a moment free? . . . I'm afraid I may be a little conspicuous here . . . could you come down, for just a moment, to my beach cabana . . .?

ANTROBUS: Why-uh . . . yes, certainly . . . for a moment . . . just for a moment.

SABINA: There's a deck-chair there. Because: you know you

do look tired. Just this morning my mother said to me: Lily, she said, I hope Mr Antrobus is getting a good rest. His fine strong face has deep lines in it. Now isn't it true, Mr Antrobus: you work too hard?

FORTUNE TELLER: Bingo! [*She goes into her shop.*]

SABINA: Now you will just stretch out. No. I shan't say a word, not a word. I shall just sit there – privileged. That's what I am.

ANTROBUS [*taking her hand*]: Miss Fairweather . . . you'll . . . spoil me.

SABINA: Just a moment. I have something I wish to say to the audience – Ladies and gentlemen. I'm not going to play this particular scene tonight. It's just a short scene and we're going to skip it. But I'll tell you what takes place and then we can continue the play from there on. Now in this scene –

ANTROBUS [*between his teeth*]: But, Miss Somerset!

SABINA: I'm sorry. I'm sorry. But I have to skip it. In this scene, I talk to Mr Antrobus, and at the end of it he decides to leave his wife, get a divorce at Reno, and marry me. that's all.

ANTROBUS: Fitz! – Fitz!

SABINA: So that now I've told you we can jump to the end of it – where you say:

[*Enter in fury* MR FITZPATRICK, *the stage manager.*]

MR FITZPATRICK: Miss Somerset, we insist on your playing this scene.

SABINA: I'm sorry, Mr Fitzpatrick, but I can't and I won't. I've told the audience all they need to know and now we can go on.

[*Other* ACTORS *begin to appear on the stage, listening.*]

MR FITZPATRICK: And *why* can't you play it?

SABINA: Because there are some lines in that scene that would hurt some people's feelings and I don't think the theatre is a place where people's feelings ought to be hurt.

MR FITZPATRICK: Miss Somerset, you can pack up your things and go home. I shall call the understudy and I shall report you to Equity.

SABINA: I sent the understudy up to the corner for a cup of coffee and if Equity tries to penalize me I'll drag the case right up to the Supreme Court. Now listen, everybody, there's no need to get excited.

MR FITZPATRICK *and* ANTROBUS: Why can't you play it . . . what's the matter with the scene?

SABINA: Well, if you must know, I have a personal guest in the auditorium tonight. Her life hasn't been exactly a happy one. I wouldn't have my friend hear some of these lines for the whole world. I don't suppose it occurred to the author that some other women might have gone through the experience of losing their husbands like this. Wild horses wouldn't drag from me the details of my friend's life, but . . . well, they'd been married twenty years, and before he got rich, why, she'd done the washing and everything.

MR FITZPATRICK: Miss Somerset, your friend will forgive you. We must play this scene.

SABINA: Nothing, nothing will make me say some of those lines . . . about 'a man outgrows a wife every seven years' and . . . and that one about 'the Mohammedans being the only people who looked the subject square in the face'. Nothing.

MR FITZPATRICK: Miss Somerset! Go to your dressing-room. I'll *read* your lines.

SABINA: Now everybody's nerves are on edge.

MR ANTROBUS: Skip the scene.

[MR FITZPATRICK *and the other* ACTORS *go off.*]

SABINA: Thank you. I knew you'd understand. We'll do just what I said. So Mr Antrobus is going to divorce his wife and marry me. Mr Antrobus, you say: 'It won't be easy to lay all this before my wife.'

[*The* ACTORS *withdraw.* ANTROBUS *walks about, his hand to his forehead muttering.*]

ANTROBUS: Wait a minute. I can't get back into it as easily as all that. 'My wife is a very obstinate woman.' Hm ... then you say ... hm ... Miss Fairweather, I mean Lily, it won't be easy to lay all this before my wife. It'll hurt her feelings a little.

SABINA: Listen, George: *other* people haven't got feelings. Not in the same way that we have – we who are presidents like you and prize-winners like me. Listen, other people haven't got feelings; they just imagine they have. Within two weeks they go back to playing bridge and going to the movies.

Listen, dear: everybody in the world except a few people like you and me are just people of straw. Most people have no insides at all. Now that you're president you'll see that. Listen, darling, there's a kind of secret society at the top of the world – like you and me – that know this. The world was made for us. What's life anyway? Except for two things, pleasure and power, what is life? Boredom! Foolishness. You know it is. Except for those two things, life's nau-se-at-ing. So – come here!

[*She moves close. They kiss.*]

So.

Now when your wife comes, it's really very simple; just tell her.

ANTROBUS: Lily, Lily: you're a wonderful woman.

SABINA: Of course I am.

[*They enter the cabana and it hides them from view. Distant*

*roll of thunder. A third black disc appears on the weather
signal. Distant thunder is heard.* MRS ANTROBUS *appears
carrying parcels. She looks about, seats herself on the bench
left, and fans herself with her handkerchief. Enter* GLADYS
right, followed by two CONVEENERS. *She is wearing red
stockings.*]

MRS ANTROBUS: Gladys!

GLADYS: Mama, here I am.

MRS ANTROBUS: Gladys Antrobus!!! Where did you get
those dreadful things?

GLADYS: Wha-a-t? Papa liked the colour.

MRS ANTROBUS: You go back to the hotel this minute!

GLADYS: I won't. I won't. Papa liked the colour.

MRS ANTROBUS: All right. All right. You stay here. I've a
good mind to let your father see you that way. You stay
right here.

GLADYS: I ... I don't want to stay if ... if you don't think
he'd like it.

MRS ANTROBUS: Oh ... it's all one to me. I don't care what
happens. I don't care if the biggest storm in the whole
world comes. Let it come. [*She folds her hands.*] Where's
your brother?

GLADYS [*in a small voice*]: He'll be here.

MRS ANTROBUS: Will he? Well, let him get into trouble.
I don't care. I don't know where your father is, I'm
sure.

[*Laughter from the cabana.*]

GLADYS [*leaning over the rail*]: I think he's ... Mama, he's
talking to the lady in the red dress.

MRS ANTROBUS: Is that so?

[*Pause.*]

We'll wait till he's through. Sit down here beside me
and stop fidgeting ... what are you crying about?

[*Distant thunder. She covers Gladys's stockings with a raincoat.*]

GLADYS: You don't like my stockings.

[*Two* CONVEENERS *rush in with a microphone on a standard and various paraphernalia. The* FORTUNE TELLER *appears at the door of her shop. Other characters gradually gather.*]

BROADCAST OFFICIAL: Mrs Antrobus! Thank God we've found you at last. Where's Mr Antrobus? We've been hunting everywhere for him. It's about time for the broadcast to the conventions of the world.

MRS ANTROBUS [*calm*]: I expect he'll be here in a minute.

BROADCAST OFFICIAL: Mrs Antrobus, if he doesn't show up in time, I hope you will consent to broadcast in his place. It's the most important broadcast of the year.

[SABINA *enters from cabana followed by* ANTROBUS.]

MRS ANTROBUS: No, I shan't. I haven't one single thing to say.

BROADCAST OFFICIAL: Then won't you help us find him, Mrs Antrobus? A storm's coming up. A hurricane. A deluge!

SECOND CONVEENER [*who has sighted Antrobus over the rail*]: Joe! Joe! Here he is.

BROADCAST OFFICIAL: In the name of God, Mr Antrobus, you're on the air in five minutes. Will you kindly please come and test the instrument? That's all we ask. If you just please begin the alphabet slowly.

[ANTROBUS, *with set face, comes ponderously up the ramp. He stops at the point where his waist is level with the stage and speaks authoritatively to the officials.*]

ANTROBUS: I'll be ready when the time comes. Until then, move away. Go away. I have something I wish to say to my wife.

BROADCAST OFFICIAL [*whimpering*]: Mr Antrobus! This is the most important broadcast of the year.

ACT TWO

[*The* OFFICIALS *withdraw to the edge of the stage.* SABINA *glides up the ramp behind Antrobus.*]

SABINA [*whispering*]: Don't let her argue. Remember arguments have nothing to do with it.

ANTROBUS: Maggie, I'm moving out of the hotel. In fact, I'm moving out of everything. For good. I'm going to marry Miss Fairweather. I shall provide generously for you and the children. In a few years you'll be able to see that it's all for the best. That's all I have to say.

BROADCAST OFFICIAL: Mr Antrobus! I hope you'll be ready. This is the most important broadcast of the year.

BINGO ANNOUNCER: A – nine; A – nine. D – forty-two; D – forty-two. C – thirty; C – thirty.
B – seventeen; B – seventeen. C – forty; C – forty.

CHORUS: Bingo!!

GLADYS: What did Papa say, Mama? I didn't hear what papa said.

BROADCAST OFFICIAL: Mr Antrobus. All we want to do is test your voice with the alphabet.

ANTROBUS: Go away. Clear out.

MRS ANTROBUS [*composedly with lowered eyes*]: George, I can't talk to you until you wipe those silly red marks off your face.

ANTROBUS: I think there's nothing to talk about. I've said what I have to say.

SABINA: Splendid!!

ANTROBUS: You're a fine woman, Maggie, but . . . but a man has his own life to lead in the world.

MRS ANTROBUS: Well, after living with you for five thousand years I guess I have a right to a word or two, haven't I?

149

ANTROBUS [*to Sabina*]: What can I answer to that?

SABINA: Tell her that conversation would only hurt her feelings. It's-kinder-in-the-long-run-to-do-it-short-and-quick.

ANTROBUS: I want to spare your feelings in every way I can, Maggie.

BROADCAST OFFICIAL: Mr Antrobus, the hurricane signal's gone up. We could begin right now.

MRS ANTROBUS [*calmly, almost dreamily*]: I didn't marry you because you were perfect. I didn't even marry you because I loved you. I married you because you gave me a promise. [*She takes off her ring and looks at it.*] That promise made up for your faults. And the promise I gave you made up for mine. Two imperfect people got married and it was the promise that made the marriage.

ANTROBUS: Maggie . . . I was only nineteen.

MRS ANTROBUS [*she puts her ring back on her finger*]: And when our children were growing up, it wasn't a house that protected them; and it wasn't our love, that protected them – it was that promise.

And when that promise is broken – this can happen!
[*With a sweep of the hand she removes the raincoat from Gladys's stockings.*]

ANTROBUS [*stretches out his arm, apoplectic*]: Gladys!! Have you gone crazy? Has everyone gone crazy? [*Turning on Sabina*] You did this. You gave them to her.

SABINA: I never said a word to her.

ANTROBUS [*to Gladys*]: You go back to the hotel and take those horrible things off.

GLADYS [*pert*]: Before I go, I've got something to tell you – it's about Henry.

MRS ANTROBUS [*claps her hands peremptorily*]: Stop your noise – I'm taking her back to the hotel, George. Before I go I have a letter. . . . I have a message to throw into the ocean.

[*Fumbling in her handbag*] Where is the plagued thing? Here it is. [*She flings something – invisible to us – far over the heads of the audience to the back of the auditorium.*] It's a bottle. And in the bottle's a letter. And in the letter is written all the things that a woman knows.

It's never been told to any man and it's never been told to any woman, and if it finds its destination, a new time will come. We're not what books and plays say we are. We're not what advertisements say we are. We're not in the movies and we're not on the radio.

We're not what you're all told and what you think we are: We're ourselves. And if any man can find one of us he'll learn why the whole universe was set in motion. And if any man harm any one of us, his soul – the only soul he's got – had better be at the bottom of that ocean – and that's the only way to put it. Gladys, come here. We're going back to the hotel.

[*She drags Gladys firmly off by the hand, but* GLADYS *breaks away and comes down to speak to her father.*]

SABINA: Such goings-on. Don't give it a minute's thought.

GLADYS: Anyway, I think you ought to know that Henry hit a man with a stone. He hit one of those coloured men that push the chairs and the man's very sick. Henry ran away and hid and some policemen are looking for him very hard. And I don't care a bit if you don't want to have anything to do with mama and me, because I'll never like you again and I hope nobody ever likes you again – so there!

[*She runs off.* ANTROBUS *starts after her.*]

ANTROBUS: I . . . I have to see what I can do about this.

SABINA: You stay right here. Don't you go now while you're excited. Gracious sakes, all these things will be forgotten in a hundred years. Come, now, you're on the air. Just

THE SKIN OF OUR TEETH

say anything – it doesn't matter what. Just a lot of birds
and fishes and things.

BROADCAST OFFICIAL: Thank you, Miss Fairweather.
Thank you very much. Ready, Mr Antrobus.

ANTROBUS [*touching the microphone*]: What is it, what is it?
Who am I talking to?

BROADCAST OFFICIAL: Why, Mr Antrobus! To our order
and to all the other orders.

ANTROBUS [*raising his head*]: What are all those birds doing?

BROADCAST OFFICIAL: Those are just a few of the birds.
Those are the delegates to our convention – two of a kind.

ANTROBUS [*pointing into the audience*]: Look at the water.
Look at them all. Those fishes jumping. The children should
see this! – there's Maggie's whales!! Here are your whales,
Maggie!!

BROADCAST OFFICIAL: I hope you're ready, Mr Antrobus.

ANTROBUS: And look on the beach! You didn't tell me these
would be here!

SABINA: Yes, George. Those are the animals.

BROADCAST OFFICIAL [*busy with the apparatus*]: Yes, Mr
Antrobus, those are the vertebrates. We hope the lion will
have a word to say when you're through. Step right up,
Mr Antrobus, we're ready. We'll just have time before the
storm. [*Pause. In a hoarse whisper*] They're wait-ing.

[*It has grown dark. Soon after he speaks a high whistling
noise begins. Strange veering lights start whirling about the stage.
The other characters disappear from the stage.*]

ANTROBUS: Friends. Cousins. Four score and ten billion
years ago our forefather brought forth upon this planet the
spark of life –

[*He is drowned out by thunder. When the thunder stops the
FORTUNE TELLER is seen standing beside him.*]

FORTUNE TELLER: Antrobus, there's not a minute to be lost.

Don't you see the four discs on the weather signal? Take your family into that boat at the end of the pier.

ANTROBUS: My family? I have no family. Maggie! Maggie! They won't come.

FORTUNE TELLER: They'll come – Antrobus! Take these animals into that boat with you. All of them – two of each kind.

SABINA: George, what's the matter with you? This is just a storm like any other storm.

ANTROBUS: Maggie!

SABINA: Stay with me, we'll go ... [*Losing conviction*] This is just another thunderstorm – isn't it? Isn't it?

ANTROBUS: Maggie!!!

[MRS ANTROBUS *appears beside him with* GLADYS.]

MRS ANTROBUS [*matter-of-fact*]: Here I am and here's Gladys.

ANTROBUS: Where've you been? Where have you been? Quick, we're going into that boat out there.

MRS ANTROBUS: I know we are. But I haven't found Henry.

[*She wanders off into the darkness calling 'Henry!'*]

SABINA [*low urgent babbling, only occasionally raising her voice*]: I don't believe it. I don't believe it's anything at all. I've seen hundreds of storms like this.

FORTUNE TELLER: There's no time to lose. Go. Push the animals along before you. Start a new world. Begin again.

SABINA: Esmeralda! George! Tell me – is it really serious?

ANTROBUS [*suddenly very busy*]: Elephants first. Gently, gently. – Look where you're going.

GLADYS [*leaning over the ramp and striking an animal on the back*]: Stop it or you'll be left behind!

ANTROBUS: Is the Kangaroo there? *There* you are! Take those turtles in your pouch, will you? [*To some other animals, pointing to his shoulder*] Here! You jump up here. You'll be trampled on.

GLADYS [*to her father, pointing below*]: Papa, look – the snakes!

MRS ANTROBUS: I can't find Henry. Hen-ry!

ANTROBUS: Go along. Go along. Climb on their backs. – Wolves! Jackals – whatever you are – tend to your own business!

GLADYS [*pointing, tenderly*]: Papa – look.

SABINA: Mr Antrobus – take me with you. Don't leave me here. I'll work. I'll help. I'll do anything.

[*Three* CONVEENERS *cross the stage, marching with a banner.*]

CONVEENERS: George! What are you scared of? – George! Fellas, it looks like rain – 'Maggie, where's my umbrella?' – George, setting up for Barnum and Bailey.

ANTROBUS [*again catching his wife's hand*]: Come on now, Maggie – the pier's going to break any minute.

MRS ANTROBUS: I'm not going a step without Henry. Henry!

GLADYS [*on the ramp*]: Mama! Papa! Hurry. The pier's cracking, Mama. It's going to break.

MRS ANTROBUS: Henry! Cain! CAIN!

[HENRY *dashes into the stage and joins his mother.*]

HENRY: Here I am, Mama.

MRS ANTROBUS: Thank God! – now come quick.

HENRY: I didn't think you wanted me.

MRS ANTROBUS: Quick!

[*She pushes him down before her into the aisle.*

All the ANTROBUSES *are now in the theatre aisle.* SABINA *stands at the top of the ramp.*]

SABINA: Mrs Antrobus, take me. Don't you remember me? I'll work. I'll help. Don't leave me here!

MRS ANTROBUS [*impatiently, but as though it were of no importance*]: Yes, yes. There's a lot of work to be done. Only hurry.

ACT TWO

FORTUNE TELLER [*now dominating the stage. To Sabina with a grim smile*]: Yes, go – back to the kitchen with you.

SABINA [*half-way down the ramp. To Fortune Teller*]: I don't know why my life's always being interrupted – just when everything's going fine!!

[*She dashes up the aisle. Now the* CONVEENERS *emerge doing a serpentine dance on the stage. They jeer at the Fortune Teller.*]

CONVEENERS: Get a canoe – there's not a minute to be lost! Tell me my future, Mrs Croaker.

FORTUNE TELLER: Paddle in the water, boys – enjoy yourselves.

VOICE [*from the Bingo Parlour*]: A – nine; A – nine. C – twenty-four; C – twenty-four.

CONVEENERS: Rags, bottles, and sacks.

FORTUNE TELLER: Go back and climb on your roofs. Put rags in the cracks under your doors – Nothing will keep out the flood. You've had your chance. You've had your day. You've failed. You've lost.

VOICE [*from the Bingo Parlour*]: B – fifteen; B – fifteen.

FORTUNE TELLER [*shading her eyes and looking out to sea*]: They're safe. George Antrobus! Think it over! A new world to make – Think it over!

CURTAIN

ACT THREE

Just before the curtain rises, two sounds are heard from the stage; a cracked bugle call.

The curtain rises on almost total darkness. Almost all the flats composing the walls of Mr Antrobus's house, as of Act I, are up, but they lean helter-skelter against one another, leaving irregular gaps. Among the flats missing are two in the back wall, leaving the frames of the window and door crazily out of line. Off stage, back right, some red Roman fire is burning. The bugle call is repeated. Enter SABINA *through the tilted door. She is dressed as a Napoleonic camp follower, 'la fille du régiment', in begrimed reds and blues.*

SABINA: Mrs Antrobus! Gladys! Where are you?

The war's over. The war's over. You can come out. The peace treaty's been signed.

Where are they? – Hmpf! Are they dead, too? Mrs Annnntrobus! Glaaaadus! Mr Antrobus'll be here this afternoon. I just saw him downtown. Huuuurry and put things in order. He says that now that the war's over we'll all have to settle down and be perfect.

[*Enter* MR FITZPATRICK, *the stage manager, followed by the whole company, who stand waiting at the edges of the stage.* MR FITZPATRICK *tries to interrupt Sabina.*]

MR FITZPATRICK: Miss Somerset, we have to stop a moment.

SABINA: They may be hiding out in the back –

MR FITZPATRICK: Miss Somerset! We have to stop a moment.

SABINA: What's the matter?

MR FITZPATRICK: There's an explanation we have to make to the audience. – Lights, please. [*To the actor who plays Mr Antrobus*] Will you explain the matter to the audience?

[*The lights go up. We now see that a balcony or elevated runway has been erected at the back of the stage, back of the wall of the Antrobus house. From its extreme right and left ends ladder-like steps descend to the floor of the stage.*]

ANTROBUS: Ladies and gentlemen, an unfortunate accident has taken place back stage. Perhaps I should say *another* unfortunate accident.

SABINA: I'm sorry. I'm sorry.

ANTROBUS: The management feels, in fact, we all feel that you are due an apology. And now we have to ask your indulgence for the most serious mishap of all. Seven of our actors have . . . have been taken ill. Apparently, it was something they ate. I'm not exactly clear what happened.

[*All the* ACTORS *start to talk at once.* ANTROBUS *raises his hand.*]

Now, now – not all at once. Fitz, do you know what it was?

MR FITZPATRICK: Why it's perfectly clear. These seven actors had dinner together, and they ate something that disagreed with them.

SABINA: Disagreed with them!!! They have ptomaine poisoning. They're in Bellevue Hospital this very minute in agony. They're having their stomachs pumped out this very minute, in perfect agony.

ANTROBUS: Fortunately, we've just heard they'll all recover.

SABINA: It'll be a miracle if they do, a downright miracle. It was the lemon meringue pie.

ACTORS: It was the fish . . . it was the canned tomatoes . . . it was the fish.

SABINA: It was the lemon meringue pie. I saw it with my own eyes; it had blue mould all over the bottom of it.

ANTROBUS: Whatever it was, they're in no condition to take part in this performance. Naturally, we haven't enough understudies to fill all these roles; but we do have a number of splendid volunteers who have kindly consented to help us out. These friends have watched our rehearsals, and they assure me that they know the lines and the business very well. Let me introduce them to you – my dresser, Mr Tremayne – himself a distinguished Shakespearean actor for many years; our wardrobe mistress, Hester; Miss Somerset's maid, Ivy; and Fred Bailey, captain of the ushers in this theatre.

[*These persons bow modestly.* IVY *and* HESTER *are coloured girls.*]

Now this scene takes place near the end of the act. And I'm sorry to say we'll need a short rehearsal, just a short run-through. And as some of it takes place in the auditorium, we'll have to keep the curtain up. Those of you who wish can go out in the lobby and smoke some more. The rest of you can listen to us, or ... or just talk quietly among yourselves, as you choose. Thank you. Now will you take it over, Mr Fitzpatrick?

MR FITZPATRICK: Thank you – Now for those of you who are listening perhaps I should explain that at the end of this act, the men have come back from the war and the family's settled down in the house. And the author wants to show the hours of the night passing by over their heads, and the planets crossing the sky ... uh ... over their heads. And he says – this is hard to explain – that each of the hours of the night is a philosopher, or a great thinker. Eleven o'clock, for instance, is Aristotle. And nine o'clock is Spinoza. Like that. I don't suppose it means anything. It's just a kind of poetic effect.

SABINA: Not mean anything! Why, it certainly does. Twelve

o'clock goes by saying those wonderful things. I think it means that when people are asleep they have all those lovely thoughts, much better than when they're awake.

IVY: Excuse me, I think it means – excuse me, Mr Fitzpatrick –

SABINA: What were you going to say, Ivy?

IVY: Mr Fitzpatrick, you let my father come to a rehearsal; and my father's a Baptist minister, and he said that the author meant that – just like the hours and stars go by over our heads at night, in the same way the ideas and thoughts of the great men are in the air around us all the time and they're working on us, even when we don't know it.

MR FITZPATRICK: Well, well, maybe that's it. Thank you, Ivy. Anyway – the hours of the night are philosophers. My friends, are you ready! Ivy, can you be eleven o'clock? 'This good estate of the mind possessing its object in energy we call divine.' Aristotle.

IVY: Yes, sir. I know that and I know twelve o'clock and I know nine o'clock.

MR FITZPATRICK: Twelve o'clock? Mr Tremayne, the Bible.

TREMAYNE: Yes.

MR FITZPATRICK: Ten o'clock? Hester – Plato?

[*She nods eagerly.*]

Nine o'clock, Spinoza – Fred?

BAILEY: Yes, sir.

[FRED BAILEY *picks up a great gilded cardboard numeral IX and starts up the steps to the platform.* MR FITZPATRICK *strikes his forehead.*]

MR FITZPATRICK: The planets! ! We forgot all about the planets.

SABINA: O my God! The planets! Are they sick too?

[ACTORS *nod.*]

MR FITZPATRICK: Ladies and gentlemen, the planets are singers. Of course, we can't replace them, so you'll have to imagine them singing in this scene. Saturn sings from the orchestra pit down here. The Moon is way up there. And Mars with a red lantern in his hand, stands in the aisle over there – Tz-tz-tz. It's too bad; it all makes a very fine effect. However! Ready – nine o'clock: Spinoza.

BAILEY [*walking slowly across the balcony, left to right*]: 'After experience had taught me that the common occurrences of daily life are vain and futile – '

FITZPATRICK: Louder, Fred. 'And I saw that all the objects of my desire and fear – '

BAILEY: 'And I saw that all the objects of my desire and fear were in themselves nothing, good nor bad save insofar as the mind was affected by them – '

FITZPATRICK: Do you know the rest? All right. Ten o'clock. Hester. Plato.

HESTER: 'Then tell me, O Critias, how will a man choose the ruler that shall rule over him? Will he not – '

FITZPATRICK: Thank you. Skip to the end, Hester.

HESTER: '. . . can be multiplied a thousand fold in its effects among the citizens.'

FITZPATRICK: Thank you. – Aristotle, Ivy?

IVY: 'This estate of the mind possessing its object in energy we call divine. This we mortals have occasionally and it is this energy which is pleasantest and best. But God has it always. It is wonderful in us; but in Him how much more wonderful.'

FITZPATRICK: Midnight. Midnight, Mr Tremayne. That's right, you've done it before. – All right, everybody. You know what you have to do. – Lower the curtain. House lights up. Act Three of THE SKIN OF OUR TEETH. [*As the curtain descends he is heard saying*] You volunteers, just wear what you have on. Don't try to put on the costumes today.

ACT THREE

[*House lights go down. The act begins again. The Bugle call.
Curtain rises. Enter* SABINA.]

SABINA: Mrs Antrobus! Gladys! Where are you?
The war's over – You've heard all this –
[*She gabbles the main points.*]
Where–are–they? Are–they–dead, too, et cetera. I–just–
saw–Mr–Antrobus–down town, et cetera. [*Slowing up*] He
says that now the war's over we'll all have to settle down
and be perfect. They may be hiding out in the back somewhere. Mrs An-tro-bus.
[*She wanders off. It has grown lighter.*
A trapdoor is cautiously raised and MRS ANTROBUS *emerges
waist-high and listens. She is dishevelled and worn; she wears
a tattered dress and a shawl half covers her head. She talks
down through the trapdoor.*]

MRS ANTROBUS: It's getting light. There's still something
burning over there – Newark, or Jersey City. What? Yes,
I could swear I heard someone moving about up here. But
I can't see anybody. I say: I can't see anybody.
[*She starts to move about the stage.* GLADYS'S *head appears
at the trapdoor. She is holding a baby.*]

GLADYS: Oh, Mama. Be careful.

MRS ANTROBUS: Now, Gladys, you stay out of sight.

GLADYS: Well, let me stay here just a minute. I want the
baby to get some of this fresh air.

MRS ANTROBUS: All right, but keep your eyes open. I'll see
what I can find. I'll have a good hot plate of soup for you
before you can say Jack Robinson. Gladys Antrobus! Do
you know what I think I see? There's old Mr Hawkins
sweeping the sidewalk in front of his A. and P. store.
Sweeping it with a broom. Why, he must have gone crazy,
like the others! I see some other people moving about, too.

GLADYS: Mama, come back, come back.

[MRS ANTROBUS *returns to the trapdoor and listens.*]

MRS ANTROBUS: Gladys, there's something in the air. Everybody's movement's sort of different. I see some women walking right out in the middle of the street.

SABINA'S VOICE: Mrs An-tro-bus!

MRS ANTROBUS *and* GLADYS: What's that?!!

SABINA'S VOICE: Glaaaadys! Mrs An-tro-bus!

[*Enter* SABINA.]

MRS ANTROBUS: Gladys, that's Sabina's voice as sure as I live – Sabina! Sabina! – Are you *alive*?!!

SABINA: Of course, I'm alive. How've you girls been? – *Don't* try and kiss me. I never want to kiss another human being as long as I live. Sh-sh, there's nothing to get emotional about. Pull yourself together, the war's over. Take a deep breath – the war's over.

MRS ANTROBUS: The war's over!! I don't believe you. I don't believe you. I can't believe you.

GLADYS: Mama!

SABINA: Who's that?

MRS ANTROBUS: That's Gladys and her baby. I don't believe you. Gladys, Sabina says the war's over. Oh, Sabina.

SABINA [*leaning over the baby*]: Goodness! Are there any babies left in the world! Can it *see*? And can it cry and everything?

GLADYS: Yes, he can. He notices everything very well.

SABINA: Where on earth did you get it? Oh, I won't ask – Lord, I've lived all these seven years around camp and I've forgotten how to behave. – Now we've got to think about the men coming home. – Mrs Antrobus, go and wash your face, I'm ashamed of you. Put your best clothes on. Mr Antrobus'll be here this afternoon. I just saw him downtown.

MRS ANTROBUS *and* GLADYS: He's alive!! He'll be here!! Sabina, you're not joking?

MRS ANTROBUS: And Henry?

SABINA [*dryly*]: Yes, Henry's alive, too, that's what they say. Now don't stop to talk. Get yourselves fixed up. Gladys, you look terrible. Have you any decent clothes?

[SABINA *has pushed them towards the trapdoor.*]

MRS ANTROBUS [*half down*]: Yes, I've something to wear just for this very day. But, Sabina – who won the war?

SABINA: Don't stop now – just wash your face.

[*A whistle sounds in the distance.*]

Oh, my God, what's that silly little noise?

MRS ANTROBUS: Why, it sounds like . . . it sounds like what used to be the noon whistle at the shoe-polish factory.

[*Exit.*]

SABINA: That's what it is. Seems to me like peacetime's coming along pretty fast – shoe polish!

GLADYS [*half down*]: Sabina, how soon after peacetime begins does the milkman start coming to the door?

SABINA: As soon as he catches a cow. Give him time to catch a cow, dear.

[*Exit* GLADYS. SABINA *walks about a moment, thinking.*]

Shoe polish! My, I'd forgotten what peacetime was like.

[*She shakes her head, then sits down by the trapdoor and starts talking down the hole.*]

Mrs Antrobus, guess what I saw Mr Antrobus doing this morning at dawn. He was tacking up a piece of paper on the door of the Town Hall. You'll die when you hear: it was a recipe for grass soup, for a grass soup that doesn't give you the diarrhoea. Mr Antrobus is still thinking up new things – He told me to give you his love. He's got all sorts of ideas for peacetime, he says. No more laziness and idiocy, he says. And oh, yes! Where are his books? What? Well, pass them up. The first thing he wants to see are his books. He says if you've burnt those books, or if the rats have eaten them, he says it isn't worth while starting over again. Everybody's going to be beautiful he says, and diligent, and very intelligent.

[*A hand reaches up with two volumes.*]

What language is that? Pu-u-gh – mould! And he's got such plans for you, Mrs Antrobus. You're going to study history and algebra – and so are Gladys and I – and philosophy. You should hear him talk. [*Taking two more volumes*] Well, these are in English, anyway. – To hear him talk, seems like he expects you to be a combination, Mrs Antrobus, of a saint and a college professor, and a dance-hall hostess, if you know what I mean.

[*Two more volumes*]

Ugh. German!

[*She is lying on the floor; one elbow bent, her cheek on her hand, meditatively.*]

Yes, peace will be here before we know it. In a week or two we'll be asking the Perkinses in for a quiet evening of bridge. We'll turn on the radio and hear how to be big successes with a new toothpaste. We'll trot down to the movies and see how girls with wax faces live – all *that* will begin again. Oh, Mrs Antrobus, God forgive me but I enjoyed the war. Everybody's at their best in wartime. I'm sorry it's over. And, oh, I forgot! Mr Antrobus sent you another message – can you hear me? –

[*Enter* HENRY, *blackened and sullen. He is wearing torn overalls, but has one gaudy admiral's epaulette hanging by a thread from his right shoulder, and there are vestiges of gold and scarlet braid running down his left trouser leg. He stands listening.*]

Listen! Henry's never to put foot in this house again, he says. He'll kill Henry on sight, if he sees him.

You don't know about Henry??? Well, where have you

been? What? Well, Henry rose right to the top. Top of *what*? Listen, I'm telling you. Henry rose from corporal to captain, to major, to general. – I don't know how to say it, but the enemy is *Henry*; Henry *is* the enemy. Everybody knows that.

HENRY: He'll kill me, will he?

SABINA: Who are *you*? I'm not afraid of you. The war's over.

HENRY: I'll kill him so fast. I've spent seven years trying to find him; the others I killed were just substitutes.

SABINA: Goodness! It's Henry! –

[*He makes an angry gesture.*]

Oh, I'm not afraid of you. The war's over, Henry Antrobus, and you're not any more important than any other unemployed. You go away and hide yourself, until we calm your father down.

HENRY: The first thing to do is to burn up those old books; it's the ideas he gets out of those old books that ... that makes the whole world so you can't live in it.

[*He reels forward and starts kicking the books about, but suddenly falls down in a sitting position.*]

SABINA: You leave those books alone!! Mr Antrobus is looking forward to them a-special. – Gracious sakes, Henry, you're so tired you can't stand up. Your mother and sister'll be here in a minute and we'll think what to do about you.

HENRY: What did they ever care about me?

SABINA: There's that old whine again. All you people think you're not loved enough, nobody loves you. Well, you start being lovable and we'll love you.

HENRY [*outraged*]: I don't want anybody to love me.

SABINA: Then stop talking about it all the time.

HENRY: I *never* talk about it. The last thing I want is anybody to pay any attention to me.

SABINA: I can hear it behind every word you say.

HENRY: I want everybody to hate me.

SABINA: Yes, you've decided that's second best, but it's still the same thing – Mrs Antrobus! Henry's here. He's so tired he can't stand up.

[MRS ANTROBUS *and* GLADYS, *with her baby, emerge. They are dressed as in Act I.* MRS ANTROBUS *carries some objects in her apron, and* GLADYS *has a blanket over her shoulder.*]

MRS ANTROBUS *and* GLADYS: Henry! Henry! Henry!

HENRY [*glaring at them*]: Have you anything to eat?

MRS ANTROBUS: Yes, I have, Henry. I've been saving it for this very day – two good baked potatoes. No! Henry! one of them's for your father. Henry!! Give me that other potato back this minute.

[SABINA *sidles up behind him and snatches the other potato away.*]

SABINA: He's so dog-tired he doesn't know what he's doing.

MRS ANTROBUS: Now you just rest there, Henry, until I can get your room ready. Eat that potato good and slow, so you can get all the nourishment out of it.

HENRY: You all might as well know right now that I haven't come back here to live.

MRS ANTROBUS: Sh. . . . I'll put this coat over you. Your room's hardly damaged at all. Your football trophies are a little tarnished, but Sabina and I will polish them up tomorrow.

HENRY: Did you hear me? I don't live here. I don't belong to anybody.

MRS ANTROBUS: Why, how can you say a thing like that! You certainly do belong right here. Where else would you want to go? Your forehead's feverish, Henry, seems to me. You'd better give me that gun, Henry. You won't need that any more.

166

GLADYS [*whispering*]: Look, he's fallen asleep already, with his potato half-chewed.

SABINA: Puh! The terror of the world.

MRS ANTROBUS: Sabina, you mind your own business, and start putting the room to rights.

[HENRY *has turned his face to the back of the sofa.* MRS ANTROBUS *gingerly puts the revolver in her apron pocket, then helps Sabina.* SABINA *has found a rope hanging from the ceiling. Grunting, she hangs all her weight on it, and as she pulls the walls begin to move into their right places.* MRS ANTROBUS *brings the overturned tables, chairs, and hassock into the positions of Act I.*]

SABINA: That's all we do – always beginning again! Over and over again. Always beginning again. [*She pulls on the rope and a part of the wall moves into place. She stops. Meditatively*] How do we know that it'll be any better than before? Why do we go on pretending? Some day the whole earth's going to have to turn cold anyway, and until that time all these other things'll be happening again: it will be more wars and more walls of ice and floods and earthquakes.

MRS ANTROBUS: Sabina!! Stop arguing and go on with your work.

SABINA: All right. I'll go on just out of *habit*, but I won't believe in it.

MRS ANTROBUS [*aroused*]: Now, Sabina. I've let you talk long enough. I don't want to hear any more of it. Do I have to explain to you what everybody knows – everybody who keeps a home going? Do I have to say to you what nobody should ever *have* to say, because they can read it in each other's eyes? Now listen to me. [MRS ANTROBUS *takes hold of the rope.*] I could live for seventy years in a cellar and make soup out of grass and bark, without ever doubting that this world has a work to do and will do it. Do you hear me?

SABINA [*frightened*]: Yes, Mrs Antrobus.

MRS ANTROBUS: Sabina, do you see this house – 216 Cedar Street – do you see it?

SABINA: Yes, Mrs Antrobus.

MRS ANTROBUS: Well, just to have known this house is to have seen the idea of what we can do someday if we keep our wits about us. Too many people have suffered and died for my children for us to start reneging now. So we'll start putting this house to rights. Now, Sabina, go and see what you can do in the kitchen.

SABINA: Kitchen! Why is it that however far I go away, I always find myself back in the kitchen?

[*Exit.*]

MRS ANTROBUS [*still thinking over her last speech, relaxes and says with a reminiscent smile*]: Goodness gracious, wouldn't you know that my father was a parson? It was just like I heard his own voice speaking and he's been dead five thousand years. There! I've gone and almost waked Henry up.

HENRY [*talking in his sleep, indistinctly*]: Fellows . . . what have they done for us? . . . Blocked our way at every step. Kept everything in their own hands. And you've stood it. When are you going to wake up?

MRS ANTROBUS: Sh, Henry. Go to sleep. Go to sleep. Go to sleep – Well, that looks better. Now let's go and help Sabina.

GLADYS: Mama, I'm going out into the backyard and hold the baby right up in the air. And show him that we don't have to be afraid any more.

[*Exit* GLADYS *to the kitchen.*

MRS ANTROBUS *glances at Henry, exits into kitchen.*
HENRY *thrashes about in his sleep. Enter* ANTROBUS, *his*

arms full of bundles, chewing the end of a carrot. He has a slight limp. Over the suit of Act I he is wearing an overcoat too long for him, its skirts trailing on the ground. He lets his bundles fall and stands looking about. Presently his attention is fixed on HENRY, *whose words grow clearer.*]

HENRY: All right! What have you got to lose? What have they done for us? That's right – nothing. Tear everything down. I don't care what you smash. We'll begin again and we'll show 'em.

[ANTROBUS *takes out his revolver and holds it pointing downwards. With his back towards the audience he moves towards the footlights.*

HENRY'S *voice grows louder and he wakes with a start. They stare at one another. Then* HENRY *sits up quickly. Throughout the following scene Henry is played, not as a misunderstood or misguided young man, but as a representation of strong unreconciled evil.*]

All right! Do something.

[*Pause.*]

Don't think I'm afraid of you, either. All right, do what you were going to do. Do it. [*Furiously*] Shoot me, I tell you. You don't have to think I'm any relation of yours. I haven't got any father or any mother, or brothers or sisters. And I don't want any. And what's more I haven't got anybody over me; and I never will have. I'm alone, and that's all I want to be: alone. So you can shoot me.

ANTROBUS: You're the last person I wanted to see. The sight of you dries up all my plans and hopes. I wish I were back at war still, because it's easier to fight you than to live with you. War's a pleasure – do you hear me? – War's a pleasure compared to what faces us now: trying to build up a peacetime with you in the middle of it.

[ANTROBUS *walks up to the window.*]

HENRY: I'm not going to be a part of any peacetime of yours. I'm going a long way from here and make my own world that's fit for a man to live in. Where a man can be free, and have a chance, and do what he wants to do in his own way.

ANTROBUS [*his attention arrested; thoughtfully. He throws the gun out of the window and turns with hope*]: . . . Henry, let's try again.

HENRY: Try what? Living *here*? – Speaking polite downtown to all the old men like you? Standing like a sheep at the street corner until the red light turns to green? Being a good boy and a good sheep, like all the stinking ideas you get out of your books? Oh, no. I'll make a world, and I'll show you.

ANTROBUS [*hard*]: How can you make a world for people to live in, unless you've first put order in yourself? Mark my words: I shall continue fighting you until my last breath as long as you mix up your idea of liberty with your idea of hogging everything for yourself. I shall have no pity on you. I shall pursue you to the far corners of the earth. You and I want the same thing; but until you think of it as something that everyone has a right to, you are my deadly enemy and I will destroy you – I hear your mother's voice in the kitchen. Have you seen her?

HENRY: I have no mother. Get it into your head. I don't belong here. I have nothing to do here. I have no home.

ANTROBUS: Then why did you come here? With the whole world to choose from, why did you come to this one place: 216 Cedar Street, Excelsior, New Jersey. . . . Well?

HENRY: What if I did? What if I wanted to look at it once more, to see if –

ANTROBUS: Oh, you're related, all right – When your mother comes in you must behave yourself. Do you hear me?

HENRY [*wildly*]: What is this? – *must behave* yourself. Don't you say *must* to me.

ANTROBUS: Quiet!

[*Enter* MRS ANTROBUS *and* SABINA.]

HENRY: Nobody can say *must* to me. All my life everybody's been crossing me – everybody, everything, all of you. I'm going to be free, even if I have to kill half the world for it. Right now, too. Let me get my hands on his throat. I'll show him.

[*He advances towards Antrobus. Suddenly* SABINA *jumps between them and calls out in her own person.*]

SABINA: Stop! Stop! Don't play this scene. You know what happened last night. Stop the play.

[*The men fall back, panting.* HENRY *covers his face with his hands.*]

Last night you almost strangled him. You became a regular savage. Stop it!

HENRY: It's true. I'm sorry. I don't know what comes over me. I have nothing against him personally. I respect him very much ... I ... I admire him. But something comes over me. It's like I become fifteen years old again. I ... I ... listen: my own father used to whip me and lock me up every Saturday night. I never had enough to eat. He never let me have enough money to buy decent clothes. I was ashamed to go downtown. I never could go to the dances. My father and my uncle put rules in the way of everything I wanted to do. They tried to prevent my living at all – I'm sorry. I'm sorry.

MRS ANTROBUS [*quickly*]: Now, go on. Finish what you were saying. Say it all.

HENRY: In this scene it's as though I were back in High School again. It's like I had some big emptiness inside me – the emptiness of being hated and blocked at every turn.

And the emptiness fills up with the one thought that you have to strike and fight and kill. Listen, it's as though you have to kill somebody else so as not to end up killing yourself.

SABINA: That's not true. I knew your father and your uncle and your mother. You imagined all that. Why, they did everything they could for you. How can you say things like that? They didn't lock you up.

HENRY: They did. They did. They wished I hadn't been born.

SABINA: That's not true.

ANTROBUS [*in his own person, with self-condemnation, but cold and proud*]: Wait a minute. I have something to say too. It's not wholly his fault that he wants to strangle me in this scene. It's my fault too. He wouldn't feel that way unless there were something in me that reminded him of all that. He talks about an emptiness. Well, there's an emptiness in me, too. Yes – work, work, work – that's all I do. I've ceased to *live*. No wonder he feels that anger coming over him.

MRS ANTROBUS: There! At least you've said it.

SABINA: We're all just as wicked as we can be, and that's the God's truth.

MRS ANTROBUS [*nods a moment, then comes forward; quietly*]: Come. Come and put your head under some cold water.

SABINA [*in a whisper*]: I'll go with him. I've known him a long while. You have to go on with the play. Come with me.

[HENRY *starts out with* SABINA, *but turns at the exit.*]

HENRY [*to Antrobus*]: Thanks. Thanks for what you said. I'll be all right tomorrow. I won't lose control in that place, I promise.

[*Exeunt* HENRY *and* SABINA.

ANTROBUS *starts towards the front door, fastens it.* MRS

ANTROBUS *goes up stage and places the chair close to table.*]

MRS ANTROBUS: George, do I see you limping?

ANTROBUS: Yes, a little. My old wound from the other war started smarting again. I can manage.

MRS ANTROBUS [*looking out of the window*]: Some lights are coming on – the first in seven years. People are walking up and down looking at them. Over in Hawkins's open lot they've built a bonfire to celebrate the peace. They're dancing around it like scarecrows.

ANTROBUS: A bonfire! As though they hadn't seen enough things burning – Maggie – the dog died?

MRS ANTROBUS: Oh, yes. Long ago. There are no dogs left in Excelsior – You're back again! All these years. I gave up counting on letters. The few that arrived were anywhere from six months to a year late.

ANTROBUS: Yes, the ocean's full of letters, along with the other things.

MRS ANTROBUS: George, sit down, you're tired.

ANTROBUS: No, you sit down. I'm tired but I'm restless. [*Suddenly, as she comes forward*] Maggie! I've lost it. I've lost it.

MRS ANTROBUS: What, George? What have you lost?

ANTROBUS: The most important thing of all: the desire to begin again, to start building.

MRS ANTROBUS [*sitting in the chair right of the table*]: Well, it will come back.

ANTROBUS [*at the window*]: I've lost it. This minute I feel like all those people dancing around the bonfire – just relief. Just the desire to settle down; to slip into the old grooves and keep the neighbours from walking over my lawn – Hm. But during the war – in the middle of all that blood and dirt and hot and cold – every day and night, I'd have moments, Maggie, when I *saw* the things that we could do when it was over. When you're at war you think about a better life; when you're at peace you think about a more comfortable one. I've lost it. I feel sick and tired.

MRS ANTROBUS: Listen! The baby's crying.

I hear Gladys talking. Probably she's quieting Henry again. George, while Gladys and I were living here – like moles, like rats, and when we were at our wits' end to save the baby's life – the only thought we clung to was that you were going to bring something good out of this suffering. In the night, in the dark, we'd whisper about it, starving and sick – Oh, George, you'll have to get it back again. Think! What else kept us alive all these years? Even now, it's not comfort we want. We can suffer whatever's necessary; only give us back that promise.

[Enter SABINA with a lighted lamp. She is dressed as in Act I.]

SABINA: Mrs Antrobus ...

MRS ANTROBUS: Yes, Sabina?

SABINA: Will you need me?

MRS ANTROBUS: No, Sabina, you can go to bed.

SABINA: Mrs Antrobus, if it's all right with you, I'd like to go to the bonfire and celebrate seeing the war's over. And, Mrs Antrobus, they've opened the Gem Movie Theatre and they're giving away a hand-painted soup tureen to every lady, and I thought one of us ought to go.

ANTROBUS: Well, Sabina, I haven't any money. I haven't seen any money for quite a while.

SABINA: Oh, you don't need money. They're taking anything you can give them. And I have some ... some ... Mrs Antrobus, promise you won't tell anyone. It's a little against the law. But I'll give you some, too.

ANTROBUS: What is it?

SABINA: I'll give you some, too. Yesterday I picked up a lot of ... of beef-cubes!

[MRS ANTROBUS *turns.*]

MRS ANTROBUS [*calmly*]: But, Sabina, you know you ought to give that in to the Centre downtown. They know who needs them most.

SABINA [*outburst*]: Mrs Antrobus, I didn't make this war. I didn't ask for it. And, in my opinion, after anybody's gone through what we've gone through, they have a right to grab what they can find. You're a very nice man, Mr Antrobus, but you'd have got on better in the world if you'd realized that dog-eat-dog was the rule in the beginning and always will be. And most of all now. [*In tears*] Oh, the world's an awful place, and you know it is. I used to think something could be done about it; but I know better now. I hate it. I hate it. [*She comes forward slowly and brings six cubes from the bag.*] All right. All right. You can have them.

ANTROBUS: Thank you, Sabina.

SABINA: Can I have ... can I have one to go to the movies?

[ANTROBUS, *in silence, gives her one.*]

Thank you.

ANTROBUS: Good night, Sabina.

SABINA: Mr Antrobus, don't mind what I say. I'm just an ordinary girl, you know what I mean, I'm just an ordinary girl. But you're a bright man, you're a very bright man, and of course you invented the alphabet and the wheel, and my God, a lot of things ... and if you've got any other plans, my God, don't let me upset them. Only every now and then I've got to go to the movies. I mean my nerves can't stand it. But if you have any ideas about improving the crazy old world, I'm really with you. I really am. Because it's ... it's ... Good night.

[*She goes out.* ANTROBUS *starts laughing softly with exhilaration.*]

ANTROBUS: Now I remember what three things always went together when I was able to see things most clearly: three things. Three things. [*He points to where Sabina has gone out.*] The voice of the people in their confusion and their need. And the thought of you and the children and this house. ... And ... Maggie! I didn't dare ask you: my books! They haven't been lost, have they?

MRS ANTROBUS: No. There are some of them right here. Kind of tattered.

ANTROBUS: Yes. – Remember, Maggie, we almost lost them once before? And when we finally did collect a few torn copies out of old cellars they ran in everyone's head like a fever. They as good as rebuilt the world. [*Pauses, book in hand, and looks up.*] Oh, I've never forgotten for long at a time that living is struggle. I know that every good and excellent thing in the world stands moment by moment on the razor-edge of danger and must be fought for – whether it's a field, or a home, or a country. All I ask is the chance to build new worlds and God has always given us that. And has given us [*opening the book*] voices to guide us; and the memory of our mistakes to warn us. Maggie, you and I will remember in peacetime all the resolves that were so clear to us in the days of war. We've come a long way. We've learned. We're learning. And the steps of our journey are marked for us here. [*He stands by the table turning the leaves of a book.*] Sometimes out there in the war – standing all night on a hill – I'd try and remember some of the words in these books. Parts of them and phrases would come back to me. And after a while I used to give names to the hours of the night. [*He sits, hunting for a passage in the book.*] Nine o'clock I used to call Spinoza. Where is it: 'After experience had taught me –'

[*The back wall has disappeared, revealing the platform.* FRED

176

ACT THREE

BAILEY *carrying his numeral has started from left to right.*
MRS ANTROBUS *sits by the table sewing.*]

BAILEY: 'After experience had taught me that the common occurrences of daily life are vain and futile; and I saw that all the objects of my desire and fear were in themselves nothing good nor bad save insofar as the mind was affected by them; I at length determined to search out whether there was something truly good and communicable to man.'

[*Almost without break* HESTER, *carrying a large Roman numeral ten, starts crossing the platform.* GLADYS *appears at the kitchen door and moves towards her mother's chair.*]

HESTER: 'Then tell me, O Critias, how will a man choose the ruler that shall rule over him? Will he not choose a man who has first established order in himself, knowing that any decision that has its spring from anger or pride or vanity can be multiplied a thousand fold in its effects upon the citizens?'

[HESTER *disappears and* IVY, *as eleven o'clock, starts speaking.*]

IVY: 'This good estate of the mind possessing its object in energy we call divine. This we mortals have occasionally and it is this energy which is pleasantest and best. But God has it always. It is wonderful in us; but in Him how much more wonderful.'

[*As* MR TREMAYNE *starts to speak,* HENRY *appears at the edge of the scene, brooding and unreconciled, but present.*]

TREMAYNE: 'In the beginning, God created the heaven and the earth. And the Earth was waste and void; and the darkness was upon the face of the deep. .... And God said, Let there be light and there was light.'

[*Sudden black-out and silence, except for the last strokes of the midnight bell. Then just as suddenly the lights go up, and* SABINA *is standing at the window, as at the opening of the play.*]

177

SABINA: Oh, oh, oh. Six o'clock and the master not home yet. Pray God nothing serious has happened to him crossing the Hudson River. But I wouldn't be surprised. The whole world's at sixes and sevens, and why the house hasn't fallen down about our ears long ago is a miracle to me. [*She comes to the footlights.*] This is where you came in. We have to go on for ages and ages yet.

You go home.

The end of this play isn't written yet.

Mr and Mrs Antrobus! Their heads are full of plans and they're as confident as the first day they began – and they told me to tell you: good night.

The Matchmaker

A FARCE

The Merchant of Yonkers was produced by Herman Shumlin and directed by Max Reinhardt. The production was designed by Boris Aronson. The cast included Jane Cowl, June Walker, Nydia Westman, Minna Phillips, Percy Waram, Tom Ewell, John Call, Joseph Sweeney, Philip Coolidge, and Edward Nannery. It was first performed on 12 December 1938 at the Colonial Theatre, Boston. The New York engagement opened at the Guild Theatre on 28 December 1938.

The Matchmaker was produced for the Edinburgh Festival by Tennent Productions. It was directed by Tyrone Guthrie and the production was designed by Tanya Moiseiwitsch. The first performance was at the Royal Lyceum Theatre, Edinburgh, on 23 August 1954.

The same production opened at the Theatre Royal, Haymarket, London, on 4 November 1954. Without changes in the principal roles – with the exception of that of Mr Vandergelder, which was played successively by Sam Levene, Eddie Mayehoff, and Loring Smith – the play was performed at the Locust Street Theatre, Philadelphia, on 27 October 1955.

The cast of the play from Edinburgh to Philadelphia, with the exceptions noted, included:

HORACE VANDERGELDER	Loring Smith
CORNELIUS HACKL	Arthur Hill
BARNABY TUCKER	Robert Morse (following Alec McCowen)
MALACHI STACK	Patrick McAlinney
AMBROSE KEMPER	Alexander Davion (following Lee Montague)
WAITERS	William Lanteau (following and followed by Timothy Findley) and John Milligan
CABMAN	Peter Bayliss
DOLLY LEVI	Ruth Gordon
IRENE MOLLOY	Eileen Herlie
MINNIE FAY	Rosamund Greenwood
ERMENGARDE	Prunella Scales
GERTRUDE	Charity Grace (following Henzie Raeburn)
FLORA VAN HUYSEN	Esme Church
COOK	Christine Thomas (following Daphne Newton)

This play is a rewritten version of
THE MERCHANT OF YONKERS,
*which was directed in 1938 by Max
Reinhardt and is again dedicated to
Max Reinhardt with deep admiration
and indebtedness*

CAST

HORACE VANDERGELDER *A merchant of Yonkers, New York*
CORNELIUS HACKL ⎫
BARNABY TUCKER   ⎬ *Clerks in his store*
MALACHI STACK   ⎭
AMBROSE KEMPER *An artist*
JOB SCANLON *A barber*
RUDOLPH ⎫
AUGUST ⎭ *Waiters*
A CABMAN
MRS DOLLY LEVI   ⎫ *Friends of Vandergelder's late*
MISS FLORA VAN HUYSEN ⎭   *wife*
MRS IRENE MOLLOY *A milliner*
MINNIE FAY *Her assistant*
ERMENGARDE *Vandergelder's niece*
GERTRUDE *Vandergelder's housekeeper*
MISS VAN HUYSEN'S COOK

Time: The early 1880s.

Act One Vandergelder's house in Yonkers, New York.

Act Two Mrs Molloy's hat shop, New York.

Act Three The Harmonia Gardens Restaurant on the Battery, New York.

Act Four Miss Van Huysen's house, New York.

This play is based upon a comedy by Johann Nestroy, *Einen Jux will es sich Machen* (Vienna, 1842), which was in turn based upon an English original, *A Day Well Spent* (London, 1835) by John Oxenford.

ACT ONE

Living-room of Mr Vandergelder's house, over his hay, feed and provision store in Yonkers, fifteen miles north of New York City. Articles from the store have overflowed into this room; it has not been cleaned for a long time and is in some disorder, but it is not sordid or gloomy.

There are three entrances. One at the centre back leads into the principal rooms of the house. One on the back right (all the directions are from the point of view of the actors) opens on steps which descend to the street door. One on the left leads to Ermengarde's room.

In the centre of the room is a trapdoor ; below it is a ladder descending to the store below.

Behind the trapdoor and to the left of it is a tall accountant's desk; to the left of it is an old-fashioned stove with a stovepipe going up into the ceiling. Before the desk is a tall stool. On the right of the stage is a table with some chairs about it.

Mr Vandergelder's Gladstone bag, packed for a journey, is beside the desk.

It is early morning.

> [VANDERGELDER, *sixty, choleric, vain, and sly, wears a soiled dressing-gown. He is seated with a towel about his neck, in a chair beside the desk, being shaved by* JOE SCANLON *(fifty; lanky, mass of grey hair falling into his eyes).* VANDERGELDER *is smoking a cigar and holding a hand mirror.* AMBROSE KEMPER, *thirty, dressed as an artist, is angrily striding about the room.*]

VANDERGELDER [*loudly*]: I tell you for the hundredth time you will never marry my niece.

AMBROSE: And I tell you for the thousandth time that I will marry your niece; and right soon, too.

185

VANDERGELDER: Never!

AMBROSE: Your niece is of age, Mr Vandergelder. Your niece has consented to marry me. This is a free country, Mr Vandergelder – not a private kingdom of your own.

VANDERGELDER: There are no free countries for fools, Mr Kemper. Thank you for the honour of your visit – good morning.

JOE: Mr Vandergelder, will you please sit still one minute? If I cut your throat it'll be practically unintentional.

VANDERGELDER: Ermengarde is not for you, nor for anybody else who can't support her.

AMBROSE: I tell you I can support her. I make a very good living.

VANDERGELDER: No, sir! A living is made, Mr Kemper, by selling something that everybody needs at least once a year. Yes, sir! And a million is made by producing something that everybody needs every day. You artists produce something that nobody needs at any time. You may sell a picture once in a while, but you'll make no living. Joe, go over there and stamp three times. I want to talk to Cornelius.

[JOE *crosses to trapdoor and stamps three times.*]

AMBROSE: Not only can I support her now, but I have considerable expectations.

VANDERGELDER: *Expectations!* We merchants don't do business with them. I don't keep accounts with people who promise somehow to pay something someday, and I don't allow my niece to marry such people.

AMBROSE: Very well, from now on you might as well know that I regard any way we can find to get married is right and fair. Ermengarde is of age, and there's no law . . .

[VANDERGELDER *rises and crosses towards Ambrose.* JOE

SCANLON *follows him complainingly and tries to find a chance to cut his hair even while he is standing.*]

VANDERGELDER: Law? Let me tell you something, Mr Kemper: most of the people in the world are fools. The law is there to prevent crime; we men of sense are there to prevent foolishness. It's I, and not the law, that will prevent Ermengarde from marrying you, and I've taken some steps already. I've sent her away to get this nonsense out of her head.

AMBROSE: Ermengarde's . . . not here?

VANDERGELDER: She's gone – east, west, north, south. I thank you for the honour of your visit.

[*Enter* GERTRUDE – *eighty; deaf; half-blind; and very pleased with herself.*]

GERTRUDE: Everything's ready, Mr Vandergelder. Ermengarde and I have just finished packing the trunk.

VANDERGELDER: Hold your tongue!

[JOE *is shaving Vandergelder's throat, so he can only wave his hands vainly.*]

GERTRUDE: Yes, Mr Vandergelder, Ermengarde's ready to leave. Her trunk's all marked, Care Miss Van Huysen, 8 Jackson Street, New York.

VANDERGELDER [*breaking away from Joe*]: Hell and damnation! Didn't I tell you it was a secret?

AMBROSE [*picking up hat and coat – kissing Gertrude*]: Care Miss Van Huysen, 8 Jackson Street, New York. Thank you very much. Good morning, Mr Vandergelder.

[*Exit* AMBROSE, *to the street.*]

VANDERGELDER: It won't help you, Mr Kemper –
[*To Gertrude*]
Deaf! And blind! At least you can do me the favour of being dumb!

GERTRUDE: Chk – chk! Such a temper! Lord save us!

[CORNELIUS *puts his head up through the trapdoor. He is thirty-three; mock-deferential – he wears a green apron and is in his shirt-sleeves.*]

CORNELIUS: Yes, Mr Vandergelder?

VANDERGELDER: Go in and get my niece's trunk and carry it over to the station. Wait! Gertrude, has Mrs Levi arrived yet?

[CORNELIUS *comes up the trapdoor, steps into the room and closes the trapdoor behind him.*]

GERTRUDE: Don't shout. I can hear perfectly well. Everything's clearly marked.

[*Exit* GERTRUDE *left.*]

VANDERGELDER: Have the buggy brought round to the front of the store in half an hour.

CORNELIUS: Yes, Mr Vandergelder.

VANDERGELDER: This morning I'm joining my lodge parade and this afternoon I'm going to New York. Before I go, I have something important to say to you and Barnaby. Good news. Fact is – I'm going to promote you. How old are you?

CORNELIUS: Thirty-three, Mr Vandergelder.

VANDERGELDER: What?

CORNELIUS: Thirty-three.

VANDERGELDER: That all? That's a foolish age to be at. I thought you were forty.

CORNELIUS: Thirty-three.

VANDERGELDER: A man's not worth a cent until he's forty. We just pay 'em wages to make mistakes – don't we, Joe?

JOE: You almost lost an ear on it, Mr Vandergelder.

VANDERGELDER: I was thinking of promoting you to chief clerk.

CORNELIUS: What am I now, Mr Vandergelder?

VANDERGELDER: You're an impertinent fool, that's what you

are. Now, if you behave yourself, I'll promote you from impertinent fool to chief clerk, with a raise in your wages. And Barnaby may be promoted from idiot apprentice to incompetent clerk.

CORNELIUS: Thank you, Mr Vandergelder.

VANDERGELDER: However, I want to see you again before I go. Go in and get my niece's trunk.

CORNELIUS: Yes, Mr Vandergelder.

[*Exit* CORNELIUS, *left*]

VANDERGELDER: Joe – the world's getting crazier every minute. Like my father used to say: the horses'll be taking over the world soon.

JOE [*presenting mirror*]: I did what I could, Mr Vandergelder, what with you flying in and out of the chair.

[*He wipes last of the soap from Vandergelder's face.*]

VANDERGELDER: Fine, fine. Joe, you do a fine job, the same job you've done me for twenty years. Joe ... I've got special reasons for looking my best today ... isn't there something a little extry you could do, something a little special? I'll pay you right up to fifty cents – see what I mean? Do some of those things you do to the young fellas. Touch me up; smarten me up a bit.

JOE: All I know is fifteen cents' worth, like usual, Mr Vandergelder; and that includes everything that's decent to do to a man.

VANDERGELDER: Now hold your horses, Joe – all I meant was ...

JOE: I've shaved you for twenty years and you never asked me no such question before.

VANDERGELDER: Hold your horses, I say, Joe! I'm going to tell you a secret. But I don't want you telling it to that riff raff down to the barber shop what I'm going to tell you now. All I ask of you is a little extry because I'm thinking

of getting married again; and this very afternoon I'm going
to New York to call on my intended, a very refined lady.

JOE: Your gettin' married is none of my business, Mr Vandergelder. I done everything to you I know, and the charge is
fifteen cents like it always was, and ...

[CORNELIUS *crosses, left to right, and exit, carrying a trunk
on his shoulder.* ERMENGARDE, *twenty-four, pretty, sentimental, and* GERTRUDE *enter from left.*]

I don't dye no hair, not even for fifty cents I don't!

VANDERGELDER: Joe Scanlon, get out!

JOE: And lastly, it looks to me like you're pretty rash to judge
which is fools and which isn't fools, Mr Vandergelder.
People that's et onions is bad judges of who's et onions and
who ain't. Good morning, ladies; good morning, Mr
Vandergelder.

[*Exit* JOE.]

VANDERGELDER: Well, what do you want?

ERMENGARDE: Uncle! You said you wanted to talk to us.

VANDERGELDER: Oh yes. Gertrude, go and get my parade
regalia – the uniform for my lodge parade.

GERTRUDE: What? Oh yes. Lord have mercy!

[*Exit* GERTRUDE, *back centre.*]

VANDERGELDER: I had a talk with that artist of yours. He's
a fool.

[ERMENGARDE *starts to cry.*]

Weeping! Weeping! You can go down and weep for a
while in New York where it won't be noticed.

[*He sits on desk chair, puts tie round neck, and calls her over
to tie it for him.*]

Ermengarde! I told him that when you were old enough
to marry you'd marry someone who could support you.
I've done you a good turn. You'll come and thank me when
you're fifty.

ERMENGARDE: But Uncle, I love him!

VANDERGELDER: I tell you you don't.

ERMENGARDE: But I *do*!

VANDERGELDER: And I tell you you don't. Leave those things to me.

ERMENGARDE: If I don't marry Ambrose I know I'll die.

VANDERGELDER: What of?

ERMENGARDE: A broken heart.

VANDERGELDER: Never heard of it. Mrs Levi is coming in a moment to take you to New York. You are going to stay two or three weeks with Miss Van Huysen, an old friend of your mother's.

[GERTRUDE *re-enters with coat, sash, and sword. Enter from the street, right,* MALACHI STACK, *fifty; sardonic; apparently innocent smile; pretence of humility*.]

You're not to receive any letters except from me. I'm coming to New York myself today and I'll call on you tomorrow.

[*To Malachi*]

Who are you?

MALACHI: Malachi Stack, your honour. I heard you wanted an apprentice in the hay, feed, provision, and hardware business.

VANDERGELDER: An apprentice at your age?

MALACHI: Yes, your honour; I bring a lot of experience to it.

VANDERGELDER: Have you any letters of recommendation?

MALACHI [*extending a sheaf of soiled papers*]: Yes, indeed, your honour! First-class recommendation.

VANDERGELDER: Ermengarde! Are you ready to start?

ERMENGARDE: Yes.

VANDERGELDER: Well, go and get ready some more. Ermengarde! Let me know the minute Mrs Levi gets here.

ERMENGARDE: Yes, Uncle Horace.

[ERMENGARDE *and* GERTRUDE *exit.*

VANDERGELDER *examines the letters, putting them down one by one.*]

VANDERGELDER: I don't want an able-seaman. Nor a type-setter. And I don't want a hospital cook.

MALACHI: No, your honour, but it's all experience. Excuse me!

[*Selects a letter.*]

This one is from your former partner, Joshua Van Tuyl, in Albany.

[*He puts letters from table back into pocket.*]

VANDERGELDER: '... for the most part honest and reliable ... occasionally willing and diligent.' There seems to be a certain amount of hesitation about these recommendations.

MALACHI: Businessmen aren't writers, your honour. There's only one businessman in a thousand that can write a good letter of recommendation, your honour. Mr Van Tuyl sends his best wishes and wants to know if you can use me in the provision and hardware business.

VANDERGELDER: Not so fast, not so fast! What's this 'your honour' you use so much?

MALACHI: Mr Van Tuyl says you're President of the Hudson River Provision Dealers' Recreational, Musical, and Burial Society.

VANDERGELDER: I am; but there's no 'your honour' that goes with it. Why did you come to Yonkers?

MALACHI: I heard that you'd had an apprentice that was a good-for-nothing, and that you were at your wit's end for another.

VANDERGELDER: Wit's end, wit's end! There's no dearth of good-for-nothing apprentices.

MALACHI: That's right, Mr Vandergelder. It's employers

there's a dearth of. Seems like you hear of a new one dying every day.

VANDERGELDER: What's that? Hold your tongue. I see you've been a barber, and a valet too. Why have you changed your place so often?

MALACHI: Changed my place, Mr Vandergelder? When a man's interested in experience ...

VANDERGELDER: Do you drink?

MALACHI: No, thanks. I've just had breakfast.

VANDERGELDER: I didn't ask you whether – Idiot! I asked you if you were a drunkard.

MALACHI: No, sir! No! Why, looking at it from all sides I don't even like liquor.

VANDERGELDER: Well, if you keep on looking at it from all sides, out you go. Remember that. Here.

[Gives him remaining letters.]

With all your faults, I'm going to give you a try.

MALACHI: You'll never regret it, Mr Vandergelder. You'll never regret it.

VANDERGELDER: Now today I want to use you in New York. I judge you know your way around New York?

MALACHI: Do I know New York? Mr Vandergelder, I know every hole and corner in New York.

VANDERGELDER: Here's a dollar. A train leaves in a minute. Take that bag to the Central Hotel on Water Street, have them save me a room. Wait for me. I'll be there about four o'clock.

MALACHI: Yes, Mr Vandergelder.

[Picks up the bag, starts out, then comes back.]

Oh, but first, I'd like to meet the other clerks I'm to work with.

VANDERGELDER: You haven't time. Hurry now. The station's across the street.

MALACHI: Yes, sir

[*Away – then back once more*]

You'll see, sir, you'll never regret it. . . .

VANDERGELDER: I regret it already. Go on. Off with you.

[*Exit* MALACHI, *right.*

The following speech is addressed to the audience. During it MR VANDERGELDER *takes off his dressing-gown, puts on his scarlet sash, his sword, and his bright-coloured coat. He is already wearing light blue trousers with a red stripe down the sides.*]

VANDERGELDER: Ninety-nine per cent of the people in the world are fools and the rest of us are in great danger of contagion. But I wasn't always free of foolishness as I am now. I was once young, which was foolish; I fell in love, which was foolish; and I got married, which was foolish; and for a while I was poor, which was more foolish than all the other things put together. Then my wife died, which was foolish of her; I grew older, which was sensible of me; then I became a rich man, which is as sensible as it is rare. Since you see I'm a man of sense, I guess you were surprised to hear that I'm planning to get married again. Well, I've two reasons for it. In the first place, I like my house run with order, comfort, and economy. That's a woman's work; but even a woman can't do it well if she's merely being paid for it. In order to run a house well, a woman must have the feeling that she owns it. Marriage is a bribe to make a housekeeper think she's a householder. Did you ever watch an ant carry a burden twice its size? What excitement! What patience! What will! Well, that's what I think of when I see a woman running a house. What giant passions in those little bodies – what quarrels with the butcher for the best cut – what fury at discovering a moth in a cupboard! Believe me! – if women could harness their

natures to something bigger than a house and a baby carriage
– tck! tck! – they'd change the world. And the second
reason, ladies and gentlemen? Well, I see by your faces
you've guessed it already. There's nothing like mixing with
women to bring out all the foolishness in a man of sense.
And that's a risk I'm willing to take. I've just turned sixty,
and I've just laid side by side the last dollar of my first half
million. So if I should lose my head a little, I still have
enough money to buy it back. After many years' caution
and hard work, I have a right to a little risk and adventure,
and I'm thinking of getting married. Yes, like all you other
fools, I'm willing to risk a little security for a certain amount
of adventure. Think it over.

[*Exit back centre.*

AMBROSE *enters from the street, crosses left, and whistles
softly.* ERMENGARDE *enters from left.*]

ERMENGARDE: Ambrose! If my uncle saw you!

AMBROSE: Sh! Get your hat.

ERMENGARDE: My hat!

AMBROSE: Quick! Your trunk's at the station. Now quick!
We're running away.

ERMENGARDE: Running away!

AMBROSE: Sh!

ERMENGARDE: Where?

AMBROSE: To New York. To get married.

ERMENGARDE: Oh, Ambrose, I can't do that. Ambrose dear
– it wouldn't be proper!

AMBROSE: Listen. I'm taking you to my friend's house. His
wife will take care of you.

ERMENGARDE: But, Ambrose, a girl can't go on a train with
a man. I can see you don't know anything about girls.

AMBROSE: But I'm telling you we're going to get married!

ERMENGARDE: Married! But what would *Uncle* say?

AMBROSE: We don't care what Uncle'd say – we're eloping.

ERMENGARDE: Ambrose Kemper! How can you use such an awful word!

AMBROSE: Ermengarde, you have the soul of a field mouse.

ERMENGARDE [crying]: Ambrose, why do you say such cruel things to me?

[Enter MRS LEVI, from the street, right. She is of uncertain age; mass of sandy hair; impoverished elegance; large, shrewd, but generous nature, an assumption of worldly cynicism conceals a tireless amused enjoyment of life. She carries a handbag and a small brown paper bag. She stands listening.]

AMBROSE: For the last time I beg you – get your hat and coat. The train leaves in a few minutes. Ermengarde, we'll get married tomorrow. . . .

ERMENGARDE: Oh, Ambrose! I see you don't understand anything about weddings. Ambrose, don't you respect me? . . .

MRS LEVI: Good morning, darling girl – how are you?

[They kiss.]

ERMENGARDE: Oh, good morning, Mrs Levi.

MRS LEVI: And who is this gentleman who is so devoted to you?

ERMENGARDE: This is Mr Kemper, Mrs Levi. Ambrose, this is . . . Mrs Levi . . . she's an old friend. . . .

MRS LEVI: Mrs Levi, born Gallagher. Very happy to meet you, Mr Kemper.

AMBROSE: Good morning, Mrs Levi.

MRS LEVI: Mr Kemper, the artist! Delighted! Mr Kemper, may I say something very frankly?

AMBROSE: Yes, Mrs Levi.

MRS LEVI: This thing you were planning to do is a very great mistake.

ERMENGARDE: Oh, Mrs Levi, please explain to Ambrose – of

course! I want to marry him, but to *elope*! ... How ...

MRS LEVI: Now, my dear girl, you go in and keep one eye on your uncle. I wish to talk to Mr Kemper for a moment. You give us a warning when you hear your Uncle Horace coming. ...

ERMENGARDE: Ye-es, Mrs Levi.

[*Exit* ERMENGARDE, *back centre*.]

MRS LEVI: Mr Kemper, I was this dear girl's mother's oldest friend. Believe me, I am on your side. I hope you two will be married very soon, and I think I can be of real service to you. Mr Kemper, I always go right to the point.

AMBROSE: What is the point, Mrs Levi?

MRS LEVI: Mr Vandergelder is a very rich man, Mr Kemper, and Ermengarde is his only relative.

AMBROSE: But I am not interested in Mr Vandergelder's money. I have enough to support a wife and family.

MRS LEVI: Enough? How much is enough when one is thinking about children and the future? The future is the most expensive luxury in the world, Mr Kemper.

AMBROSE: Mrs Levi, what is the point?

MRS LEVI: Believe me, Mr Vandergelder wishes to get rid of Ermengarde, and if you follow my suggestions he will even permit her to marry you. You see, Mr Vandergelder is planning to get married himself.

AMBROSE: What? That monster!

MRS LEVI: Mr Kemper!

AMBROSE: Married! To you, Mrs Levi?

MRS LEVI [*taken aback*]: Oh, no, no ... NO! I am merely arranging it. I am helping him find a suitable bride.

AMBROSE: For Mr Vandergelder there are no suitable brides.

MRS LEVI: I think we can safely say that Mr Vandergelder will be married to someone by the end of next week.

AMBROSE: What are you suggesting, Mrs Levi?

MRS LEVI: I am taking Ermengarde to New York on the next train. I shall not take her to Miss Van Huysen's, as is planned; I shall take her to my house. I wish you to call for her at my house at five-thirty. Here is my card.

AMBROSE: 'Mrs Dolly Gallagher Levi. Varicose veins reduced.'

MRS LEVI [*trying to take back card*]: I beg your pardon. . . .

AMBROSE [*holding card*]: I beg *your* pardon. 'Consultations free.'

MRS LEVI: I meant to give you my other card. Here.

AMBROSE: 'Mrs Dolly Gallagher Levi. Aurora Hosiery. Instruction in the guitar and mandolin.' You do all these things, Mrs Levi?

MRS LEVI: Two and two make four, Mr Kemper – always did. So you will come to my house at five-thirty. At about six I shall take you both with me to the Harmonia Gardens Restaurant on the Battery; Mr Vandergelder will be there and everything will be arranged.

AMBROSE: How?

MRS LEVI: Oh, I don't know. One thing will lead to another.

AMBROSE: How do I know that I can trust you, Mrs Levi? You could easily make our situation worse.

MRS LEVI: Mr Kemper, your situation could not possibly be worse.

AMBROSE: I wish I knew what you get out of this, Mrs Levi.

MRS LEVI: That is a very proper question. I get two things: profit and pleasure.

AMBROSE: How?

MRS LEVI: Mr Kemper, I am a woman who arranges things. At present I am arranging Mr Vandergelder's domestic affairs. Out of it I get – shall we call it: little pickings? I need little pickings, Mr Kemper, and especially just now, when I haven't got my train fare back to New York. You see: I am frank with you.

AMBROSE: That's your profit, Mrs Levi; but where do you get your pleasure?

MRS LEVI: My pleasure? Mr Kemper, when you artists paint a hillside or a river you change everything a little, you make thousands of little changes, don't you? Nature is never completely satisfactory and must be corrected. Well, I'm like you artists. Life as it is is never quite interesting enough for me – I'm bored, Mr Kemper, with life as it is – and so I do things. I put my hand in here, and I put my hand in there, and I watch and I listen – and often I'm very much amused.

AMBROSE [rising]: Not in my affairs, Mrs Levi.

MRS LEVI: Wait, I haven't finished. There's another thing. I'm very interested in this household here – in Mr Vandergelder and all that idle, frozen money of his. I don't like the thought of it lying in great piles, useless, motionless, in the bank, Mr Kemper. Money should circulate like rain water. It should be flowing down among the people, through dressmakers and restaurants and cabmen, setting up a little business here, and furnishing a good time there. Do you see what I mean?

AMBROSE: Yes, I do.

MRS LEVI: New York should be a very happy city, Mr Kemper, but it isn't. My late husband came from Vienna; now there's a city that understands this. I want New York to be more like Vienna and less like a collection of nervous and tired ants. And if you and Ermengarde get a good deal of Mr Vandergelder's money, I want you to see that it starts flowing in and around a lot of people's lives. And for that reason I want you to come with me to the Harmonia Gardens Restaurant tonight.

[Enter ERMENGARDE.]

ERMENGARDE: Mrs Levi, Uncle Horace is coming.

MRS LEVI: Mr Kemper, I think you'd better be going. . . .

[AMBROSE *crosses to trapdoor and disappears down the ladder, closing trap as he goes.*]

Darling girl, Mr Kemper and I have had a very good talk. You'll see: Mr Vandergelder and I will be dancing at your wedding very soon –

[*Enter* VANDERGELDER *at back. He has now added a splendid plumed hat to his costume and is carrying a standard or small flag bearing the initials of his lodge.*]

Oh, Mr Vandergelder, how handsome you look! You take my breath away. Yes, my dear girl, I'll see you soon.

[*Exit* ERMENGARDE *back centre.*]

Oh, Mr Vandergelder, I wish Irene Molloy could see you now. But then! I don't know what's come over you lately. You seem to be growing younger every day.

VANDERGELDER: Allowing for exaggeration, Mrs Levi. If a man eats careful there's no reason why he should look old.

MRS LEVI: You never said a truer word.

VANDERGELDER: I'll never see fifty-five again.

MRS LEVI: Fifty-five! Why, I can see at a glance that you're the sort that will be stamping about at a hundred – and eating five meals a day, like my Uncle Harry. At fifty-five my Uncle Harry was a mere boy. I'm a judge of hands, Mr Vandergelder – show me your hand.

[*Looks at it.*]

Lord in heaven! What a life line!

VANDERGELDER: Where?

MRS LEVI: From *here* to *here*. It runs right off your hand. I don't know where it goes. They'll have to hit you on the head with a mallet. They'll have to stifle you with a sofa pillow. You'll bury us all! However, to return to our business – Mr Vandergelder, I suppose you've changed your mind again. I suppose you've given up all idea of getting married.

VANDERGELDER [*complacently*]: Not at all, Mrs Levi. I have news for you.

MRS LEVI: News?

VANDERGELDER: Mrs Levi, I've practically decided to ask Mrs Molloy to be my wife.

MRS LEVI [*taken aback*]: You have?

VANDERGELDER: Yes, I have.

MRS LEVI: Oh, you have! Well, I guess that's just about the best news I ever heard. So there's nothing more for me to do but wish you every happiness under the sun and say good-bye.

[*Crosses as if to leave.*]

VANDERGELDER [*stopping her*]: Well – Mrs Levi – Surely I thought –

MRS LEVI: Well, I did have a little suggestion to make – but I won't. You're going to marry Irene Molloy, and that closes the matter.

VANDERGELDER: What suggestion was that, Mrs Levi?

MRS LEVI: Well – I *had* found *another* girl for you.

VANDERGELDER: Another?

MRS LEVI: The most wonderful girl, the ideal wife.

VANDERGELDER: Another, eh? What's her name?

MRS LEVI: Her name?

VANDERGELDER: Yes!

MRS LEVI [*groping for it*]: Err . . . er . . . her *name*? – Ernestina – Simple. *Miss* Ernestina Simple. But now of course all that's too late. After all, you're engaged – you're practically engaged to marry Irene Molloy.

VANDERGELDER: Oh, I ain't engaged to Mrs Molloy!

MRS LEVI: Nonsense! You can't break poor Irene's heart now and change to another girl. . . . When a man at your time of life calls four times on an attractive widow like that – and sends her a pot of geraniums – that's practically an engagement!

VANDERGELDER: That ain't an engagement!

MRS LEVI: And yet –! If only you were free! I've found this treasure of a girl. Every moment I felt like a traitor to Irene Molloy – but let me tell you: I couldn't help it. I told this girl all about you, just as though you were a free man. Isn't that dreadful? The fact is, she has fallen in love with you already.

VANDERGELDER: Ernestina?

MRS LEVI: Ernestina Simple.

VANDERGELDER: Ernestina Simple.

MRS LEVI: Of course she's a very different idea from Mrs Molloy, Ernestina is. Like her name – simple, domestic, practical.

VANDERGELDER: Can she cook?

MRS LEVI: Cook, Mr Vandergelder? I've had two meals from her hands, and – as I live – I don't know what I've done that God should reward me with such meals.

(*The following passage – adapted from a scene in Molière's L'Avare – has been cut in recent performances:*

MRS LEVI [*continuing*]: Her duck! Her steak!

VANDERGELDER: Eh! Eh! In this house we don't eat duck and steak every day, Mrs Levi.

MRS LEVI: But didn't I tell you? – that's the wonderful part about it. Her duck – what was it? Pigeon! I'm alive to tell you. I don't know how she does it. It's a secret that's come down in her family. The greatest chefs would give their right hands to know it. And the steaks? Shoulder of beef – four cents a pound. Dogs wouldn't eat. But when Ernestina passes her hands over it –!!

VANDERGELDER: Allowing for exaggeration, Mrs Levi.

MRS LEVI: No exaggeration.)

I'm the best cook in the world myself, and I *know* what's good.

VANDERGELDER: Hm. How old is she, Mrs Levi?

MRS LEVI: Nineteen, well – say twenty.

VANDERGELDER: Twenty, Mrs Levi? Girls of twenty are apt to favour young fellows of their own age.

MRS LEVI: But you don't listen to me. And you don't know the girl. Mr Vandergelder, she has a positive horror of flighty, brainless young men. A fine head of grey hair, she says, is worth twenty shined up with goose grease. No, sir. 'I like a man that's *settled*' – in so many words she said it.

VANDERGELDER: That's ... that's not usual, Mrs Levi.

MRS LEVI: Usual? I'm not wearing myself to the bone hunting up *usual* girls to interest you, Mr Vandergelder. Usual, indeed. Listen to me. Do you know the sort of pictures she has on her wall? Is it any of these young Romeos and Lochinvars? No! – it's Moses on the Mountain – that's what she's got. If you want to make her happy, you give her a picture of Methuselah surrounded by his grand-children. That's my advice to you.

(*Following passage – also based on Molière – has generally been cut in performance:*

VANDERGELDER: I hope ... hm ... that she has some means, Mrs Levi. I have a large household to run.

MRS LEVI: Ernestina? She'll bring you five thousand dollars a year.

VANDERGELDER: Eh! Eh!

MRS LEVI: Listen to me, Mr Vandergelder. You're a man of sense, I hope. A man that can reckon. In the first place, she's an orphan. She's been brought up with a great saving of food. What does she eat herself? Apples and lettuce. It's what she's been used to eat and what she likes best. She saves

203

you two thousand a year right there. Secondly, she makes her own clothes – out of old tablecloths and window curtains. And she's the best-dressed woman in Brooklyn this minute. She saves you a thousand dollars right there. Thirdly, her health is of iron –

VANDERGELDER: But, Mrs Levi, that's not money in the pocket.

MRS LEVI: We're talking about marriage, aren't we, Mr Vandergelder? The money she saves while she's in Brooklyn is none of your affair – but if she were your wife that would be *money*. Yes, sir, that's money.)

VANDERGELDER: What's her family?

MRS LEVI: Her father? – God be good to him! He was the best – what am I trying to say? – the best undertaker in Brooklyn, respected, esteemed. He knew all the best people – knew them well, even before they died. So – well, that's the way it is.

[Lowering her voice, intimately]

Now let me tell you a little more of her appearance. Can you hear me: as I say, a beautiful girl, beautiful, I've seen her go down the street – you know what I mean? – the young men get dizzy. They have to lean against lamp-posts. And she? Modest, eyes on the ground – I'm not going to tell you any more. .... Couldn't you come to New York today?

VANDERGELDER: I was thinking of coming to New York this afternoon. ...

MRS LEVI: You were? Well now, I wonder if something could be arranged – oh, she's so eager to see you! Let me see ...

VANDERGELDER: Could I ... Mrs Levi, could I give you a little dinner, maybe?

MRS LEVI: Really, come to think of it, I don't see where I could get the time. I'm so busy over that wretched lawsuit of mine. Yes. If I win it, I don't mind telling you, I'll be what's called a very rich woman. I'll own half of Long Island, that's a fact. But just now I'm at my wit's end for a little help, just enough money to finish it off. My wit's end!

[*She looks in her handbag.*

In order not to hear this, VANDERGELDER *has a series of coughs, sneezes, and minor convulsions.*]

But perhaps I could arrange a little dinner; I'll see. Yes, for that lawsuit all I need is fifty dollars, and Staten Island's as good as mine. I've been trotting all over New York for you, trying to find you a suitable wife.

VANDERGELDER: Fifty dollars!!

MRS LEVI: Two whole months I've been . . .

VANDERGELDER: Fifty dollars, Mrs Levi . . . is no joke.

[*Producing purse*]

I don't know where money's gone to these days. It's in hiding. . . . There's twenty . . . well, there's twenty-five. I can't spare no more, not now I can't.

MRS LEVI: Well, this will help – will help somewhat. Now let me tell you what we'll do. I'll bring Ernestina to that restaurant on the Battery. You know it: the Harmonia Gardens. It's good, but it's not flashy. Now, Mr Vandergelder, I think it'd be nice if just this once you'd order a real nice dinner. I guess you can afford it.

VANDERGELDER: Well, just this once.

MRS LEVI: A chicken wouldn't hurt.

VANDERGELDER: Chicken!! – Well, just this once.

MRS LEVI: And a little wine.

VANDERGELDER: Wine? Well, just this once.

MRS LEVI: Now about Mrs Molloy – what do you think? Shall we call that subject closed?

VANDERGELDER: No, not at all, Mrs Levi, I want to have dinner with Miss . . . with Miss . . .

MRS LEVI: Simple.

VANDERGELDER: With Miss Simple; but first I want to make another call on Mrs Molloy.

MRS LEVI: Dear, dear, dear! And Miss Simple? What races you make me run! Very well; I'll meet you on one of those benches in front of Mrs Molloy's hat store at four-thirty, as usual.

[*Trapdoor rises, and* CORNELIUS's *head appears.*]

CORNELIUS: The buggy's here ready for the parade, Mr Vandergelder.

VANDERGELDER: Call Barnaby. I want to talk to both of you.

CORNELIUS: Yes, Mr Vandergelder.

[*Exit* CORNELIUS *down trapdoor. Leaves trap open.*]

MRS LEVI: Now do put your thoughts in order, Mr Vandergelder. I can't keep upsetting and disturbing the finest women in New York City unless you mean business.

VANDERGELDER: Oh, I mean business all right!

MRS LEVI: I hope so. Because, you know, you're playing a very dangerous game.

VANDERGELDER: Dangerous? – Dangerous, Mrs Levi?

MRS LEVI: Of course, it's dangerous – and there's a name for it! You're tampering with these women's affections, aren't you? And the only way you can save yourself now is to be married to *someone* by the end of next week. So think that over!

[*Exit centre back.*

Enter CORNELIUS *and* BARNABY, *by the trapdoor. Barnaby is seventeen; round-faced, wide-eyed innocence; wearing a green apron.*]

VANDERGELDER: This morning I'm joining my lodge parade, and this afternoon I'm going to New York. When I come back there are going to be some changes in the house here. I'll tell you what the change is, but I don't want you discussing it amongst yourselves: you're going to have a mistress.

BARNABY: I'm too young, Mr Vandergelder!!

VANDERGELDER: Not yours! Death and damnation! Not yours, idiot – *mine*!

[*Then realizing*]

Hey! Hold your tongue until you're spoken to! I'm thinking of getting married.

CORNELIUS [*crossing, hand outstretched*]: Many congratulations, Mr Vandergelder, and my compliments to the lady.

VANDERGELDER: That's none of your business. Now go back to the store.

[*The* BOYS *start down the ladder*, BARNABY *first.*]

Have you got any questions you want to ask before I go?

CORNELIUS: Mr Vandergelder – er – Mr Vandergelder, does the chief clerk get one evening off every week?

VANDERGELDER: So that's the way you begin being chief clerk, is it? When I was your age I got up at five; I didn't close the shop until ten at night, and then I put in a good hour at the account books. The world's going to pieces. You elegant laddies lie in bed until six and at nine o'clock at night you rush to close the door so fast the line of customers bark their noses. No, sir – you'll attend to the store as usual, and on Friday and Saturday nights you'll remain open until ten – now hear what I say! This is the first time I've been away from the store overnight. When I come back I want to hear that you've run the place perfectly in my absence. If I hear of any foolishness, I'll discharge you. An evening free! Do you suppose that *I* had evenings free?

[*At the top of his complacency*]

If I'd had evenings free I wouldn't be what I am now!

[*He marches out, right.*]

BARNABY [*watching him go*]: The horses nearly ran away when they saw him. What's the matter, Cornelius?

CORNELIUS [*sitting in dejected thought*]: Chief clerk! Promoted from chief clerk to chief clerk.

BARNABY: Don't you like it?

CORNELIUS: Chief clerk! – and if I'm good, in ten years I'll be promoted to chief clerk again. Thirty-three years old and I still don't get an evening free? When am I going to begin to live?

BARNABY: Well – ah . . . you can begin to live on Sundays, Cornelius.

CORNELIUS: That's not living. Twice to church, and old Wolf-trap's eyes on the back of my head the whole time. And as for holidays! What did we do last Christmas? All those canned tomatoes went bad and exploded. We had to clean up the mess all afternoon. Was that living?

BARNABY [*holding his nose at the memory of the bad smell*]: No!!!

CORNELIUS [*rising, with sudden resolution*]: Barnaby, how much money have you got – where you can get at it?

BARNABY: Oh – three dollars. Why, Cornelius?

CORNELIUS: You and I are going to New York.

BARNABY: Cornelius!!! We can't! Close the store?

CORNELIUS: Some more rotten-tomato cans are going to explode.

BARNABY: Holy cabooses! How do you know?

CORNELIUS: I know they're rotten. All you have to do is to light a match under them. They'll make such a smell that customers can't come into the place for twenty-four hours. That'll get us an evening free. We're going to New York too, Barnaby, we're going to live! I'm going to have enough adventures to last me until I'm *partner*. So go and get your Sunday clothes on.

BARNABY: Wha-a-a-t?

CORNELIUS: Yes, I mean it. We're going to have a good meal; and we're going to be in danger; and we're going to get almost arrested; and we're going to spend all our money.

BARNABY: Holy cabooses!!

CORNELIUS: And one more thing: we're not coming back to Yonkers until we've kissed a girl.

BARNABY: Kissed a girl! Cornelius, you can't do that. You don't know any girls.

CORNELIUS: I'm thirty-three. I've got to begin sometime.

BARNABY: I'm only seventeen, Cornelius. It isn't so urgent for me.

CORNELIUS: Don't start backing down now – if the worst comes to the worst and we get discharged from here we can always join the Army.

BARNABY: Uh – did I hear you say that you'd be old Wolf-trap's partner?

CORNELIUS: How can I help it? He's growing old. If you go to bed at nine and open the store at six, you get promoted upwards whether you like it or not.

BARNABY: My! Partner.

CORNELIUS: Oh, there's no way of getting away from it. You and I will be Vandergelders.

BARNABY: I? Oh, no – I may rise a little, but I'll never be a Vandergelder.

CORNELIUS: Listen – everybody thinks when he gets rich he'll be a different kind of rich person from the rich people he sees around him; later on he finds out there's only one kind of rich person, and he's it.

BARNABY: Oh, but I'll –

CORNELIUS: No. The best of all would be a person who has all the good things a poor person has, and all the good meals a rich person has, but that's never been known. No, you and I are going to be Vandergelders; all the more reason, then, for us to try and get some living and some adventure into us now – will you come, Barnaby?

BARNABY [*in a struggle with his fears, a whirlwind of words*]: But Wolf-trap – KRR-pt, Gertrude-KRR-pt –

[*With a sudden cry of agreement.*]

Yes, Cornelius!

[*Enter* MRS LEVI, ERMENGARDE, *and* GERTRUDE *from back centre. The* BOYS *start down the ladder,* CORNELIUS *last.*]

MRS LEVI: Mr Hackl, is the trunk waiting at the station?

CORNELIUS: Yes, Mrs Levi.

[*Closes the trapdoor.*]

MRS LEVI: Take a last look, Ermengarde.

ERMENGARDE: What?

MRS LEVI: Take a last look at your girlhood home, dear. I remember when I left my home. I gave a whinny like a young colt, and off I went.

[ERMENGARDE *and* GERTRUDE *exit.*]

ERMENGARDE [*as they go*]: Oh, Gertrude, do you think I ought to get married this way? A young girl has to be so careful!

[MRS LEVI *is alone. She addresses the audience.*]

MRS LEVI: You know, I think I'm going to have this room with *blue* wallpaper – yes in blue!

[*Hurries out after the others.*

BARNABY *comes up trapdoor, looks off right, then lies on floor, gazing down through the trapdoor.*]

BARNABY: All clear up here, Cornelius! Cornelius – hold the candle steady a minute – the bottom row's all right – but try the top now . . . they're swelled up like they are ready to bust! *BANG.* Holy CABOOSES! *BANG, BANG.* Cornelius! I can smell it up here!

[*Rises and dances about, holding his nose.*]

CORNELIUS [*rushing up the trapdoor*]: Get into your Sunday clothes, Barnaby. We're going to New York!

[*As they run out . . . there is a big explosion. A shower of tomato cans comes up from below, as –*

THE

CURTAIN

FALLS]

ACT TWO

Mrs Molloy's hat shop, New York City.

There are two entrances. One door at the extreme right of the back wall, to Mrs Molloy's workroom; one at the back left corner, to the street. The whole left wall is taken up with the show windows, filled with hats. It is separated from the shop by a low brass rail, hung with net; during the act both MRS MOLLOY *and* BARNABY *stoop under the rail and go into the shop window. By the street door stands a large cheval glass. In the middle of the back wall is a large wardrobe or clothes cupboard, filled with ladies' coats, large enough for* CORNELIUS *to hide in. At the left, beginning at the back wall, between the wardrobe and the workroom door, a long counter extends towards the audience, almost to the footlights. In the centre of the room is a large round table with a low-hanging red cloth. There is a small gilt chair by the wardrobe and two chairs in front of the counter. Over the street door and the workroom door are bells which ring when the doors are opened.*

> [*As the curtain rises,* MRS MOLLOY *is in the window, standing on a box, reaching up to put hats on the stand.* MINNIE FAY *is sewing by the counter.* MRS MOLLOY *has a pair of felt overshoes, to be removed later.*]

MRS MOLLOY: Minnie, you're a fool. Of course I shall marry Horace Vandergelder.

MINNIE: Oh, Mrs Molloy! I didn't ask you. I wouldn't dream of asking you such a personal question.

MRS MOLLOY: Well, it's what you meant, isn't it? And there's your answer. I shall certainly marry Horace Vandergelder if he asks me.

> [*Crawls under window rail, into the room, singing loudly.*]

MINNIE: I know it's none of my business . . .

MRS MOLLOY: Speak up, Minnie, I can't hear you.

MINNIE: ... but do you ... do you ...?

MRS MOLLOY [*having crossed the room, is busy at the counter*]: Minnie, you're a fool. Say it: Do I love him? Of course, I don't love him. But I have two good reasons for marrying him just the same. Minnie, put something on that hat. It's not ugly enough.

[*Throws hat over counter.*]

MINNIE [*catching and taking hat to table*]: Not ugly enough!

MRS MOLLOY: I couldn't sell it. Put a ... put a sponge on it.

MINNIE: Why, Mrs Molloy, you're in such a *mood* today.

MRS MOLLOY: In the first place I shall marry Mr Vandergelder to get away from the millinery business. I've hated it from the first day I had anything to do with it. Minnie, I hate hats.

[*Sings loudly again.*]

MINNIE: Why, what's the matter with the millinery business?

MRS MOLLOY [*crossing to window with two hats*]: I can no longer stand being suspected of being a wicked woman, while I have nothing to show for it. I can't stand it.

[*She crawls under rail into window.*]

MINNIE: Why, no one would dream of suspecting you –

MRS MOLLOY [*on her knees, looking over the rail*]: Minnie, you're a fool. All millineresses are suspected of being wicked women. Why, half the time all those women come into the shop merely to look at me.

MINNIE: Oh!

MRS MOLLOY: They enjoy the suspicion. But they aren't certain. If they were *certain* I was a wicked woman, they wouldn't put foot in this place again. Do I go to restaurants? No, it would be bad for business. Do I go to balls, or theatres, or operas? No, it would be bad for business. The only men I ever meet are feather merchants.

[*Crawls out of window, but gazes intently into the street.*]

What are those two young men doing out there on that park bench? Take my word for it, Minnie, either I marry Horace Vandergelder, or I break out of this place like a fire engine. I'll go to every theatre and ball and opera in New York City.

[MRS MOLLOY *returns to counter, singing again.*]

MINNIE: But Mr Vandergelder's not ...

MRS MOLLOY: Speak up, Minnie, I can't hear you.

MINNIE: ... I don't think he's attractive.

MRS MOLLOY: But what I think he is – and it's very important – I think he'd make a good fighter.

MINNIE: Mrs Molloy!

MRS MOLLOY: Take my word for it, Minnie: the best part of married life is the fights. The rest is merely so-so.

MINNIE [*fingers in ears*]: I won't listen.

MRS MOLLOY: Peter Molloy – God rest him! – was a fine arguing man. I pity the woman whose husband slams the door and walks out of the house at the beginning of an argument. Peter Molloy would stand up and fight for hours on end. He'd even throw things, Minnie, and there's no pleasure to equal that. When I felt tired I'd start a good bloodwarming fight and it'd take ten years off my age; now Horace Vandergelder would put up a good fight; I know it. I've a mind to marry him.

MINNIE: I think they're just awful, the things you're saying today.

MRS MOLLOY: Well, I'm enjoying them myself, too.

MINNIE [*at the window*]: Mrs Molloy, those two men out in the street –

MRS MOLLOY: What?

MINNIE: Those men. It looks as if they meant to come in here.

MRS MOLLOY: Well now, it's time some men came into this place. I give you the younger one, Minnie.

MINNIE: Aren't you terrible!

[MRS MOLLOY *sits on centre table, while* MINNIE *takes off her felt overshoes.*]

MRS MOLLOY: Wait till I get my hands on that older one! Mark my words, Minnie, we'll get an adventure out of this yet. Adventure, adventure! Why does everybody have adventures except me, Minnie? Because I have no spirit, I have no gumption. Minnie, they're coming in here. Let's go into the workroom and make them wait for us for a minute.

MINNIE: Oh, but Mrs Molloy ... my work! ...

MRS MOLLOY [*running to workroom*]: Hurry up, be quick now, Minnie!

[*They go out to workroom.*

BARNABY *and* CORNELIUS *run in from street, leaving front door open. They are dressed in the stiff discomfort of their Sunday clothes.* CORNELIUS *wears a bowler hat,* BARNABY *a straw hat too large for him.*]

BARNABY: No one's here.

CORNELIUS: Some women were here a minute ago. I saw them.

[*They jump back to the street door and peer down the street.*]
That's Wolf-trap all right!
[*Coming back*]
Well, we've got to hide here until he passes by.

BARNABY: He's sitting down on that bench. It may be quite a while.

CORNELIUS: When these women come in, we'll have to make conversation until he's gone away. We'll pretend we're buying a hat. How much money have you got now?

BARNABY [*counting his money*]: Forty cents for the train – seventy cents for dinner – twenty cents to see the whale – and a dollar I lost – I have seventy cents.

CORNELIUS: And I have a dollar seventy-five. I wish I knew how much hats cost!

BARNABY: Is this an adventure, Cornelius?

CORNELIUS: No, but it may be.

BARNABY: I think it is. There we wander around New York all day and nothing happens; and then we come to the quietest street in the whole city and suddenly Mr Vandergelder turns the corner.

[*Going to door*]

I think that's an adventure. I think ... Cornelius! That Mrs Levi is there now. She's sitting down on the bench with him.

CORNELIUS: What do you know about that! We know only one person in all New York City, and there she is!

BARNABY: Even if our adventure came along now I'd be too tired to enjoy it. Cornelius, why isn't this an adventure?

CORNELIUS: Don't be asking that. When you're in an adventure, you'll know it all right.

BARNABY: Maybe I wouldn't. Cornelius, let's arrange a signal for you to give me when an adventure's really going on. For instance, Cornelius, you say ... uh ... *pudding*; you say *pudding* to me if it's an adventure we're in.

CORNELIUS: I wonder where the lady who runs this store is? What's her name again?

BARNABY: 'Mrs Molloy, hats for ladies.'

CORNELIUS: Oh yes. I must think over what I'm going to say when she comes in.

[*Speaking to counter*]

'Good afternoon, Mrs Molloy, wonderful weather we're having. We've been looking everywhere for some beautiful hats.'

BARNABY: That's fine, Cornelius!

CORNELIUS: 'Good afternoon, Mrs Molloy; wonderful weather. ....' We'll make her think we're very rich.

[*One hand in trouser pocket, the other on back of chair*]

'Good afternoon, Mrs Molloy. ....' You keep one eye on the door the whole time. 'We've been looking everywhere for ...'

[*Enter* MRS MOLLOY *from the workroom.*]

MRS MOLLOY [*behind the counter*]: Oh, I'm sorry. Have I kept you waiting? Good afternoon, gentlemen.

CORNELIUS [*hat off*]: Here, Cornelius Hackl.

BARNABY [*hat off*]: Here, Barnaby Tucker.

MRS MOLLOY: I'm very happy to meet you, Perhaps I can help you. Won't you sit down?

CORNELIUS: Thank you, we will.

[*The* BOYS *place their hats on the table, then sit down at the counter facing Mrs Molloy.*]

You see, Mrs Molloy, we're looking for hats. We've looked everywhere. Do you know what we heard? Go to Mrs Molloy's, they said. So we came here. Only place we *could* go ...

MRS MOLLOY: Well now, that's *very* complimentary.

CORNELIUS: ... and we were right. Everybody was right.

MRS MOLLOY: You wish to choose some hats for a friend?

CORNELIUS: Yes, exactly.

[*Kicks Barnaby.*]

BARNABY: Yes, exactly.

CORNELIUS: We were thinking of five or six, weren't we, Barnaby?

BARNABY: Er – five.

CORNELIUS: You see, Mrs Molloy, money's no object with us. None at all.

MRS MOLLOY: Why, Mr Hackl. ...

CORNELIUS [*rising and going towards street door*]: ... I beg your pardon, what an interesting street! Something happening every minute. Passers-by, and ...

[BARNABY *runs to join him.*]

MRS MOLLOY: You're from out of town, Mr Hackl?

CORNELIUS [*coming back*]: Yes, ma'am – Barnaby, just keep your eye on the street, will you? You won't see that in Yonkers every day.

[BARNABY *remains kneeling at street door.*]

BARNABY: Oh yes, I will.

CORNELIUS: Not all of it.

MRS MOLLOY: Now this friend of yours – couldn't she come in with you someday and choose her hats herself?

CORNELIUS [*sitting at counter*]: No. Oh, no. It's a surprise for her.

MRS MOLLOY: Indeed? That may be a little difficult, Mr Hackl. It's not entirely customary – Your friend's very interested in the street, Mr Hackl.

CORNELIUS: Oh yes. Yes. He has reason to be.

MRS MOLLOY: You said you were from out of town?

CORNELIUS: Yes, we're from Yonkers.

MRS MOLLOY: Yonkers?

CORNELIUS: Yonkers ... yes, Yonkers.

[*He gazes rapt into her eyes.*]

You should know Yonkers, Mrs Molloy. Hudson River; Palisades; drives; some say it's the most beautiful town in the world; that's what they say.

MRS MOLLOY: Is that so!

CORNELIUS [*rising*]: Mrs Molloy, if you ever had a Sunday free, I'd ... we'd like to show you Yonkers. Y'know, it's very historic, too.

MRS MOLLOY: That's very kind of you. Well, perhaps ... now about those hats.

[*Takes two hats from under counter, and crosses to back centre of the room.*]

CORNELIUS [*following*]: Is there . . . Have you a . . . Maybe Mr Molloy would like to see Yonkers too?

MRS MOLLOY: Oh, I'm a widow, Mr Hackl.

CORNELIUS [*joyfully*]: You are!

[*With sudden gravity*]

Oh, that's too bad. Mr Molloy would have enjoyed Yonkers.

MRS MOLLOY: Very likely. Now about these hats. Is your friend dark or light?

CORNELIUS: Don't think about that for a minute. Any hat you'd like would be perfectly all right with her.

MRS MOLLOY: Really!

[*She puts one on.*]

Do you like this one?

CORNELIUS [*in awe-struck admiration*]: Barnaby!

[*In sudden anger*]

Barnaby! Look!

[BARNABY *turns; unimpressed, he laughs vaguely, and turns to the door again.*]

Mrs Molloy, that's the most beautiful hat I ever saw.

[BARNABY *now crawls under the rail into the window.*]

MRS MOLLOY: Your friend is acting very strangely, Mr Hackl.

CORNELIUS: Barnaby, stop acting strangely. When the street's quiet and empty, come back and talk to us. What was I saying? Oh yes: Mrs Molloy, you should know Yonkers.

MRS MOLLOY [*hat off*]: The fact is, I have a friend in Yonkers. Perhaps you know him. It's always so foolish to ask in cases like that, isn't it?

[*They both laugh over this with increasing congeniality.* MRS MOLLOY *goes to counter with hats from table.* CORNELIUS *follows.*]

It's a Mr Vandergelder.

CORNELIUS [*stopping abruptly*]: What was that you said?

MRS MOLLOY: Then you do know him?

CORNELIUS: Horace Vandergelder?

MRS MOLLOY: Yes, that's right.

CORNELIUS: Know him!

[*Looks to Barnaby.*]

Why, no. No!

BARNABY: No! No!

CORNELIUS [*starting to glide about the room, in search of a hiding-place*]: I beg your pardon, Mrs Molloy – what an attractive shop you have!

[*Smiling fixedly at her he moves to the workshop door.*]

And where does this door lead to?

[*Opens it, and is alarmed by the bell which rings above it.*]

MRS MOLLOY: Why, Mr Hackl, that's my workroom.

CORNELIUS: Everything here is so interesting.

[*Looks under counter.*]

Every corner. Every door, Mrs Molloy. Barnaby, notice the interesting doors and cupboards.

[*He opens the cupboard door.*]

Deeply interesting. Coats for ladies.

[*Laughs.*]

Barnaby, make a note of the table. Precious piece of furniture, with a low-hanging cloth, I see.

[*Stretches his leg under table.*]

MRS MOLLOY [*taking a hat from box left of wardrobe*]: Perhaps your friend might like some of this new Italian straw. Mr Vandergelder's a substantial man and very well liked, they tell me.

CORNELIUS: A lovely man, Mrs Molloy.

MRS MOLLOY: Oh yes – charming, charming!

CORNELIUS [*smiling sweetly*]: Has only one fault, as far as I know; he's hard as nails; but apart from that, as you say, a charming nature, ma'am.

MRS MOLLOY: And a large circle of friends –?

CORNELIUS: Yes, indeed, yes, indeed – five or six.

BARNABY: Five!

CORNELIUS: He comes and calls on you here from time to time, I suppose.

MRS MOLLOY [*turning from mirror where she has been putting a hat on*]: This summer we'll be wearing ribbons down our back. Yes, as a matter of fact I am expecting a call from him this afternoon.

[*Hat off*]

BARNABY: I think ... Cornelius I think ... !!

MRS MOLLOY: Now to show you some more hats –

BARNABY: Look out!

[*He takes a flying leap over the rails and flings himself under the table.*]

CORNELIUS: Begging your pardon, Mrs Molloy.

[*He jumps into the cupboard.*]

MRS MOLLOY: Gentlemen! Mr Hackl! Come right out of there this minute!

CORNELIUS [*sticking his head out of the wardrobe door*]: Help us just this once, Mrs Molloy! We'll explain later!

MRS MOLLOY: Mr Hackl!

BARNABY: We're as innocent as can be, Mrs Molloy.

MRS MOLLOY: But really! Gentlemen! I can't have this! *What are you doing?*

BARNABY: Cornelius! Cornelius! Pudding?

CORNELIUS [*shouting*]: Pudding!

[*They disappear. Enter from the street* MRS LEVI, *followed by* MR VANDERGELDER. VANDERGELDER *is dressed in a too-bright checked suit, and wears a green derby – or bowler – hat.*

He is carrying a large ornate box of chocolates in one hand, and a cane in the other.]

MRS LEVI: Irene, my darling child, how *are* you? Heaven be good to us, how well you look!

[*They kiss.*]

MRS MOLLOY: But what a surprise! And Mr Vandergelder in New York – what a pleasure!

VANDERGELDER [*swaying back and forth on his heels complacently*]: Good afternoon, Mrs Molloy.

[*They shake hands.* MRS MOLLOY *brings chair from counter for him. He sits at left of table.*]

MRS LEVI: Yes, Mr Vandergelder's in New York. Yonkers lies up there – *decimated* today. Irene, we thought we'd pay you a very short call. Now you'll tell us if it's inconvenient, won't you?

MRS MOLLOY [*placing a chair for Mrs Levi at right of table*]: Inconvenient, Dolly! The idea! Why, it's sweet of you to come.

[*She notices the boys' hats on the table – sticks a spray of flowers into crown of Cornelius's bowler and winds a piece of chiffon round Barnaby's panama.*]

VANDERGELDER: We waited outside a moment.

MRS LEVI: Mr Vandergelder thought he saw two customers coming in – two men.

MRS MOLLOY: Men! Men, Mr Vandergelder? Why, what will you be saying next?

MRS LEVI: Then we'll sit down for a minute or two. . . .

MRS MOLLOY [*wishing to get them out of the shop into the workroom*]: Before you sit down –

[*She pushes them both.*]

Before you sit down, there's something I want to show you. I want to show Mr Vandergelder my workroom, too.

ACT TWO

MRS LEVI: I've seen the workroom a hundred times. I'll stay right here and try on some of these hats.

MRS MOLLOY: No, Dolly, you come too. I have something for you. Come along, everybody.

[*Exit* MRS LEVI *to workroom.*]

Mr Vandergelder, I want your advice. You don't know how helpless a woman in business is. Oh, I feel I need advice every minute from a fine business head like yours.

[*Exit* VANDERGELDER *to workroom.* MRS MOLLOY *shouts this line and then slams the workroom door.*]

Now I shut the door!!

[*Exit* MRS MOLLOY.

CORNELIUS *puts his head out of the wardrobe door and gradually comes out into the room, leaving door open.*]

CORNELIUS: Hsst!

BARNABY [*poking his head out from under the table*]: Maybe she wants us to go, Cornelius?

CORNELIUS: Certainly I won't go. Mrs Molloy would think we were just thoughtless fellows. No, all I want is to stretch a minute.

BARNABY: What are you going to do when he's gone, Cornelius? Are we just going to run away?

CORNELIUS: Well ... I don't know yet. I like Mrs Molloy a lot. I wouldn't like her to think badly of me. I think I'll buy a hat. We can walk home to Yonkers, even if it takes us all night. I wonder how much hats cost. Barnaby, give me all the money you've got.

[*As he leans over to take the money, he sneezes. Both return to their hiding-places in alarm; then emerge again.*]

My, all those perfumes in that cupboard tickle my nose! But I like it in there ... it's a woman's world, and very different.

BARNABY: I like it where I am, too; only I'd like it better if I had a pillow.

CORNELIUS [*taking coat from wardrobe*]: Here, take one of these coats. I'll roll it up for you so it won't get mussed. Ladies don't like to have their coats mussed.

BARNABY: That's fine. Now I can just lie here and hear Mr Vandergelder talk.

[CORNELIUS *goes slowly above table towards cheval mirror, repeating Mrs Molloy's line dreamily*.]

CORNELIUS: This summer we'll be wearing ribbons down our back. . . .

BARNABY: Can I take off my shoes, Cornelius?

[CORNELIUS *does not reply. He comes to the footlights and addresses the audience, in completely simple naïve sincerity*.]

CORNELIUS: Isn't the world full of wonderful things. There we sit cooped up in Yonkers for years and years and all the time wonderful people like Mrs Molloy are walking around in New York and we don't know them at all. I don't know whether – from where you're sitting – you can see – well, for instance, the way [*pointing to the edge of his right eye*] her eye and forehead and cheek come together, up here. Can you? And the kind of fireworks that shoot out of her eyes all the time. I tell you right now: a fine woman is the greatest work of God. You can talk all you like about Niagara Falls and the Pyramids; they aren't in it at all. Of course, up there at Yonkers they came into the store all the time, and bought this and that, and I said 'Yes, ma'am', and 'That'll be seventy-five cents, ma'am'; and I *watched* them. But today I've talked to one, equal to equal, equal to equal, and to the finest one that ever existed, in my opinion. They're so different from men! Everything that they say and do is so different that you feel like laughing all the time.

[*He laughs.*]

Golly, they're different from men. And they're awfully mysterious, too. You never can be really sure what's going on in their heads. They have a kind of wall around them all the time – of pride and a sort of play-acting: I bet you could know a woman a hundred years without ever being really sure whether she liked you or not. This minute I'm in danger. I'm in danger of losing my job and my future and everything that people think is important; but I don't care. Even if I have to dig ditches for the rest of my life, I'll be a ditch-digger who once had a wonderful day.

Barnaby!

BARNABY: Oh, you woke me up!

CORNELIUS [*kneeling*]: Barnaby, we can't go back to Yonkers yet and you know why.

BARNABY: Why not?

CORNELIUS: We've had a good meal. We've had an adventure. We've been in danger of getting arrested. There's only one more thing we've got to do before we go back to be successes in Yonkers.

BARNABY: Cornelius! You're never going to kiss Mrs Molloy!

CORNELIUS: Maybe.

BARNABY: But she'll scream.

CORNELIUS: Barnaby, you don't know anything at all. You might as well know right now that everybody except us goes through life kissing right and left all the time.

BARNABY [*pausing for reflection; humbly*]: Well, thanks for telling me, Cornelius. I often wondered.

[*Enter* MRS LEVI *from workroom.*]

MRS LEVI: Just a minute, Irene. I must find my handkerchief. [CORNELIUS, *caught by the arrival of Mrs Levi, drops to his hands and knees, and starts very slowly to crawl back to the wardrobe, as though the slowness rendered him invisible.* MRS

LEVI, *leaning over the counter, watches him. From the cupboard he puts his head out of it and looks pleadingly at her.*] Why, Mr Hackl, I thought you were up in Yonkers.

CORNELIUS: I almost always am, Mrs Levi. Oh, Mrs Levi, don't tell Mr Vandergelder! I'll explain everything later.

BARNABY [*putting head out*]: We're terribly innocent, Mrs Levi.

MRS LEVI: Why, who's that?

BARNABY: Barnaby Tucker – just paying a call.

MRS LEVI [*looking under counter and even shaking out her skirts*]: Well, who else is here?

CORNELIUS: Just the two of us, Mrs Levi, that's all.

MRS LEVI: Old friends of Mrs Molloy's, is that it?

CORNELIUS: We never knew her before a few minutes ago, but we like her a lot – don't we, Barnaby? In fact, I think she's . . . I think she's the finest person in the world. I'm ready to tell that to anybody.

MRS LEVI: And does she think *you're* the finest person in the world?

CORNELIUS: Oh, no. I don't suppose she even notices that I'm alive.

MRS LEVI: Well, I think she must notice that you're alive in that cupboard, Mr Hackl. Well, if I were you, I'd get back into it right away. Somebody could be coming in any minute.

[CORNELIUS *disappears. She sits unconcernedly in chair right. Enter* MRS MOLLOY.]

MRS MOLLOY [*leaving door open and looking about in concealed alarm*]: Can I help you, Dolly?

MRS LEVI: No, no, no. I was just blowing my nose.

[*Enter* VANDERGELDER *from workroom.*]

VANDERGELDER: Mrs Molloy, I've got some advice to give you about your business.

[MRS MOLLOY *comes to the centre of the room and puts Barnaby's hat on floor in window, then Cornelius's hat on the counter.*]

MRS LEVI: Oh, advice from Mr Vandergelder! The whole city should hear this.

VANDERGELDER [*standing in the workroom door, pompously*]: In the first place, the aim of business is to make profit.

MRS MOLLOY: Is that so?

MRS LEVI: I never heard it put so clearly before. Did you hear it?

VANDERGELDER [*crossing the room to the left*]: You pay those girls of yours too much. You pay them as much as men. Girls like that enjoy their work. Wages, Mrs Molloy, are paid to make people do work they don't want to do.

MRS LEVI: Mr Vandergelder thinks so ably. And that's exactly the way his business is run up in Yonkers.

VANDERGELDER [*patting her hand*]: Mrs Molloy, I'd like for you to come up to Yonkers.

MRS MOLLOY: That would be very nice.

[*He hands her the box of chocolates.*]

Oh, thank you. As a matter of fact I know someone from Yonkers, someone else.

VANDERGELDER [*hanging hat on the cheval mirror*]: Oh? Who's that?

[MRS MOLLOY *puts chocolates on table and brings gilt chair forward and sits centre at table facing the audience.*]

MRS MOLLOY: Someone quite well-to-do, I believe, though a little free and easy in his behaviour. Mr Vandergelder do you know Mr Cornelius Hackl in Yonkers?

VANDERGELDER: I know him like I know my own boot. He's my head clerk.

MRS MOLLOY: Is that so?

VANDERGELDER: He's been in my store for ten years.

MRS MOLLOY: Well, I never!

VANDERGELDER: Where would you have known him?

[MRS MOLLOY *is in silent confusion. She looks for help to Mrs Levi, seated at the right end of table.*]

MRS LEVI [*groping for means to help Mrs Molloy*]: Err . . . blah . . . err . . . bl . . . er . . . Oh, just one of those chance meetings, I suppose.

MRS MOLLOY: Yes, oh yes! One of those chance meetings.

VANDERGELDER: What? Chance meetings? Cornelius Hackl has no right to chance meetings. Where was it?

MRS MOLLOY: Really, Mr Vandergelder, it's very unlike you to question me in such a way. I think Mr Hackl is better known than you think he is.

VANDERGELDER: Nonsense.

MRS MOLLOY: He's in New York often and he's very well liked.

MRS LEVI [*having found her idea, with decision*]: Well, the truth might as well come out now as later. Mr Vandergelder, Irene is quite right. Your head clerk is often in New York. Goes everywhere; has an army of friends. Everybody knows Cornelius Hackl.

VANDERGELDER [*laughing blandly and sitting in chair at left of table*]: He never comes to New York. He works all day in my store and at nine o'clock at night he goes to sleep in the bran room.

MRS LEVI: So you think. But it's not true.

VANDERGELDER: Dolly Gallagher, you're crazy.

MRS LEVI: Listen to me. You keep your nose so deep in your account books you don't know what goes on. Yes, by day Cornelius Hackl is your faithful trusted clerk – that's true; but by night! Well, he leads a double life, that's all! He's here at the opera; at the great restaurants; in all the fashionable homes . . . why, he's at the Harmonia Gardens Restaurant three nights a week. The fact is, he's the wittiest, gayest, naughtiest, most delightful man in New York. Well, he's just *the* famous Cornelius Hackl!

VANDERGELDER [*sure of himself*]: It ain't the same man. If I ever thought Cornelius Hackl came to New York, I'd discharge him.

MRS LEVI: Who took the horses out of Jenny Lind's carriage and pulled her through the streets?

MRS MOLLOY: Who?

MRS LEVI: Cornelius Hackl! Who dressed up as a waiter at the Fifth Avenue Hotel the other night and took an oyster and dropped it right down Mrs . . .

[*Rises.*]

No, it's too wicked to tell you!

MRS MOLLOY: Oh yes, Dolly, tell it! Go on!

MRS LEVI: No. But it *was* Cornelius Hackl.

VANDERGELDER [*loudly*]: It ain't the same man. Where'd he get the money?

MRS LEVI: But he's very rich.

VANDERGELDER [*rising*]: Rich! I keep his money in my own safe. He has a hundred and forty-six dollars and thirty-five cents.

MRS LEVI: Oh, Mr Vandergelder, you're killing me! Do come to your senses He's one of *the* Hackls.

[MRS MOLLOY *sits at chair right of table where Mrs Levi has been sitting.*]

VANDERGELDER: *The* Hackls?

MRS LEVI: They built the Raritan Canal.

VANDERGELDER: Then why should he work in my store?

MRS LEVI: Well, I'll tell you.

[*Sits at the centre of the table, facing the audience.*]

VANDERGELDER [*striding about*]: I don't want to hear! I've got a headache! I'm going home. *It ain't the same man!!* He sleeps in my bran room. You can't get away from facts. I just made him my chief clerk.

MRS LEVI: If you had any sense you'd make him partner.

[*Rises, crosses to Mrs Molloy.*]

Now Irene, I can see you were as taken with him as everybody else is.

MRS MOLLOY: Why, I only met him once, very hastily.

MRS LEVI: Yes, but I can see that you were taken with him. Now don't you be thinking of marrying him!

MRS MOLLOY [*her hands on her cheeks*]: Dolly! What are you saying! Oh!

MRS LEVI: Maybe it'd be fine. But think it over carefully. He breaks hearts like hickory nuts.

VANDERGELDER: Who?

MRS LEVI: Cornelius Hackl!

VANDERGELDER: Mrs Molloy, how often has he called on you?

MRS MOLLOY: Oh, I'm telling the truth. I've only seen him once in my life. Dolly Levi's been exaggerating so. I don't know where to look!

[*Enter* MINNIE *from workroom and crosses to window.*]

MINNIE: Excuse me, Mrs Molloy. I must get together that order for Mrs Parkinson.

MRS MOLLOY: Yes, we must get that off before closing.

MINNIE: I want to send it off by the errand girl.

[*Having taken a hat from the window.*]

Oh, I almost forgot the coat.

[*She starts for the wardrobe.*]

MRS MOLLOY [*running to the wardrobe to prevent her*]: Oh, oh! I'll do that, Minnie!

[*But she is too late.* MINNIE *opens the right-hand cupboard door and falls back in terror, and screams.*]

MINNIE: Oh, Mrs Molloy! Help! There's a man!

[MRS MOLLOY *with the following speech pushes her back to
the workroom door.* MINNIE *walks with one arm pointing at
the cupboard. At the end of each of Mrs Molloy's sentences she
repeats – at the same pitch and degree – the words:* 'There's
a man!']

MRS MOLLOY [*slamming cupboard door*]: Minnie, you imagined
it. You're tired, dear. You go back in the workroom and
lie down. Minnie, you're a fool; hold your tongue!

MINNIE: There's a man!

[*Exit* MINNIE *to workroom.*

MRS MOLLOY *returns to the front of the stage.*

VANDERGELDER *raises his stick threateningly.*]

VANDERGELDER: If there's a man there, we'll get him out.
Whoever you are, come out of there!

[*Strikes table with his stick.*]

MRS LEVI [*going masterfully to the cupboard – sweeping her
umbrella around among the coats and closing each door as
she does so*]: Nonsense! There's no man there. See! Miss
Fay's nerves have been playing tricks on her. Come
now, let's sit down again. What were you saying, Mr
Vandergelder?

[*They sit,* MRS MOLLOY *right,* MRS LEVI *centre,* VANDER-
GELDER *left.*

*A sneeze is heard from the cupboard. They all rise, look towards
cupboard, then sit again.*]

Well now . . .

[*Another tremendous sneeze.*

With a gesture that says, 'I can do no more.']

God bless you!

[*They all rise.* MRS MOLLOY *stands with her back to the
cupboard.*]

MRS MOLLOY [*to Vandergelder*]: Yes, there is a man in there.
I'll explain it all to you another time. Thank you very much

231

for coming to see me. Good afternoon, Dolly. Good afternoon, Mr Vandergelder.

VANDERGELDER: You're protecting a man in there!

MRS MOLLOY [*with back to cupboard*]: There's a very simple explanation, but for the present, good afternoon.

[BARNABY *now sneezes twice, lifting the table each time.* VANDERGELDER, *right of table, jerks off the tablecloth.* BARNABY *pulls cloth under table and rolls himself up in it.* MRS MOLLOY *picks up the box of chocolates, which has rolled on to the floor.*]

MRS LEVI: Lord, the whole room's *crawling* with men! I'll never get over it.

VANDEGELDER: The world is going to pieces! I can't believe my own eyes!

MRS LEVI: Come, Mr Vandergelder. Ernestina Simple is waiting for us.

VANDERGELDER [*finding his hat and putting it on*]: Mrs Molloy, I shan't trouble you again, and *vice versa*.

[MRS MOLLOY *is standing transfixed in front of cupboard, clasping the box of chocolates.* VANDERGELDER *snatches the box from her and goes out.*]

MRS LEVI [*crossing to her*]: Irene, when I think of all the interesting things you have in this room!

[*Kisses her.*]

Make the most of it, dear.

[*Raps cupboard.*]

Good-bye!

[*Raps on table with umbrella.*]

Good-bye!

[*Exit* MRS LEVI.

MRS MOLLOY *opens door of cupboard.* CORNELIUS *steps out.*]

MRS MOLLOY: So that was one of your practical jokes, Mr Hackl?

CORNELIUS: No, no. Mrs Molloy!

MRS MOLLOY: Come out from under that, Barnaby Tucker, you troublemaker!

[*She snatches the cloth and spreads it back on table.* MINNIE *enters.*]

There's nothing to be afraid of, Minnie, I know all about these gentlemen.

CORNELIUS: Mrs Molloy, we realize that what happened here –

MRS MOLLOY: You think because you're rich you can make up for all the harm you do, is that it?

CORNELIUS: No, no!

BARNABY [*on the floor putting shoes on*]: No, no!

MRS MOLLOY: Minnie, this is the famous Cornelius Hackl who goes round New York tying people into knots; and that's Barnaby Tucker, another troublemaker.

BARNABY: How d'you do?

MRS MOLLOY: Minnie, choose yourself any hat and coat in the store. We're going out to dinner. If this Mr Hackl is so rich and gay and charming, he's going to be rich and gay and charming to us. He dines three nights a week at the Harmonia Gardens Restaurant, does he? Well, he's taking us there now.

MINNIE: Mrs Molloy, are you sure it's safe?

MRS MOLLOY: Minnie, hold your tongue. We're in a position to put these men into jail if they so much as squeak.

CORNELIUS: Jail, Mrs Molloy?

MRS MOLLOY: Jail, Mr Hackl. Officer Cogarty does everything I tell him to do. Minnie, you and I have been respectable for years; now we're in disgrace, we might as well make the most of it. Come into the workroom with me; I know some ways we can perk up our appearances. Gentlemen, we'll be back in a minute.

CORNELIUS: Uh – Mrs Molloy, I hear there's an awfully good restaurant at the railway station.

MRS MOLLOY [*in high indignation*]: Railway station? Railway station? Certainly not! No, sir! You're going to give us a good dinner in the heart of the fashionable world. Go on in, Minnie! Don't you boys forget that you've made us lose our reputations, and now the fashionable world's the only place we *can* eat.

[MRS MOLLOY *exits to workroom.*]

BARNABY: She's angry at us, Cornelius. Maybe we'd better run away now.

CORNELIUS: No, I'm going to go through with this if it kills me. Barnaby, for a woman like that a man could consent to go back to Yonkers and be a success.

BARNABY: All I know is no woman's going to make a success out of me.

CORNELIUS: Jail or no jail, we're going to take those ladies out to dinner. So grit your teeth.

[*Enter* MRS MOLLOY *and* MINNIE *from workroom dressed for the street.*]

MRS MOLLOY: Gentlemen, the cabs are at the corner, so forward march!

[*She takes a hat – which will be Barnaby's at the end of Act III – and gives it to* MINNIE.]

CORNELIUS: Yes, ma'am.

[BARNABY *stands shaking his empty pockets warningly.*]

Oh, Mrs Molloy . . . is it far to the restaurant? Couldn't we walk?

MRS MOLLOY [*pauses a moment, then says*]: Minnie, take off your things. We're not going.

OTHERS: Mrs Molloy!

MRS MOLLOY: Mr Hackl, I don't go anywhere I'm not wanted. Good night. I'm not very happy to have met you.

[*She crosses the stage as though going to the workroom door.*]

OTHERS: Mrs Molloy!

MRS MOLLOY: I suppose you think we're not fashionable enough for you? Well, I won't be a burden to you. Good night, Mr Tucker.

[*The others follow her behind counter:* CORNELIUS, BARNABY, *then* MINNIE.]

CORNELIUS: We want you to come with us more than anything in the world, Mrs Molloy.

[MRS MOLLOY *turns and pushes the three back. They are now near the centre of the stage, to the right of the table,* MRS MOLLOY *facing the audience.*]

MRS MOLLOY: No, you don't! Look at you! Look at the pair of them, Minnie! Scowling, both of them!

CORNELIUS: Please, Mrs Molloy!

MRS MOLLOY: Then smile.

[*To Barnaby*]

Go on, smile! No, that's not enough. Minnie, you come with me and we'll get our own supper.

CORNELIUS. Smile, Barnaby, you lout!

BARNABY: My face can't smile any stronger than that.

MRS MOLLOY: Then do something! Show some interest. Do something lively: sing!

CORNELIUS: I can't sing, really I can't.

MRS MOLLOY: We're wasting our time, Minnie. They don't want us.

CORNELIUS: Barnaby, what can you sing? Mrs Molloy, all we know are sad songs.

MRS MOLLOY: That doesn't matter. If you want us to go out with you, you've got to sing something.

[*All this has been very rapid; the boys turn up to counter, put their heads together, confer and abruptly turn, stand stiffly and sing 'Tenting tonight; tenting tonight; tenting on the old camp*

235

ground'. *The four of them now repeat the refrain, softly harmonizing.*

At the end of the song, after a pause, MRS MOLLOY, *moved, speaks.*]

MRS MOLLOY: We'll come!

[*The* BOYS *shout joyfully.*]

You boys go ahead.

[CORNELIUS *gets his hat from counter; as he puts it on he discovers the flowers on it.* BARNABY *gets his hat from window. They go out whistling.*

MINNIE *turns and puts her hat on at the mirror.*]

Minnie, get the front-door key – I'll lock the workroom.

[MRS MOLLOY *goes to workroom.*

MINNIE *takes key from hook left on wardrobe and goes to Mrs Molloy, at the workroom door. She turns her around.*]

MINNIE: Why, Mrs Molloy, you're crying!

[MRS MOLLOY *flings her arms round Minnie.*]

MRS MOLLOY: Oh, Minnie, the world is full of wonderful things. Watch me, dear, and tell me if my petticoat's showing.

[*She crosses to door, followed by* MINNIE, *as –*

THE

CURTAIN

FALLS]

ACT THREE

Veranda at the Harmonia Gardens Restaurant on the Battery, New York.

This room is informal and rustic. The main restaurant is indicated to be off stage back right.

There are three entrances: swinging double doors at the centre of the back wall leading to the kitchen; one on the right wall (perhaps up a few steps and flanked by potted palms) to the street; one on the left wall to the staircase leading to the rooms above.

On the stage are two tables, left and right, each with four chairs. It is now afternoon and they are not yet set for dinner.

Against the back wall is a large folding screen. Also against the back wall are hat and coat racks.

> [*As the curtain rises,* VANDERGELDER *is standing, giving orders to* RUDOLPH, *a tall 'snob' waiter, alternating between cold superiority and rage. German accent.* MALACHI STACK *sits at table left.*]

VANDERGELDER: Now, hear what I say. I don't want you to make any mistakes. I want a table for three.

RUDOLPH: For three.

VANDERGELDER: There'll be two ladies and myself.

MALACHI: It's a bad combination, Mr Vandergelder. You'll regret it.

VANDERGELDER: And I want a chicken.

MALACHI: A chicken! You'll regret it.

VANDERGELDER: Hold your tongue. Write it down: chicken.

RUDOLPH: Yes, sir. Chicken Esterhazy? Chicken cacciatore? Chicken à la crème –?

VANDERGELDER [*exploding*]: A chicken! A chicken like

everybody else has. And with the chicken I want a bottle of wine.

RUDOLPH: Moselle? Chablis? Vouvray?

MALACHI: He doesn't understand you, Mr Vandergelder. You'd better speak louder.

VANDERGELDER [*spelling*]: W-I-N-E.

RUDOLPH: Wine.

VANDERGELDER: Wine! And I want this table removed. We'll eat at that table alone.

[*Exit* RUDOLPH *through service door at back.*]

MALACHI: There are some people coming in here now, Mr Vandergelder.

[VANDERGELDER *goes to back right to look at the newcomers.*]

VANDERGELDER: What! Thunder and damnation! It's my niece Ermengarde! What's she doing here? – Wait till I get my hands on her.

MALACHI [*running up to him*]: Mr Vandergelder! You must keep your temper!

VANDERGELDER: And there's that rascal artist with her. Why, it's a plot. I'll throw them in jail.

MALACHI: Mr Vandergelder! They're old enough to come to New York. You can't throw people into jail for coming to New York.

VANDERGELDER: And there's Mrs Levi! What's she doing with them? It's a plot. It's a conspiracy! What's she saying to the cabman? Go up and hear what she's saying.

MALACHI [*listening at entrance, right*]: She's telling the cabman to wait, Mr Vandergelder. She's telling the young people to come in and have a good dinner, Mr Vandergelder.

VANDERGELDER: I'll put an end to this.

MALACHI: Now, Mr Vandergelder, if you lose your temper, you'll make matters worse. Mr Vandergelder, come here and take my advice.

VANDERGELDER: Stop pulling my coat. What's your advice?

MALACHI: Hide, Mr Vandergelder. Hide behind this screen, and listen to what they're saying.

VANDERGELDER [*being pulled behind the screen*]: Stop pulling at me.

[*They hide behind the screen as* MRS LEVI, ERMENGARDE, *and* AMBROSE *enter from the right.* AMBROSE *is carrying Ermengarde's luggage.*]

ERMENGARDE: But I don't want to eat in a restaurant. It's not proper.

MRS LEVI: Now, Ermengarde, dear, there's nothing wicked about eating in a restaurant. There's nothing wicked, even, about being in New York. Clergymen just make those things up to fill out their sermons.

ERMENGARDE: Oh, I wish I were in Yonkers, where *nothing* ever happens!

MRS LEVI: Ermengarde, you're hungry. That's what's troubling you.

ERMENGARDE: Anyway, after dinner you must promise to take me to Aunt Flora's. She's been waiting for me all day and she must be half dead of fright.

MRS LEVI: All right, but of course, you know at Miss Van Huysen's you'll be back in your uncle's hands.

AMBROSE [*hands raised to heaven*]: I can't stand it.

MRS LEVI [*to Ambrose*]: Just keep telling yourself how pretty she is. Pretty girls have very little opportunity to improve their other advantages.

AMBROSE: Listen, Ermengarde! You don't want to go back to your uncle. Stop and think! That old man with one foot in the grave!

MRS LEVI: And the other three in the cashbox.

AMBROSE: Smelling of oats –

MRS LEVI: And axle grease.

MALACHI: That's not true. It's only partly true.

VANDERGELDER [*loudly*]: Hold your tongue! I'm going to teach them a lesson.

MALACHI [*whispering*]: Keep your temper, Mr Vandergelder. Listen to what they say.

[MRS LEVI *hears this; throws a quick glance towards the screen; her whole manner changes.*]

MRS LEVI: Oh dear, what was I saying? The Lord be praised, how glad I am that I found you two dreadful children just as you were about to break poor dear Mr Vandergelder's heart.

AMBROSE: He's got no heart to break!

MRS LEVI [*vainly signalling*]: Mr Vandergelder's a much kinder man than you think.

AMBROSE: Kinder? He's a wolf.

MRS LEVI: Remember that he leads a very lonely life. Now you're going to have dinner upstairs. There are some private rooms up there – just meant for shy, timid girls like Ermengarde. Come with me.

[*She pushes the young people out left,* AMBROSE *carrying the luggage.*]

VANDERGELDER [*coming forward*]: I'll show them!

[*He sits at table right.*]

MALACHI: Everybody should eavesdrop once in a while, I always say. There's nothing like eavesdropping to show you that the world outside your head is different from the world inside your head.

VANDERGELDER [*producing a pencil and paper*]: I want to write a note. Go and call that cabman in here. I want to talk to him.

MALACHI: No one asks advice of a cabman, Mr Vandergelder. They see so much of life that they have no ideas left.

VANDERGELDER: Do as I tell you.

MALACHI: Yes sir. Advice of a cabman!

[*Exit right.*

VANDERGELDER *writes his letter.*]

VANDERGELDER: 'My dear Miss Van Huysen' –

[*To audience*]

Everybody's dear in a letter. It's enough to make you give up writing 'em. 'My dear Miss Van Huysen. This is Ermengarde and that rascal Ambrose Kemper. They are trying to run away. Keep them in your house until I come.'

[MALACHI *returns with an enormous* CABMAN *in a high hat and a long coat. He carries a whip.*]

CABMAN [*entering*]: What's he want?

VANDERGELDER: I want to talk to you.

CABMAN: I'm engaged. I'm waiting for my parties.

VANDERGELDER [*folding letter and writing address*]: I know you are. Do you want to earn five dollars?

CABMAN: Eh?

VANDERGELDER: I asked you, do you want to earn five dollars?

CABMAN: I don't know. I never tried.

VANDERGELDER: When those parties of yours come downstairs, I want you to drive them to this address. Never mind what they say, drive them to this address. Ring the bell: give this letter to the lady of the house: see that they get in the door and keep them there.

CABMAN: I can't make people go into a house if they don't want to.

VANDERGELDER [*producing purse*]: Can you for ten dollars?

CABMAN: Even for ten dollars, I can't do it alone.

VANDERGELDER: This fellow here will help you.

MALACHI [*sitting at table left*]: Now I'm pushing people into houses.

VANDERGELDER: There's the address: Miss Flora Van Huysen, 8 Jackson Street.

241

CABMAN: Even if I get them in the door I can't be sure they'll stay there.

VANDERGELDER: For fifteen dollars you can.

MALACHI: Murder begins at twenty-five.

VANDERGELDER: Hold your tongue!

[*To cabman*]

The lady of the house will help you. All you have to do is to sit in the front hall and see that the man doesn't run off with the girl. I'll be at Miss Van Huysen's in an hour or two and I'll pay you then.

CABMAN: If they call the police, I can't do anything.

VANDERGELDER: It's perfectly honest business. Perfectly honest.

MALACHI: Every man's the best judge of his own honesty.

VANDERGELDER: The young lady is my niece.

[*The* CABMAN *laughs, sceptically.*]

The young lady is my niece!!

[*The* CABMAN *looks at Malachi and shrugs.*]

She's trying to run away with a good-for-nothing and we're preventing it.

CABMAN: Oh, I know them, sir. They'll win in the end. Rivers don't run uphill.

MALACHI: What did I tell you, Mr Vandergelder? Advice of a cabman.

VANDERGELDER [*hitting table with his stick*]: Stack! I'll be back in half an hour. See that the table's set for three. See that nobody else eats here. Then go and join the cabman on the box.

MALACHI: Yes, sir.

[*Exit* VANDERGELDER *right.*]

CABMAN: Who's your friend?

MALACHI: Friend!! That's not a friend; that's an employer I'm trying out for a few days.

CABMAN: You won't like him.

MALACHI: I can see you're in business for yourself because you talk about liking employers. No one's ever liked an employer since business began.

CABMAN: *Aw* –!

MALACHI: No, sir. I suppose you think *your horse* likes you?

CABMAN: My old Clementine? She'd give her right feet for me.

MALACHI: That's what all employers think. You imagine it. The streets of New York are full of cab horses winking at one another. Let's go in the kitchen and get some whisky. I can't push people into houses when I'm sober. No, I've had about fifty employers in my life. but this is the most employer of them all. He talks to everybody as though he were paying them.

CABMAN: I had an employer once. He watched me from eight in the morning until six at night – just sat there and watched me. Oh, dear! Even my mother didn't think I was as interesting as that.

[CABMAN *exits through service door.*]

MALACHI [*following him off*]: Yes, being employed is like being loved: you know that somebody's thinking about you the whole time.

[*Exits.*

Enter right, MRS MOLLOY, MINNIE, BARNABY, *and* CORNELIUS.]

MRS MOLLOY: See! Here's the place I meant! Isn't it fine? Minnie, take off your things; we'll be here for hours.

CORNELIUS [*stopping at door*]: Mrs Molloy, are you sure you'll like it here? I think I feel a draught.

MRS MOLLOY: Indeed, I do like it. We're going to have a fine dinner right in this room; it's private, and it's elegant. Now we're all going to forget our troubles and call each other by our first names. Cornelius! Call the waiter.

CORNELIUS: Wait – wait – I can't make a sound. I must have caught a cold on that ride. Wai – No! it won't come.

MRS MOLLOY: I don't believe you. Barnaby, you call him.

BARNABY [*boldly*]: Waiter! Waiter!

[CORNELIUS *threatens him.* BARNABY *runs left.*]

MINNIE: I never thought I'd be in such a place in my whole life. Mrs Molloy, is this what they call a 'café'?

MRS MOLLOY [*sitting at table left, facing audience*]: Yes, this a café. Sit down, Minnie. Cornelius, Mrs Levi gave us to understand that every waiter in New York knew you.

CORNELIUS: They will.

[BARNABY *sits at chair left;* MINNIE *in chair back to audience.*

Enter RUDOLPH *from service door.*]

RUDOLPH: Good evening, ladies and gentlemen.

CORNELIUS [*shaking his hand*]: How are you, Fritz? How are you, my friend?

RUDOLPH: I am Rudolph.

CORNELIUS: Of course. Rudolph, of course. Well, Rudolph, these ladies want a little something to eat – you know what I mean? Just if you can find the time – we know how busy you are.

MRS MOLLOY: Cornelius, there's no need to be so familiar with the waiter.

[*Takes menu from Rudolph.*]

CORNELIUS: Oh, yes there is.

MRS MOLLOY [*passing menu across*]: Minnie, what do you want to eat?

MINNIE: Just anything, Irene.

MRS MOLLOY: No, speak up, Minnie. What do you want?

MINNIE: No, really, I have no appetite at all.

[*Swings round in her chair and studies the menu, horrified at the prices.*]

Oh ... Oh ... I'd like some sardines on toast and a glass of milk.

CORNELIUS [*taking menu from her*]: Great grindstones! What a sensible girl. Barnaby, shake Minnie's hand. She's the most sensible girl in the world. Rudolph, bring us gentlemen two glasses of beer, a loaf of bread and some cheese.

MRS MOLLOY [*taking menu*]: I never heard such nonsense. Cornelius, we've come here for a good dinner and a good time. Minnie, have you ever eaten pheasant?

MINNIE: Pheasant? No-o-o-o!

MRS MOLLOY: Rudolph, have you any pheasant?

RUDOLPH: Yes, ma'am. Just in from New Jersey today.

MRS MOLLOY: Even the pheasants are leaving New Jersey.

[*She laughs loudly, pushing Cornelius, then Rudolph.*
Orders, not from menu]

Now, Rudolph, write this down: mock-turtle soup; pheasant; mashed chestnuts; green salad; and some nice red wine.

[RUDOLPH *repeats each item after her.*]

CORNELIUS [*losing all his fears, boldly*]: All right, Barnaby, you watch me.

[*He reads from the bill of fare.*]

Rudolph, write this down: Neapolitan ice-cream; hothouse peaches; champagne ...

ALL: Champagne!

[BARNABY *spins round in his chair.*]

CORNELIUS [*holding up a finger*]: ... and a German band. Have you got a German band?

MRS MOLLOY: No, Cornelius, I won't let you be extravagant. Champagne, but no band. Now, Rudolph, be quick about this. We're hungry.

[*Exit* RUDOLPH *to kitchen.* MRS MOLLOY *crosses to right.*]
Minnie, come upstairs. I have an idea about your hair. I
think it'd be nice in two wee horns –

MINNIE [*hurrying after her, turning and looking at the boys*]: Oh!
Horns!

[*They go out right.*

There is a long pause. CORNELIUS *sits staring after them.*]

BARNABY: Cornelius, in the Army you have to peel potatoes
all the time.

CORNELIUS [*not turning*]: Oh, that doesn't matter. By the
time we get out of jail we can move right over to the Old
Men's Home.

[*Another waiter,* AUGUST, *enters from service door bearing a
bottle of champagne in cooler, and five glasses.* AUGUST *is a
young waiter; baby face; continually bursting into tears.* MRS
MOLLOY *re-enters right, followed by* MINNIE, *and stops
August.*]

MRS MOLLOY: Waiter! What's that? What's that you
have?

AUGUST: It's some champagne, ma'am.

MRS MOLLOY: Cornelius, it's our champagne.

[*All gather round August.*]

AUGUST: No, no. It's for His Honour the Mayor of New
York and he's very impatient.

MRS MOLLOY: Shame on him! The Mayor of New York has
more important things to be impatient about. Cornelius,
open it.

[CORNELIUS *takes the bottle, opens it, and fills the glasses.*]

AUGUST: Ma'am, he'll kill me.

MRS MOLLOY: Well, have a glass first and die happy.

AUGUST [*sitting at table right, weeping*]: He'll kill me.

[RUDOLPH *lays the cloth on the table, left.*]

MRS MOLLOY: I go to a public restaurant for the first time in

ten years and all the waiters burst into tears. There, take
that and stop crying, love.

[*She takes a glass to August and pats his head, then comes back.*]
Barnaby, make a toast!

BARNABY [*centre of the group, with naïve sincerity*]: I? . . . uh . . .
To all the ladies in the world . . . may I get to know more
of them . . . and . . . may I get to know them better.

[*There is a hushed pause.*]

CORNELIUS [*softly*]: To the ladies!

MRS MOLLOY: That's *very* sweet and *very* refined. Minnie, for
that I'm going to give Barnaby a kiss.

MINNIE: Oh!

MRS MOLLOY: Hold your tongue, Minnie. I'm old enough to
be his mother, and [*indicating a height three feet from the floor*]
a dear wee mother I would have been too. Barnaby, this is
for you from all the ladies in the world.

[*She kisses him.* BARNABY *is at first silent and dazed, before
he speaks.*]

BARNABY: Now I can go back to Yonkers, Cornelius. Pudding. Pudding. Pudding!

[*He spins round and falls on his knees.*]

MRS MOLLOY: Look at Barnaby. He's not strong enough for
a kiss. His head can't stand it.

[*Exit* AUGUST, *right service door, with tray and cooler.*
The sound of 'Les Patineurs' waltz comes from off left.
CORNELIUS *sits in chair facing audience, top of table.*
MINNIE *at left.* BARNABY *at right and* MRS MOLLOY *back
to audience.*]

Minnie, I'm enjoying myself. To think that this goes on in
hundreds of places every night, while I sit at home darning
my stockings.

[MRS MOLLOY *rises and dances, alone, slowly about the stage.*]
Cornelius, dance with me.

CORNELIUS [*rising*]: Irene, the Hackls don't dance. We're Presbyterian.

MRS MOLLOY: Minnie, you dance with me.

[MINNIE *joins her.* CORNELIUS *sits again.*]

MINNIE: Lovely music.

MRS MOLLOY: Why, Minnie, you dance beautifully.

MINNIE: We girls dance in the workroom when you're not looking, Irene.

MRS MOLLOY: You thought I'd be angry! Oh dear, no one in the world understands anyone else in the world.

[*The girls separate.* MINNIE *dances off to her place at the table.* MRS MOLLOY *sits thoughtfully at table right. The music fades away.*]

Cornelius! Jenny Lind and all those other ladies – do you see them all the time?

CORNELIUS [*rising and joining her at table right*]: Irene, I've put them right out of my head. I'm interested in . . .

[RUDOLPH *has entered by the service door. He now flings a tablecloth between them on table.*]

MRS MOLLOY: Rudolph, what are you doing?

RUDOLPH: A table's been reserved here. Special orders.

MRS MOLLOY: Stop right where you are. That party can eat inside. This veranda's ours.

RUDOLPH: I'm very sorry. This veranda is open to anybody who wants it. Ah, there comes the man who brought the order.

[*Enter* MALACHI *from the kitchen, drunk.*]

MRS MOLLOY [*to Malachi*]: Take your table away from here. We got here first, Cornelius throw him out.

MALACHI: Ma'am, my employer reserved this room at four o'clock this afternoon. You can go and eat in the restaurant. My employer said it was very important that he have a table alone.

MRS MOLLOY: No, sir. We got here first and we're going to stay here – alone, too.

[MINNIE *and* BARNABY *come forward.*]

RUDOLPH: Ladies and gentlemen!

MRS MOLLOY: Shut up, you!

[*To Malachi*]

You're an impertinent, idiotic kill-joy.

MALACHI [*very pleased*]: That's an insult!

MRS MOLLOY: All the facts about you are insults.

[*To Cornelius*]

Cornelius, do something. Knock it over! The table.

CORNELIUS: Knock it over.

[*After a shocked struggle with himself* CORNELIUS *calmly overturns the table.* AUGUST *rights the table and picks up cutlery, weeping copiously.*]

RUDOLPH [*in cold fury*]: I'm sorry, but this room can't be reserved for anyone. If you want to eat alone, you must go upstairs. I'm sorry, but that's the rule.

MRS MOLLOY: We're having a nice dinner alone and we're going to stay here. Cornelius, knock it over.

[CORNELIUS *overturns the table again. The girls squeal with pleasure. The waiter* AUGUST *again scrambles for the silver.*]

MALACHI: Wait till you see my employer!

RUDOLPH [*bringing screen down*]: Ladies and gentlemen! I tell you what we'll do. There's a big screen here. We'll put the screen up between the tables. August, come and help me.

MRS MOLLOY: I won't eat behind a screen. I won't. Minnie, make a noise. We're not animals in a menagerie. Cornelius, no screen. Minnie, there's a fight. I feel ten years younger. No screen! No screen!

[*During the struggle with the screen all talk at once.*]

MALACHI [*loud and clear and pointing to entrance right*]: Now you'll learn something. There comes my employer now, getting out of that cab.

CORNELIUS [*coming to him, taking off his coat*]: Where? I'll knock him down too.

[BARNABY *has gone up to right entrance. He turns and shouts clearly.*]

BARNABY: Cornelius, it's Wolf-trap. Yes, it is!

CORNELIUS: Wolf-trap! Listen, everybody. I think the screen's a good idea. Have you got any more screens, Rudolph? We could use three or four.

[*He pulls the screen forward again.*]

MRS MOLLOY: Quiet down, Cornelius, and stop changing your mind. Hurry up, Rudolph, we're ready for the soup.

[*During the following scene* RUDOLPH *serves the meal at the table left, as unobtrusively as possible.*

The stage is now divided in half. The quartet's table is at the left. Enter VANDERGELDER *from the right. Now wears overcoat and carries the box of chocolates.*]

VANDERGELDER: Stack! What's the meaning of this? I told you I wanted a table alone. What's that?

[VANDERGELDER *hits the screen twice with his stick.* MRS MOLLOY *hits back twice with a spoon. The four young people sit:* BARNABY *facing audience;* MRS MOLLOY *right,* MINNIE *left, and* CORNELIUS *back to audience.*]

MALACHI: Mr Vandergelder, I did what I could. Mr Vandergelder, you wouldn't believe what wild savages the people of New York are. There's a woman over there, Mr Vandergelder – civilization hasn't touched her.

VANDERGELDER: Everything's wrong. You can't even manage a thing like that. Help me off with my coat. Don't kill me. Don't kill me.

[*During the struggle with the overcoat* MR VANDERGELDER'S

purse flies out of his pocket and falls by the screen. VANDER-
GELDER *goes to the coat tree and hangs his coat up.*]

MRS MOLLOY: Speak up! I can't hear you.

CORNELIUS: My voice again. Barnaby, how's your throat?
Can you speak?

BARNABY: Can't make a sound.

MRS MOLLOY: Oh, all right. Bring your heads together, and
we'll whisper.

VANDERGELDER: Who are those people over there?

MALACHI: Some city sparks and their girls, Mr Vandergelder.
What goes on in big cities, Mr Vandergelder – best not think
of it.

VANDERGELDER: Has that couple come down from upstairs
yet? I hope they haven't gone off without your seeing
them.

MALACHI: No, sir. Myself and the cabman have kept our eyes
on everything.

VANDERGELDER [*sitting at right of table right, profile to the
audience*]: I'll sit here and wait for my guests. You go out to
the cab.

MALACHI: Yes, sir.

[VANDERGELDER *unfurls newspaper and starts to read.*
MALACHI *sees the purse on the floor and picks it up.*]
Eh? What's that? A purse. Did you drop something, Mr
Vandergelder?

VANDERGELDER: No. Don't bother me any more. Do as I
tell you.

MALACHI [*stooping over. Coming centre*]: A purse. That fellow
over there must have let it fall during the misunderstanding
about the screen. No, I won't look inside. Twenty-dollar
bills, dozens of them. I'll go over and give it to him.

[*Starts towards Cornelius, then turns and speaks to audience.*]
You're surprised? You're surprised to see me getting rid

of this money so quickly, eh? I'll explain it to you. There was a time in my life when my chief interest was picking up money that didn't belong to me. The law is there to protect property, but – sure, the law doesn't care whether a property owner deserves his property or not, and the law has to be corrected. There are several thousands of people in this country engaged in correcting the law. For a while I, too, was engaged in the redistribution of superfluities. A man works all his life and leaves a million to his widow. She sits in hotels and eats great meals and plays cards all afternoon and evening, with ten diamonds on her fingers. Call in the robbers! Call in the robbers! Or a man leaves it to his son who stands leaning against bars all night boring a bartender. Call in the robbers! Stealing's a weakness. There are some people who say you shouldn't have any weaknesses at all – no vices. But if a man has no vices, he's in great danger of making vices out of his virtues, and there's a spectacle. We've all seen them: men who were monsters of philanthropy and women who were dragons of purity. We've seen people who told the truth, though the Heavens fall – and the Heavens fell. No, no – nurse one vice in your bosom. Give it the attention it deserves and let your virtues spring up modestly around it. Then you'll have the miser who's no liar; and the drunkard who's the benefactor of a whole city. Well, after I'd had that weakness of stealing for a while, I found another: I took to whisky – whisky took to me. And then I discovered an important rule that I'm going to pass on to you: Never support two weaknesses at the same time. It's your combination sinners – your lecherous liars and your miserly drunkards – who dishonour the vices and bring them into bad repute. So now you see why I want to get rid of this money: I want to keep my mind free to do the credit to whisky that it deserves. And

my last word to you, ladies and gentlemen, is this: one vice
at a time.

[*Goes over to Cornelius.*]

Can I speak to you for a minute?

CORNELIUS [*rising*]: You certainly can. We all want to
apologize to you about that screen – that little misunderstanding.

[*They all rise, with exclamations of apology.*]

What's your name, sir?

MALACHI: Stack, sir. Malachi Stack. If the ladies will excuse
you, I'd like to speak to you for a minute.

[*Draws Cornelius down to front of stage.*]

Listen, boy, have you lost . . . ? Come here . . .

[*Leads him farther down, out of Vandergelder's hearing.*]

Have you lost something?

CORNELIUS: Mr Stack, in this one day I've lost everything I
own.

MALACHI: There it is.

[*Gives him purse.*]

Don't mention it.

CORNELIUS: Why, Mr Stack . . . you know what it is? It's a
miracle.

[*Looks towards the ceiling.*]

MALACHI: Don't mention it.

CORNELIUS: Barnaby, come here a minute. I want you to
shake hands with Mr Stack.

[BARNABY, *napkin tucked into his collar, joins them.*]

Mr Stack's just found the purse I lost, Barnaby. You
know – the purse full of money.

BARNABY [*shaking his hand vigorously*]: You're a wonderful
man, Mr Stack.

MALACHI: Oh, it's nothing – nothing.

CORNELIUS: I'm certainly glad I went to church all these

years. You're a good person to know, Mr Stack. In a way.
Mr Stack, where do you work?

MALACHI: Well, I've just begun. I work for a Mr Vandergelder in Yonkers.

[CORNELIUS *is thunderstruck. He glances at Barnaby and
turns to Malachi with awe. All three are swaying slightly, back
and forth.*]

CORNELIUS: You do? It's a miracle.

[*He points to the ceiling.*]

Mr Stack, I know you don't need it – but can I give you
something for . . . the good work?

MALACHI [*putting out his hand*]: Don't mention it. It's nothing.

[*Starts to go left.*]

CORNELIUS: Take that.

[*Hands him a note.*]

MALACHI [*taking note*]: Don't mention it.

CORNELIUS: And that.

[*Another note*]

MALACHI [*taking it and moving away*]: I'd better be going.

CORNELIUS: Oh, here. And that.

MALACHI [*handing third note back*]: No . . . I might get to like
them.

[*Exit left.*

CORNELIUS *bounds exultantly back to table.*]

CORNELIUS: Irene, I feel a lot better about everything. Irene,
I feel so well that I'm going to tell the truth.

MRS MOLLOY: I'd forgotten that, Minnie. Men get drunk so
differently from women. All right, what is the truth?

CORNELIUS: If I tell the truth, will you let me . . . will you
let me put my arm around your waist?

[MINNIE *screams and flings her napkin over her face.*]

MRS MOLLOY: Hold your tongue, Minnie. All right, you can
put your arm around my waist just to show it can be done

254

in a gentlemanly way; but I might as well warn you: a corset is a corset.

CORNELIUS [*his arm around her; softly*]: You're a wonderful person, Mrs Molloy.

MRS MOLLOY: Thank you.

[*She removes his hand from around her waist.*]

All right, now that's enough. What is the truth?

CORNELIUS: Irene, I'm not rich as Mrs Levi said I was.

MRS MOLLOY: Not rich!

CORNELIUS: I almost never came to New York. And I'm not like she said I was, – bad. And I think you ought to know that at this very minute Mr Vandergelder's sitting on the other side of that screen.

MRS MOLLOY: What!! Well, he's not going to spoil any party of mine. So *that's* why we've been whispering? Let's forget all about Mr Vandergelder and have some more wine.

[*They start to sing softly 'The Sidewalks of New York'. Enter* MRS LEVI, *from the street, in an elaborate dress.* VANDERGELDER *rises.*]

MRS LEVI: Good evening, Mr Vandergelder.

VANDERGELDER: Where's – where's Miss Simple?

MRS LEVI: Mr Vandergelder, I'll never trust a woman again as long as I live.

VANDERGELDER: Well? What is it?

MRS LEVI: She ran away this afternoon and got married!

VANDERGELDER: She did?

MRS LEVI: Married, Mr Vandergelder, to a young boy of fifty.

VANDERGELDER: She did?

MRS LEVI: Oh, I'm as disappointed as you are. I-can't-eat-a-thing-what-have-you-ordered?

VANDERGELDER: I ordered what you told me to, a chicken.

[*Enter* AUGUST. *He goes to Vandergelder's table.*]

MRS LEVI: I don't think I could face a chicken. Oh, waiter. How do you do? What's your name?

AUGUST: August, ma'am.

MRS LEVI: August, this is Mr Vandergelder of Yonkers – Yonkers' most influential citizen, in fact. I want you to see that he's served with the best you have and served promptly. And there'll only be the two of us.

> [MRS LEVI *gives one set of cutlery to August.*
>
> VANDERGELDER *puts chocolate box under table.*]

Mr Vandergelder's been through some trying experiences today – what with men hidden all over Mrs Molloy's store – like Indians in ambush.

VANDERGELDER [*between his teeth*]: Mrs Levi, you don't have to tell him everything about me.

> [*The quartet commences singing again very softly.*]

MRS LEVI: Mr Vandergelder, if you're thinking about getting married, you might as well learn right now you have to let women be women. Now, August, we want excellent service.

AUGUST: Yes, ma'am.

> [*Exits to kitchen.*]

VANDERGELDER: You've managed things very badly. When I plan a thing it takes place.

> [MRS LEVI *rises.*]

Where are you going?

MRS LEVI: Oh, I'd just like to see who's on the other side of that screen.

> [MRS LEVI *crosses to the other side of the stage and sees the quartet. They are frightened and fall silent.*]

CORNELIUS [*rising*]: Good evening, Mrs Levi.

> [MRS LEVI *takes no notice, but, taking up the refrain where they left off, returns to her place at the table right.*]

VANDERGELDER: Well, who was it?

MRS LEVI: Oh, just some city sparks entertaining their girls, I guess.

VANDERGELDER: Always wanting to know everything; always curious about everything; always putting your nose into other people's affairs. Anybody who lived with you would get as nervous as a cat.

MRS LEVI: What? What's that you're saying?

VANDERGELDER: I said anybody who lived with you would –

MRS LEVI: Horace Vandergelder, get that idea right out of your head this minute. I'm surprised that you even mentioned such a thing. Understand once and for all that I have no intention of marrying you.

VANDERGELDER: I didn't mean that.

MRS LEVI: You've been hinting around at such a thing for some time, but from now on put such ideas right out of your head.

VANDERGELDER: Stop talking that way. That's not what I meant at all.

MRS LEVI: I hope not. I should hope not. Horace Vandergelder, you go your way [*pointing a finger*] and I'll go mine.
[*Points again in same direction.*]
I'm not some Irene Molloy, whose head can be turned by a pot of geraniums. Why, the idea of your even suggesting such a thing.

VANDERGELDER: Mrs Levi, you misunderstood me.

MRS LEVI: I certainly hope I did. If I had any intention of marrying again it would be to a far more pleasure-loving man than you. Why, I'd marry Cornelius Hackl before I'd marry you.
[CORNELIUS *raises his head in alarm. The others stop eating and listen.*]
However, we won't discuss it any more.
[*Enter* AUGUST *with a tray.*]

Here's August with our food I'll serve it, August.

AUGUST: Yes, ma'am.

[*Exit* AUGUST.]

MRS LEVI: Here's some white meat for you, and some giblets, very tender and very good for you. No, as I said before, you go your way and I'll go mine – Start right in on the wine. I think you'll feel better at once. However, since you brought the matter up, there's one more thing I think I ought to say.

VANDERGELDER [*rising in rage*]: I didn't bring the matter up at all.

MRS LEVI: We'll have forgotten all about it in a moment, but – sit down, sit down, we'll close the matter forever in just a moment, but there's one more thing I ought to say –

[VANDERGELDER *sits down*.]

It's true, I'm a woman who likes to know everything that's going on; who likes to manage things, you're perfectly right about that. But I wouldn't like to manage anything as disorderly as your household, as out of control, as untidy. You'll have to do that yourself, God helping you.

VANDERGELDER: It's not out of control.

MRS LEVI: Very well, let's not say another word about it. Take some more of that squash, it's good. No, Horace, a complaining, quarrelsome, friendless soul like you is no sort of companion for me. You go your way [*peppering her own plate*] and I'll go mine.

[*Peppers his plate*.]

VANDERGELDER: Stop saying that.

MRS LEVI: I won't say another word.

VANDERGELDER: Besides . . . I'm not those things you said I am.

MRS LEVI: What? – Well, I guess you're friendless, aren't you? Ermengarde told me this morning you'd even quarrelled

with your barber – a man who's held a razor to your throat
for twenty years! Seems to me that that's sinking pretty
low.

VANDERGELDER: Well, ... but ... my clerks, they ...

MRS LEVI: They like you? Cornelius Hackl and that Barnaby?
Behind your back they call you Wolf-trap.

[*Quietly the quartet at the other table have moved up to the
screens – bringing chairs for Mrs Molloy and Minnie.
Wine glasses in hand, they overhear this conversation.*]

VANDERGELDER [*blanching*]: They don't.

MRS LEVI: No, Horace. It looks to me as though I were the
last person in the world that liked you, and even I'm just
so-so. No, for the rest of my life I intend to have a good
time. You'll be able to find some housekeeper who can
prepare you three meals for a dollar a day – it can be done,
you know, if you like cold baked beans. You'll spend your
last days listening at keyholes, for fear someone's cheating
you. Take some more of that.

VANDERGELDER: Dolly, you're a damned exasperating
woman.

MRS LEVI: There! You see? That's the difference between us.
I'd be nagging you all day to get some spirit into you. You
could be a perfectly charming, witty, amiable man, if you
wanted to.

VANDERGELDER [*rising, bellowing*]: I don't want to be
charming.

MRS LEVI: But you are. Look at you now. You can't hide it.

VANDERGELDER [*sitting*]: Listening at keyholes! Dolly, you
have no right to say such things to me.

MRS LEVI: At your age you ought to enjoy hearing the honest
truth.

VANDERGELDER: My age! My age! You're always talking
about my age.

MRS LEVI: I don't know what your age is, but I do know that up at Yonkers with bad food and bad temper you'll double it in six months. Let's talk of something else; but before we leave the subject there's one more thing I *am* going to say.

VANDERGELDER: Don't!

MRS LEVI: Sometimes, just sometimes, I think I'd be tempted to marry you out of sheer pity; and if the confusion in your house gets any worse I may *have* to.

VANDERGELDER: I haven't asked you to marry me.

MRS LEVI: Well, *please don't*.

VANDERGELDER: And my house is not in confusion.

MRS LEVI: What? With your niece upstairs in the restaurant right now?

VANDERGELDER: I've fixed that better than you know.

MRS LEVI: And your clerks skipping around New York behind your back?

VANDERGELDER: They're in Yonkers where they always are.

MRS LEVI: Nonsense!

VANDERGELDER: What do you mean, nonsense?

MRS LEVI: Cornelius Hackl's the other side of that screen this very minute.

VANDERGELDER: It ain't the same man!

MRS LEVI: All right. Go on. Push it, knock it down. Go and see.

[VANDERGELDER *goes to screen, pauses in doubt, then returns to his chair again.*]

VANDERGELDER: I don't believe it.

MRS LEVI: All right. All right. Eat your chicken. Of course, Horace, if your affairs went from bad to worse and you became actually miserable, I might feel that it was my duty to come up to Yonkers and be of some assistance to you. After all, I was your wife's oldest friend.

VANDERGELDER: I don't know how you ever got any such notion. Now understand, once and for all, I have *no intention of marrying anybody*. Now, I'm tired and I don't want to talk.

[CORNELIUS *crosses to extreme left,* MRS MOLLOY *following him.*]

MRS LEVI: I won't say another word, either.

CORNELIUS: Irene, I think we'd better go. You take this money and pay the bill. Oh, don't worry, it's not mine.

MRS MOLLOY: No, no, I'll tell you what we'll do. You boys put on our coats and veils, and if he comes stamping over here, he'll think you're girls.

CORNELIUS: What! Those things!

MRS MOLLOY: Yes. Come one.

[*She and* MINNIE *take the clothes from the stand.*]

VANDERGELDER [*rising*]: I've got a headache. I've had a bad day. I'm going to Flora Van Huysen's, and then I'm going back to my hotel.

[*Reaches for his purse.*]

So, here's the money to pay for the dinner.

[*Searching another pocket*]

Here's the money to pay for the . . .

[*Going through all his pockets*]

Here's the money . . . I've lost my purse!!

MRS LEVI: Impossible! I can't imagine you without your purse.

VANDERGELDER: It's been stolen.

[*Searching overcoat*]

Or I left it in the cab. What am I going to do? I'm new at the hotel; they don't know me. I've never been here before. . . . Stop eating the chicken, I can't pay for it!

MRS LEVI [*laughing gaily*]: Horace, I'll be able to find some money. Sit down and calm yourself.

VANDERGELDER: Dolly Gallagher, I gave you twenty-five dollars this morning.

MRS LEVI: I haven't a cent. I gave it to my lawyer. We can borrow it from Ambrose Kemper, upstairs.

VANDERGELDER: I wouldn't take it.

MRS LEVI: Cornelius Hackl will lend it to us.

VANDERGELDER: He's in Yonkers – Waiter!

[CORNELIUS *comes forward dressed in Mrs Molloy's coat, thrown over his shoulder like a cape.*

MRS LEVI *is enjoying herself immensely.* VANDERGELDER *again goes to back wall to examine the pockets of his overcoat.*]

MRS MOLLOY: Cornelius, is that Mr Vandergelder's purse?

CORNELIUS: I didn't know it myself. I thought it was money just wandering around loose that didn't belong to anybody.

MRS MOLLOY: Goodness! That's what politicians think!

VANDERGELDER: Waiter!

[*A band off left starts playing a polka.* BARNABY *comes forward dressed in Minnie's hat, coat, and veil.*]

MINNIE: Irene, doesn't Barnaby make a lovely girl? He just ought to stay that way.

[MRS LEVI *and* VANDERGELDER *move their table upstage while searching for the purse.*]

MRS MOLLOY: Why should we have our evening spoiled? Cornelius, I can teach you to dance in a few minutes. Oh, he won't recognize you.

MINNIE: Barnaby, it's the easiest thing in the world.

[*They move their table up against the back wall.*]

MRS LEVI: Horace, you danced with me at your wedding and you danced with me at mine. Do you remember?

VANDERGELDER: No. Yes.

MRS LEVI: Horace, you were a good dancer then. Don't confess to me that you're too old to dance.

VANDERGELDER: I'm not too old. I just don't want to dance

MRS LEVI: Listen to that music. Horace, do you remember the dances in the firehouse at Yonkers on Saturday nights? You gave me a fan. Come, come on!

[VANDERGELDER *and* MRS LEVI *start to dance.* CORNE-LIUS, *dancing with* MRS MOLLOY, *bumps into Vandergelder, back to back.* VANDERGELDER, *turning, fails at first to recognize him, then does and roars.*]

VANDERGELDER: You're discharged! Not a word! You're fired! Where's that idiot, Barnaby Tucker? He's fired, too.

[*The four young people, laughing, start rushing out of the door to the street.* VANDERGELDER, *pointing at Mrs Molloy, shouts.*]

You're discharged!

MRS MOLLOY [*pointing at him*]: You're discharged!

[*Exit.*]

VANDERGELDER: You're discharged!

[*Enter from left,* AMBROSE *and* ERMENGARDE.

To Ermengarde]

I'll lock you up for the rest of your life, young lady.

ERMENGARDE: Uncle!

[*She faints in Ambrose's arms.*]

VANDERGELDER [*to Ambrose*]: I'll have you arrested. Get out of my sight. I never want to see you again.

AMBROSE [*carrying Ermengarde across to exit right*]: You can't do anything to me, Mr Vandergelder.

[*Exit* AMBROSE *and* ERMENGARDE.

MRS LEVI, *who has been laughing heartily, follows the distraught* VANDERGELDER *about the stage as he continues to hunt for his purse.*]

MRS LEVI: Well, there's your life, Mr Vandergelder! Without niece – without clerks – without bride – and without your purse. *Will you marry me now?*

VANDERGELDER: No!

[*To get away from her, he dashes into the kitchen.* MRS LEVI,
still laughing, exclaims to the audience]

MRS LEVI: Damn!!

[*And rushes off right.*]

THE

CURTAIN

FALLS

ACT FOUR

Miss Flora Van Huysen's house.

This is a prosperous spinster's living-room and is filled with knick-knacks, all in bright colours, and hung with family portraits, bird cages, shawls, etc.

There is only one entrance – a large double door in the centre of the back wall. Beyond it one sees the hall which leads left to the street door and right to the kitchen and the rest of the house. On the left are big windows hung with lace curtains on heavy draperies. Front left is Miss Van Huysen's sofa, covered with bright-coloured cushions, and behind it a table. On the right is another smaller sofa.

> [MISS VAN HUYSEN *is lying on the sofa. The* COOK *is at the window, left.* MISS VAN HUYSEN, *fifty, florid, stout, and sentimental, is sniffing at smelling salts.* COOK *(enormous) holds a china mixing bowl.*]

COOK: No, ma'am. I could swear I heard a cab drawing up to the door.

MISS VAN H.: You imagined it. Imagination. Everything in life ... like that ... disappointment ... illusion. Our plans ... our hopes ... what becomes of them? Nothing. The story of my life.

> [*She sings for a moment.*]

COOK: Pray God nothing's happened to the dear girl. Is it a long journey from Yonkers?

MISS VAN H.: No; but long enough for a thousand things to happen.

COOK: Well, we've been waiting all day. Don't you think we ought to call the police about it?

MISS VAN H.: The police! If it's God's will, the police can't prevent it. Oh, in three days, in a week, in a year, we'll

265

know what's happened ... And if anything *has* happened to Ermengarde, it'll be a lesson to *him* – that's what it'll be.

COOK: To who?

MISS VAN H.: To that cruel uncle of hers, of course – to Horace Vandergelder, and to everyone else who tries to separate young lovers. Young lovers have enough to contend with as it is. Who should know that better than I? No one. The story of my life.

[*Sings for a moment.*]

There! Now I hear a cab. Quick!

COOK: No. No, ma'am. I don't see anything.

MISS VAN H.: There! What did I tell you? Everything's imagination – illusion.

COOK: But surely, if they'd changed their plans Mr Vandergelder would have sent you a message.

MISS VAN H.: Oh, I know what's the matter. That poor child probably thought she was coming to another prison – to another tyrant. If she'd known that I was her friend, and a friend of all young lovers, she'd be here by now. Oh, yes, she would. Her life shall not be crossed with obstacles and disappointments as ... Cook, a minute ago my smelling salts were on this table. Now they've completely disappeared.

COOK: Why, there they are, ma'am, right there in your hand.

MISS VAN H.: Goodness! How did they get there? I won't inquire. Stranger things have happened!

COOK: I suppose Mr Vandergelder was sending her down with someone?

MISS VAN H.: Two can go astray as easily as ...

[*She sneezes.*]

COOK: God bless you!

[*Runs to window.*]

Now, here's a carriage stopping.

[*The doorbell rings.*]

MISS VAN H.: Well, open the door, Cook.

[COOK *exits.*]

It's probably some mistake ...

[*Sneezes again.*]

God bless you!

[*Sounds of altercation off in hall*]

It almost sounds as though I heard voices.

CORNELIUS [*off*]: I don't want to come in. This is a free country, I tell you.

CABMAN [*off*]: Forward march!

MALACHI [*off*]: In you go. We have orders.

CORNELIUS [*off*]: You can't make a person go where he doesn't want to go.

[*Enter* MALACHI, *followed by* COOK. *The* CABMAN *bundles* BARNABY *and* CORNELIUS *into the room, but they fight their way back into the hall.* CORNELIUS *has lost Mrs Molloy's coat, but* BARNABY *is wearing Minnie's clothes.*]

MALACHI: Begging your pardon, ma'am, are you Miss Van Huysen?

MISS VAN H.: Yes, I am, unfortunately. What's all this noise about?

MALACHI: There are two people here that Mr Vandergelder said must be brought to this house and kept here until he comes. And here's his letter to you.

MISS VAN H.: No one has any right to tell me whom I'm to keep in my house if they don't want to stay.

MALACHI: You're right, ma'am. Everybody's always talking about people breaking into houses, ma'am; but there are more people in the world who want to break out of houses, that's what I always say – Bring them in, Joe.

[*Enter* CORNELIUS *and* BARNABY *being pushed by the* CABMAN.]

CORNELIUS: This young lady and I have no business here. We jumped into a cab and asked to be driven to the station and these men brought us to the house and forced us to come inside. There's been a mistake.

CABMAN: Is your name Miss Van Huysen?

MISS VAN H.: Everybody's asking me if my name's Miss Van Huysen. I think that's a matter I can decide for myself. Now will you all be quiet while I read this letter? . . . 'This is Ermengarde and that rascal Ambrose Kemper . . .' Now I know who you two are, anyway. 'They are trying to run away . . .' Story of my life. 'Keep them in your house until I come.' Mr Kemper, you have nothing to fear.

[*To cabman*]

Who are you?

CABMAN: I'm Joe. I stay here until the old man comes. He owes me fifteen dollars.

MALACHI: That's right, Miss Van Huysen, we must stay here to see they don't escape.

MISS VAN H. [*to Barnaby*]: My dear child, take off your things. We'll all have some coffee.

[*To Malachi and cabman*]

You two go out and wait in the hall. I'll send coffee out to you. Cook, take them.

[COOK *pushes* MALACHI *and* CABMAN *into the hall.*]

CORNELIUS: Ma'am, we're not the people you're expecting, and there's no reason . . .

MISS VAN H.: Mr Kemper, I'm not the tyrant you think I am. . . . You don't have to be afraid of me. . . . I know you're trying to run away with this innocent girl. . . . All my life I have suffered from the interference of others. You shall not suffer as I did. So put yourself entirely in my hands.

[*She lifts Barnaby's veil.*]

Ermengarde!

[*Kisses him on both cheeks.*]

Where's your luggage?

BARNABY: It's – uh – uh – it's . . .

CORNELIUS: Oh, I'll find it in the morning. It's been mislaid.

MISS VAN H.: Mislaid! How like life! Well, Ermengarde; you shall put on some of my clothes.

BARNABY: Oh, I know I wouldn't be happy, really.

MISS VAN H.: She's a shy little thing, isn't she? Timid little darling! . . . Cook! Put some gingerbread in the oven and get the coffee ready . . .

COOK: Yes, ma'am.

[*Exits to kitchen.*]

MISS VAN H.: . . . while I go and draw a good hot bath for Ermengarde.

CORNELIUS: Oh, oh – Miss Van Huysen . . .

MISS VAN H.: Believe me, Ermengarde, your troubles are at an end. You two will be married tomorrow.

[*To Barnaby*]

My dear, you look just like I did at your age, and your sufferings have been as mine. While you're bathing, I'll come and tell you the story of my life.

BARNABY: Oh, I don't want to take a bath. I always catch cold.

MISS VAN H.: No, dear, you won't catch cold. I'll slap you all over. I'll be back in a minute.

[*Exit.*]

CORNELIUS [*looking out of window*]: Barnaby, do you think we could jump down from this window?

BARNABY: Yes – we'd kill ourselves.

CORNELIUS: We'll just have to stay here and watch for something to happen. Barnaby, the situation's desperate.

BARNABY: It began getting desperate about half past four and

it's been getting worse ever since. Now I have to take a bath
and get slapped all over.

[*Enter* MISS VAN HUYSEN *from kitchen*.]

MISS VAN H.: Ermengarde, you've still got those wet things
on. Your bath's nearly ready. Mr Kemper, you come into
the kitchen and put your feet in the oven.

[*The doorbell rings. Enter* COOK.]

What's that? It's the doorbell. I expect it's your uncle.

COOK: There's the doorbell.

[*At window*]

It's *another* man and a girl in a cab!

MISS VAN H.: Well, go and let them in, Cook. Now, come
with me, you two. Come, Ermengarde.

[*Exit* COOK. MISS VAN HUYSEN *drags* CORNELIUS *and
the protesting* BARNABY *off into the kitchen*.]

COOK [*off*]: No, that's impossible. Come in, anyway.

[*Enter* ERMENGARDE, *followed by* AMBROSE, *carrying the
two pieces of luggage*.]

There's some mistake. I'll tell Miss Van Huysen, but
there's some mistake.

ERMENGARDE: But, I tell you I *am* Mr Vandergelder's niece;
I'm Ermengarde.

COOK: Beg your pardon, Miss, but you *can't* be Miss
Ermengarde.

ERMENGARDE: But – but – I *am*. And that's my baggage.

COOK: Well, I'll tell Miss Van Huysen who you *think* you are,
but she won't like it.

[*Exits*.]

AMBROSE: You'll be all right now, Ermengarde. I'd better go
before she sees me.

ERMENGARDE: Oh, no. You must stay. I feel so strange here.

AMBROSE: I know, but Mr Vandergelder will be here in a
minute. . . .

ERMENGARDE: Ambrose, you can't go. You can't leave me in this crazy house with those drunken men in the hall. Ambrose ... Ambrose, let's say you're someone else that my uncle sent down to take care of me. Let's say you're – you're Cornelius Hackl!

AMBROSE: Who's Cornelius Hackl?

ERMENGARDE: You know. He's chief clerk in Uncle's store.

AMBROSE: I don't want to be Cornelius Hackl. No, no, Ermengarde, come away with me now. I'll take you to my friend's house. Or I'll take you to Mrs Levi's house.

ERMENGARDE: Why, it was Mrs Levi who threw us right at Uncle Horace's face. Oh, I wish I were back in Yonkers where nothing ever happens.

[*Enter* MISS VAN HUYSEN.]

MISS VAN H.: What's all this I hear? Who do you say you are?

ERMENGARDE: Aunt Flora ... don't you remember me? I'm Ermengarde.

MISS VAN H.: And you're Mr Vandergelder's niece?

ERMENGARDE: Yes, I am.

MISS VAN H.: Well, that's very strange indeed, because he has just sent me another niece named Ermengarde. She came with a letter from him, explaining everything. Have you got a letter from him?

ERMENGARDE: No ...

MISS VAN H.: Really! – And who is this?

ERMENGARDE: This is Cornelius Hackl, Aunt Flora.

MISS VAN H.: Never heard of him.

ERMENGARDE: He's chief clerk in Uncle's store.

MISS VAN H.: Never heard of him. The other Ermengarde came with the man she's in love with, and that *proves* it. She came with Mr Ambrose Kemper.

AMBROSE [*shouting*]: Ambrose Kemper!

MISS VAN H.: Yes, Mr Hackl, and Mr Ambrose Kemper is in the kitchen there now *with his feet in the oven*.

[ERMENGARDE *starts to cry.* MISS VAN HUYSEN *takes her to the sofa. They both sit.*]

Dear child, what is your trouble?

ERMENGARDE: Oh, dear! I don't know what to do.

MISS VAN H. [*in a low voice*]: Are you in love with this man?

ERMENGARDE: Yes, I am.

MISS VAN H.: I could see it – and are people trying to separate you?

ERMENGARDE: Yes, they are.

MISS VAN H.: I could see it – who? Horace Vandergelder?

ERMENGARDE: Yes.

MISS VAN H.: That's enough for me. I'll put a stop to Horace Vandergelder's goings on.

[MISS VAN HUYSEN *draws Ambrose down to sit on her other side.*]

Mr Hackl, think of me as your friend. Come in the kitchen and get warm. . . .

[*She rises and starts to go out.*]

We can decide later who everybody is. My dear, would you like a good hot bath?

ERMENGARDE: Yes, I would.

MISS VAN H.: Well, when Ermengarde comes out you can go in.

[*Enter* CORNELIUS *from the kitchen.*]

CORNELIUS: Oh, Miss Van Huysen . . .

ERMENGARDE: Why, Mr Hack – !!

CORNELIUS [*sliding up to her, urgently*]: Not yet! I'll explain. I'll explain everything.

MISS VAN H.: Mr Kemper! – Mr Kemper! This is Mr Cornelius Hackl.

[*To Ambrose*]

Mr Hackl, this is Mr Ambrose Kemper.

[*Pause, while the men glare at one another*]

Perhaps you two know one another?

AMBROSE: No!

CORNELIUS: No, we don't.

AMBROSE [*hotly*]: Miss Van Huysen, I know that man is not Ambrose Kemper.

CORNELIUS [*ditto*]: And he's not Cornelius Hackl.

MISS VAN H.: My dear young men, what does it matter what your names are? The important thing is that you are you.

[*To Ambrose.*]

You are alive and breathing, aren't you, Mr Hackl?

[*Pinches Ambrose's left arm.*]

AMBROSE: Ouch, Miss Van Huysen.

MISS VAN H.: This dear child imagines she is Horace Vandergelder's niece Ermengarde.

ERMENGARDE: But I am.

MISS VAN H.: The important thing is that you're all in love. Everything else is illusion.

[*She pinches Cornelius's arm.*]

CORNELIUS: Ouch! Miss Van Huysen!

MISS VAN H. [*coming down and addressing the audience*]: Everybody keeps asking me if I am Miss Van Huys. . . .

[*She seems suddenly to be stricken with doubt as to who she is; her face shows bewildered alarm. She pinches herself on the upper arm and is abruptly and happily relieved.*]

Now, you two gentlemen sit down and have a nice chat while this dear child has a good hot bath.

[*The doorbell rings.* ERMENGARDE *exit*, MISS VAN HUYSEN *about to follow her, but stops. Enter* COOK.]

COOK: There's the doorbell again.

MISS VAN H.: Well, answer it.

[*She and* ERMENGARDE *exit to kitchen.*]

COOK [*at window, very happy about all these guests*]: It's a cab and three ladies. I never saw such a night.

[*Exit to front door.*]

MISS VAN H.: Gentlemen, you can rest easy. I'll see that Mr Vandergelder lets his nieces marry you both.

[*Enter* MRS LEVI.]

MRS LEVI: Flora, how are you?

MISS VAN H.: Dolly Gallagher! What brings you here?

MRS LEVI: Great Heavens, Flora, what are those two drunken men doing in your hall?

MISS VAN H.: I don't know. Horace Vandergelder sent them to me.

MRS LEVI: Well, I've brought you two girls in much the same condition. Otherwise they're the finest girls in the world.

[*She goes up to the door and leads in* MRS MOLLOY. MINNIE *follows.*]

I want you to meet Irene Molloy and Minnie Fay.

MISS VAN H.: Delighted to know you.

MRS LEVI: Oh, I see you two gentlemen are here, too. Mr Hackl, I was about to look for you [*pointing about the room*] *somewhere* here.

CORNELIUS: No, Mrs Levi. I'm ready to face anything now.

MRS LEVI: Mr Vandergelder will be here in a minute. He's downstairs trying to pay for a cab without any money.

MRS MOLLOY [*holding Vandergelder's purse*]: Oh, I'll help him.

MRS LEVI: Yes, will you, dear? You had to pay the restaurant bills. You must have hundreds of dollars there it seems.

MRS MOLLOY: This is his own purse he lost. I can't give it back to him without seeming ...

MRS LEVI: I'll give it back to him – There, you help him with this now.

[*She gives Mrs Molloy a bill and puts the purse airily under her arm.*]

VANDERGELDER [*off*]: Will somebody please pay for this cab?

[MRS MOLLOY *exits to front door.*]

MRS MOLLOY [*off stage*]: I'll take care of that, Mr Vandergelder.

[*As* MR VANDERGELDER *enters*, MALACHI *and the* CABMAN *follow him in.* VANDERGELDER *carries overcoat, stick, and box of chocolates.*]

CABMAN: Fifteen dollars, Mr Vandergelder.

MALACHI: Hello, Mr Vandergelder.

VANDERGELDER [*to Malachi*]: You're discharged!

[*To cabman*]

You too!

[MALACHI *and* CABMAN *go out and wait in the hall.*]

So I've caught up with you at last!

[*To Ambrose*]

I never want to see you again!

[*To Cornelius*]

You're discharged! Get out of the house, both of you.

[*He strikes sofa with his stick; a second after,* MISS VAN HUYSEN *strikes him on the shoulder with a folded newspaper or magazine.*]

MISS VAN H. [*forcefully*]: Now then you. Stop ordering people out of my house. You can shout and carry on in Yonkers, but when you're in my house you'll behave yourself.

VANDERGELDER: They're both dishonest scoundrels.

MISS VAN H.: Take your hat off. Gentlemen, you stay right where you are.

CORNELIUS: Mr Vandergelder, I can explain –

MISS VAN H.: There aren't going to be any explanations. Horace, stop scowling at Mr Kemper and forgive him.

VANDERGELDER: That's not Kemper, that's a dishonest rogue named Cornelius Hackl.

MISS VAN H.: You're crazy.

[*Points to Ambrose.*]

That's Cornelius Hackl.

VANDERGELDER: I guess I know my own chief clerk.

MISS VAN H.: I don't care what their names are. You shake hands with them both, or out you go.

VANDERGELDER: Shake hands with those dogs and scoundrels!

MRS LEVI: Mr Vandergelder, you've had a hard day. You don't want to go out in the rain now. Just for form's sake, you shake hands with them. You can start quarrelling with them tomorrow.

VANDERGELDER [*giving Cornelius one finger to shake*]: There. Don't regard that as a handshake.

[*He turns to* AMBROSE, *who mockingly offers him one finger.*]

Hey! I never want to see you again.

[MRS MOLLOY *enters from front door.*]

MRS MOLLOY: Miss Van Huysen.

MISS VAN H.: Yes, dear?

MRS MOLLOY: Do I smell coffee?

MISS VAN H.: Yes, dear.

MRS MOLLOY: Can I have some, good and black?

MISS VAN H.: Come along, everybody. We'll all go into the kitchen and have some coffee.

[*As they all go.*]

Horace, you'll be interested to know there are two Ermengardes in there. . . .

VANDERGELDER: Two!!

[*Last to go is* MINNIE, *who revolves about the room dreamily waltzing, a finger on her forehead.* MRS LEVI *has been standing at one side. She now comes forward, in thoughtful mood.* MINNIE *continues her waltz round the left sofa and out to the kitchen.*]

276

ACT FOUR

MRS LEVI, *left alone, comes to front, addressing an imaginary Ephraim.*]

MRS LEVI: Ephraim Levi, I'm going to get married again. Ephraim, I'm marrying Horace Vandergelder for his money. I'm going to send his money out doing all the things you taught me. Oh, it won't be a marriage in the sense that we had one – but I shall certainly make him happy, and Ephraim – I'm tired. I'm tired of living from hand to mouth, and I'm asking your permission, Ephraim – will you give me away?

[*Now addressing the audience, she holds up the purse.*]

Money! Money! – it's like the sun we walk under; it can kill or cure – Mr Vandergelder's money! Vandergelder's never tired of saying most of the people in the world are fools, and in a way he's right, isn't he? Himself, Irene, Cornelius, myself! But there comes a moment in everybody's life when he must decide whether he'll live among human beings or not – a fool among fools or a fool alone.

As for me, I've decided to live among them.

I wasn't always so. After my husband's death I retired into myself. Yes, in the evenings, I'd put out the cat, and I'd lock the door, and I'd make myself a little rum toddy; and before I went to bed I'd say a little prayer, thanking God that I was independent – that no one else's life was mixed up with mine. And when ten o'clock sounded from Trinity Church tower, I fell off to sleep and I was a perfectly contented woman. And one night, after two years of this, an oak leaf fell out of my Bible. I had placed it there on the day my husband asked me to marry him; a perfectly good oak leaf – but without colour and without life. And suddenly I realized that for a long time I had not shed one tear; nor had I been filled with the wonderful hope that something or other would turn out well. I saw that I was like that oak leaf, and on that night I decided to rejoin the human race.

Yes, we're all fools and we're all in danger of destroying the world with our folly. But the surest way to keep us out of harm is to give us the four or five human pleasures that are our right in the world – and that takes a little *money*!

The difference between a little money and no money at all is enormous – and can shatter the world. And the difference between a little money and an enormous amount of money is very slight – and that, also, can shatter the world.

Money, I've always felt, money – pardon my expression – is like manure; it's not worth a thing unless it's spread about encouraging young things to grow.

Anyway – that's the opinion of the second Mrs Vandergelder.

[VANDERGELDER *enters with two cups of coffee. With his back, he closes both doors.*]

VANDERGELDER: Miss Van Huysen asked me to bring you this.

MRS LEVI: Thank you both. Sit down and rest yourself. What's been going on in the kitchen?

VANDERGELDER: A lot of foolishness. Everybody falling in love with everybody. I forgave 'em; Ermengarde and that artist.

MRS LEVI: I knew you would.

VANDERGELDER: I made Cornelius Hackl my partner.

MRS LEVI: You won't regret it.

VANDERGELDER: Dolly, you said some mighty unpleasant things to me in the restaurant tonight ... all that about my house ... and everything.

MRS LEVI: Let's not say another word about it.

VANDERGELDER: Dolly, you have a lot of faults –

MRS LEVI: Oh, I know what you mean.

VANDERGELDER: You're bossy, scheming, inquisitive ...

MRS LEVI: Go on.

278

VANDERGELDER: But you're a wonderful woman. Dolly, marry me.

MRS LEVI: Horace!

[*Rises.*]

Stop right there.

VANDERGELDER: I know I've been a fool about Mrs Molloy, and that other woman. But, Dolly, forgive me and marry me.

[*He goes on his knees.*]

MRS LEVI: Horace, I don't dare. No. I don't dare.

VANDERGELDER: What do you mean?

MRS LEVI: You know as well as I do that you're the first citizen of Yonkers. Naturally, you'd expect your wife to keep open house, to have scores of friends in and out all the time. Any wife of yours should be used to that kind of thing.

VANDERGELDER [*after a brief struggle with himself*]: Dolly, you can live any way you like.

MRS LEVI: Horace, you can't deny it, your wife would have to be a *somebody*. Answer me: am I a somebody?

VANDERGELDER: You are . . . you are. Wonderful woman.

MRS LEVI: Oh, you're partial.

[*She crosses, giving a big wink at the audience, and sits on sofa right.*

VANDERGELDER *follows her on his knees.*]

Horace, it won't be enough for you to load your wife with money and jewels; to insist that she be a benefactress to half the town.

[*He rises and still struggling with himself, coughs so as not to hear this.*]

No, she must be a somebody. Do you really think I have it in me to be a credit to you?

VANDERGELDER: Dolly, everybody knows that you could do anything you wanted to do

MRS LEVI: I'll try. With your help, I'll try – and by the way, I found your purse.

[*Holds it up.*]

VANDERGELDER: Where did you – ? Wonderful woman!

MRS LEVI: It just walked into my hand. I don't know how I do it. Sometimes I frighten myself. Horace, take it. Money walks out of my hands, too.

VANDERGELDER: Keep it. Keep it.

MRS LEVI: Horace!

[*Half-laughing, half-weeping, and with an air of real affection for him*]

I never thought . . . I'd ever . . . hear you say a thing like that!

[BARNABY *dashes in from the kitchen in great excitement. He has discarded Minnie's clothes.*]

BARNABY: Oh! Excuse me. I didn't know anybody was here.

VANDERGELDER [*bellowing*]: Didn't know anybody was here. Idiot!

MRS LEVI [*putting her hand on Vandergelder's arm; amiably*]: Come in, Barnaby. Come in.

[VANDERGELDER *looks at her a minute; then speaks, imitating her tone.*]

VANDERGELDER: Come in, Barnaby. Come in.

BARNABY: Cornelius is going to marry Mrs Molloy!!

MRS LEVI: Isn't that fine! Horace! . . .

[MRS LEVI *rises, and indicates that he has an announcement to make.*]

VANDERGELDER: Barnaby, go in and tell the rest of them that Mrs Levi has consented –

MRS LEVI: *Finally* consented!

VANDERGELDER: Finally consented to become my wife.

BARNABY: Holy cabooses.

[*Dashes back to the doorway.*]

Hey! Listen, everybody! Wolf-trap – I mean – Mr Vandergelder is going to marry Mrs Levi.

[MISS VAN HUYSEN *enters followed by all the people in this act. She is now carrying the box of chocolates.*]

MISS VAN H.: Dolly, that's the best news I ever heard.

[*She addresses the audience.*]

There isn't any more coffee; there isn't any more ginger bread; but there are three couples in my house and they're all going to get married. And do you know, one of those Ermengardes wasn't a dear little girl at all – she was a boy; Well, that's what life is: disappointment, illusion.

MRS LEVI [*to audience*]: There isn't any more coffee; there isn't any more gingerbread, and there isn't any more play – but there is one more thing we have to do. . . . Barnaby, come here.

[*She whispers to him, pointing to the audience. Then she speaks to the audience.*]

I think the youngest person here ought to tell us what the moral of the play is.

[BARNABY *is reluctantly pushed forward to the footlights.*]

BARNABY: Oh, I think it's about . . . I think it's about adventure. The test of an adventure is that when you're in the middle of it, you say yourself, 'Oh, now I've got myself into an awful mess; I wish I were sitting quietly at home.' And the sign that something's wrong with you is when you sit quietly at home wishing you were out having lots of adventure. What we would like for you is that you have just the right amount of sitting quietly at home, and just the right amount of – adventure! So that now we all want to thank you for coming tonight, and we all hope that in your lives you have just the right amount of – adventure!

THE
CURTAIN
FALLS

FOR THE BEST IN PAPERBACKS, LOOK FOR THE

In every corner of the world, on every subject under the sun, Penguin represents quality and variety – the very best in publishing today.

For complete information about books available from Penguin – including Puffins, Penguin Classics and Arkana – and how to order them, write to us at the appropriate address below. Please note that for copyright reasons the selection of books varies from country to country.

In the United Kingdom: Please write to *Dept E.P., Penguin Books Ltd, Harmondsworth, Middlesex, UB7 0DA.*

If you have any difficulty in obtaining a title, please send your order with the correct money, plus ten per cent for postage and packaging, to *PO Box No 11, West Drayton, Middlesex*

In the United States: Please write to *Dept BA, Penguin, 299 Murray Hill Parkway, East Rutherford, New Jersey 07073*

In Canada: Please write to *Penguin Books Canada Ltd, 2801 John Street, Markham, Ontario L3R 1B4*

In Australia: Please write to the *Marketing Department, Penguin Books Australia Ltd, P.O. Box 257, Ringwood, Victoria 3134*

In New Zealand: Please write to the *Marketing Department, Penguin Books (NZ) Ltd, Private Bag, Takapuna, Auckland 9*

In India: Please write to *Penguin Overseas Ltd, 706 Eros Apartments, 56 Nehru Place, New Delhi, 110019*

In the Netherlands: Please write to *Penguin Books Netherlands B.V., Postbus 195, NL–1380AD Weesp*

In West Germany: Please write to *Penguin Books Ltd, Friedrichstrasse 10–12, D–6000 Frankfurt/Main 1*

In Spain: Please write to *Longman Penguin España, Calle San Nicolas 15, E–28013 Madrid*

In Italy: Please write to *Penguin Italia s.r.l., Via Como 4, I-20096 Pioltello (Milano)*

In France: Please write to *Penguin Books Ltd, 39 Rue de Montmorency, F-75003 Paris*

In Japan: Please write to *Longman Penguin Japan Co Ltd, Yamaguchi Building, 2–12–9 Kanda Jimbocho, Chiyoda-Ku, Tokyo 101*

CLASSICS OF THE TWENTIETH CENTURY

The Outsider Albert Camus

Meursault leads an apparently unremarkable bachelor life in Algiers, until his involvement in a violent incident calls into question the fundamental values of society. 'The protagonist of *The Outsider* is undoubtedly the best achieved of all the central figures of the existential novel' – *Listener*

Dark as the Grave wherein my Friend is Laid Malcolm Lowry

A Dantesque descent into hell: into Lowry's infernal landscape of Mexico – the Mexico of his masterpiece, *Under the Volcano* – and into Lowry's own personal abyss, reverberating with mental terrors and spiritual chasms.

I'm Dying Laughing Christina Stead

A dazzling novel set in the 1930s and 1940s when fashionable Hollywood Marxism was under threat from the savage repression of McCarthyism. 'The Cassandra of the modern novel in English … reading her seems like plunging into the mess of life itself' – Angela Carter

The Desert of Love François Mauriac

Two men, father and son, share a passion for the same woman – attractive, intelligent and proud, but an outcast from respectable society because of her position as a 'kept woman'. 'He writes with an intense, almost tempestuous force about the life of the emotions' – Olivia Manning

The Expelled and Other Novellas Samuel Beckett

Rich in verbal and situational humour, these four stories offer the reader a fascinating insight into Beckett's preoccupation with the helpless individual consciousness, a preoccupation which has remained constant throughout his work.

Chance Acquaintances and Julie de Carneilhan Colette

Two contrasting works in one volume. Colette's last full-length novel, *Julie de Carneilhan* was 'as close a reckoning with the elements of her second marriage as she ever allowed herself'. In *Chance Acquaintances*, Colette visits a health resort, accompanied only by her cat.

FOR THE BEST IN PAPERBACKS, LOOK FOR THE 🐧

CLASSICS OF THE TWENTIETH CENTURY

Thirst for Love   Yukio Mishima

Before her husband's death Etsuko had already learnt that jealousy is useless unless it can be controlled. Love, hatred, and a new, secret passion – she can control them all as long as there is hope. But as that hope fades, her frustrated desire gathers a momentum that can be checked only by an unspeakable act of violence.

The Collected Dorothy Parker

Dorothy Parker, more than any of her contemporaries, captured in her writing the spirit of the Jazz Age. Here, in a single volume, is the definitive Dorothy Parker: poetry, prose, articles and reviews. 'A good, fat book … greatly to be welcomed' – Richard Ingrams

Remembrance of Things Past (3 volumes)   Marcel Proust

'What an extraordinary world it is, the universe that Proust created! Like all great novels, À la Recherche has changed and enlarged our vision of the "real" world in which we live' – Peter Quennell. Terence Kilmartin's flawless translation is 'as near to the real Proust as we can hope for' – Angus Wilson

The Sword of Honour Trilogy   Evelyn Waugh

A glorious fusion of comedy, satire and farcical despair, Waugh's magnificently funny trilogy is also a bitter attack on a world where chivalry and nobility were betrayed at every hand. 'Unquestionably the finest novels to have come out of the war' – Cyril Connolly

Buddenbrooks   Thomas Mann

Published in 1902, Mann's 'immortal masterpiece' was already a classic before it was banned and burned by Hitler. 'The richness and complexity … the interplay of action and ideas … has never been surpassed in German fiction' – J. P. Stern

Sanctuary   William Faulkner

Faulkner draws America's Deep South exactly as he saw it – seething with life and corruption. In Sanctuary he asserts a compulsive and unsparing vision of human nature.

The Ides of March

Love affairs and treacherous friendships sweep in and out of Thornton Wilder's imaginative reconstruction of the diaries, letters and political pamphlets of a dying dictatorship.

Set in Rome in 45 B.C., and inspired in part by the conspiratorial chain-letters against Mussolini that circulated in Italy under the twentieth-century fascist regime, *The Ides of March* is a 'fantasia on certain events and persons of the last days of the Roman Republic'.

Julius Caesar is portrayed through the eyes of friends, lovers, enemies and himself as he waits for his inevitable assassination, measuring his political strengths and his fatal weaknesses. With tenderness, wit and wisdom, Thornton Wilder has written one of the best historical novels of this century.

The Bridge of San Luis Rey

On 20 July 1714 the finest bridge in all Peru collapsed, and five people plummeted to their deaths in the gorge below.

Hundreds had crossed the bridge every day – why should such a catastrophe have happened to those particular people? Did it reveal a latent pattern in human life?

Thornton Wilder's beautiful, searching and vividly written investigation of the unhappy Marquesa de Montemayor, the orphans Pepita and Esteban, the remarkable Uncle Pio, and Don Jaime sheds subtle light on the tragedy, and has long been acclaimed as a twentieth-century masterpiece.

Also published

THE EIGHTH DAY
THEOPHILUS NORTH